THE BEAUTY OF HER AGE

A Tale of Sex, Scandal and Money in Victorian England

Jenifer Roberts

AMBERLEY

First published 2016
This edition published 2018

Amberley Publishing
The Hill, Stroud
Gloucestershire, GL5 4EP

www.amberley-books.com

Copyright © Jenifer Roberts, 2016, 2018

The right of Jenifer Roberts to be identified as
the Author of this work has been asserted in
accordance with the Copyrights, Designs and
Patents Act 1988.

ISBN 978 1 4456 7719 4 (print)
ISBN 978 1 4456 5321 1 (ebook)

British Library Cataloguing in Publication Data.
A catalogue record for this book is available
from the British Library.

Typesetting and Origination by Amberley Publishing
Printed in the UK.

For my stepdaughters, Mandy and Emma,
with love and gratitude

CONTENTS

The Lyne Stephens family.

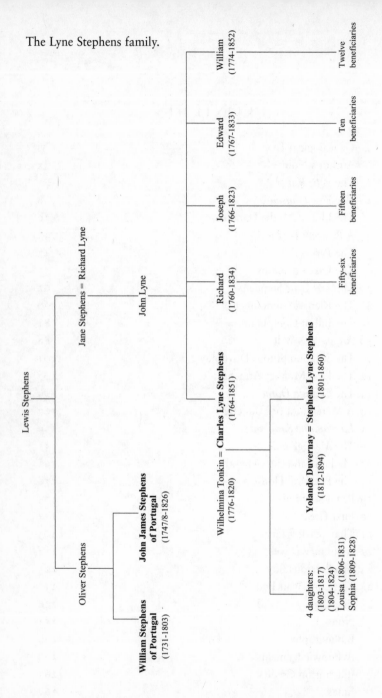

The Claremont family.

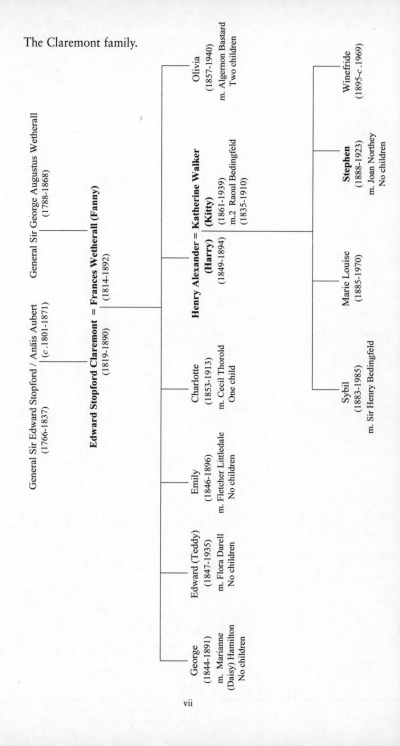

General Sir Edward Stopford / Anäis Aubert (c.1801-1871)
(1766-1837)

General Sir George Augustus Wetherall (1788-1868)

Edward Stopford Claremont = Frances Wetherall (Fanny)
(1819-1890)   (1814-1892)

George   Edward (Teddy)   Emily   Charlotte   Henry Alexander = Katherine Walker   Olivia
(1844-1891)   (1847-1935)   (1846-1896)   (1853-1913)   (Harry)   (Kitty)   (1857-1940)
m. Marianne   m. Flora Darell   m. Fletcher Littledale m. Cecil Thorold   (1849-1894)   (1861-1939)   m. Algernon Bastard
(Daisy) Hamilton   No children   No children   One child   m.2 Raoul Bedingfeld   Two children
No children   (1835-1910)

                                                                  Sybil   Marie Louise   Stephen   Winefride
                                                                  (1883-1985)   (1885-1970)   (1888-1923)   (1895-c.1969)
                                                                  m. Sir Henry Bedingfeld   m. Joan Northey   No children

AUTHOR'S NOTE

When I was a child, my mother told me of a great fortune in the family. Her grandfather, a lawyer in Cornwall, was one of the beneficiaries, but he invested unwisely in tin mines and sold his interest to pay off his debts. Over the years, I met a number of distant cousins who also remembered a family fortune, some of them with boxes tucked away in lofts and garages containing papers proving their lineage.

Details had been lost down the generations. We knew only that the wealth was made by relatives in Portugal, and when their second cousin (my great-grandfather's great-uncle) inherited the fortune in 1826, he added their name to his. After my mother's death, I found a few old newspaper cuttings among her papers. These explained how the fortune was divided after the death of a Mrs Yolande Lyne Stephens, the richest woman in England. She too had disappeared from history.

During the next few years, I unearthed the story of the fortune from its beginnings in Portugal in the mid-eighteenth century to its distribution among a large number of beneficiaries more than 150 years later. This led to the publication of *Glass: The Strange History of the Lyne Stephens Fortune*. The extraordinary rags-to-riches story of Yolande Lyne Stephens featured in a few short chapters at the end of the book. Now I have been able to bring her centre stage.

Contemporary values of the pound sterling are relevant to this story of great wealth. To obtain present-day values, I have used Bank of England figures for 2015 taken from 'The Composite Price Index' compiled by the Office for National Statistics. These provide multiplication factors ranging between 96 and 126 during the course of the story. To convey the magnitude of sums of money, I have occasionally added present-day values in brackets.

This dancer's story is a legend and the Alexandre Dumas of the future will write long novels in many volumes about it.

Albéric Second
L'Entr'acte, 9 June 1857

I

THE *PETIT RAT*

*Duvernay was one of the most ravishing women you could wish to
see ... with charming eyes, an adorably turned leg, and a figure of
perfect elegance.*

Charles Séchan, 1883

One of the brightest stars of the Paris Opéra, Yolande Marie Louise
Duvernay, was born on a cold winter day in the Passage Saulnier,
a narrow street in the ninth arrondissement. It was December
1812. Napoleon's Grande Armée was in retreat from Moscow.
Her family had endured more than twenty years of revolution and
wars; her grandmother would tell her how, in the autumn of 1792,
she had seen a mob parade through the streets with the severed
head of the Princesse de Lamballe, friend and confidante of Marie
Antoinette, impaled on a pike.

Yolande's father, Jean-Louis Duvernay, was described as a teacher
of dance. Her mother, known to history only as Madame Duvernay,
had been a performer in her youth and her only child was destined
for the stage. Her first six years in the Passage Saulnier saw the
defeat of Napoleon, the restoration of the Bourbon monarchy,
and a three-year occupation of Paris by allied troops under the

command of the Duke of Wellington. In early 1819, a few months after the last foreign soldiers left the city, she was enrolled in the School of Dance in the Salle Louvois, close to the Salle Montansier, the opera house in the Rue de Richelieu.

Less than a year later, the king's nephew was assassinated outside the Salle Montansier during an evening performance. In retribution, the building was demolished and a new opera house, the Salle le Peletier, opened its doors in August 1821. Built of wood and plaster in the narrow Rue le Peletier, it was intended to be a temporary structure but would remain the home of the Paris Opéra for more than fifty years. The School of Dance also moved to new premises in the Rue Richer, close to the new theatre and a few minutes' walk from the Passage Saulnier.

Almost all pupils in the School of Dance came from poor families and began their training at a young age. 'I was barely seven when I was sent to the Rue Richer,' explained one of Yolande's fellow pupils:

I left home in the morning fortified only by a cup of coffee. I had neither clogs for my feet, nor a shawl for my shoulders, and more often than not my poor cotton dress was full of holes. I arrived shivering and often starving. Then began the daily suffering ...

Every morning, my teacher imprisoned my feet in a grooved box. There, heel to heel, with knees pointing outwards, my martyred feet became used to remaining in a parallel line by themselves. They call this 'turning out'. After half an hour of the box, I had to endure another form of torture. This time I had to place my foot on a *barre* which I had to hold with the opposite hand to the foot in exercise. This was called 'breaking in' ...

After being turned out and broken in, we were forced, under pain of our teacher's reprimands and our mothers' chastisement, to study *assemblés, jetés, balancés, pirouettes sur le cou-de-pied, sauts de basque, pas de bourrée,* and, finally, *entrechats quatre, six* and *huit* ... and do not imagine that such brutal fatigues last only for a short time. They must continue for ever and be constantly renewed.[1]

These underfed, poorly clad little girls in the School of Dance were known as the *petits rats*. They spent their days in the Rue Richer and their evenings in the opera house, appearing on stage in a variety of juvenile roles. According to Nestor Roqueplan, an *habitué* of the theatre:

> The *rat* is a child of the building … a little girl who wears cast-off shoes, faded shawls and soot-coloured hats, warms herself over smoky oil-lamps, has bread sticking out of her pockets, and begs you for ten *sous* to buy sweets. A *rat* makes holes in the scenery to watch the performance, rushes about behind the backcloths, and plays puss-in-the-corner in the wings. She is supposed to earn twenty *sous* a night, but with the fines which her pranks entail, she receives only eight to ten francs a month and thirty kicks from her mother.[2]

Each *petit rat* was under the control of her mother, 'herself perhaps a decayed celebrity', who sat in the wings:

> ready to throw a shawl over her offspring as she left the stage; coming, night after night, with her little basket containing *eau sucré*, or diluted *vin ordinaire*, and the invariable four-legged stool on which she sat during the performance, abusing the director … for his want of discernment in not bringing forward more prominently the child on whom all her hopes were centred.[3]

Yolande's mother was the most domineering and ambitious of these stage mothers, ready to fight 'tooth and nail' for the advancement of her daughter. She was venal, bossy, controlling and manipulative, a woman happy to pimp Yolande for her own financial gain. Mothers of *petit rats* who had reached puberty were not only in charge of their daughter's performances on stage, they were also in charge of their sexual availability. Men of society kept an eye on the ballet pupils and, through their mothers, made assignations with the *petit rat* of their choice.

In 1829, when Yolande was sixteen, her mother wrote three letters to the director of the Opéra, Émile Lubbert, asking that her daughter be transferred to the *classe de perfectionnement* taught by the ballet-master Auguste Vestris, a class intended for pupils who showed promise of progressing beyond the *corps de ballet*.

Her first letter, written in August, was forwarded to Vestris for his opinion. There was no reply. She wrote again on 25 October, asking that Yolande be granted leave of several months because of her 'altered health' and reminding him about her request for the *classe de perfectionnement*. This time Lubbert replied, granting the leave but making no mention of the transfer. On 2 November she wrote for a third time, thanking Lubbert for granting the leave and 'also to request the class of M. Vestris. There has never been the least favour from the administration, so I think that this request could perhaps be granted.'[4]

At the end of the year, Lubbert agreed that Yolande should enter the class taught by Vestris when she returned from 'sick leave'. This was a euphemism for pregnancy, the result of an assignation arranged by her mother. There is no further mention of a child in the records. Yolande may have had a miscarriage or an abortion, but the months of absence from class would suggest a full-term pregnancy. If the child of an opera-dancer survived, it was normally given away to relatives or to a family in the country.

Recovered from childbirth, Yolande joined the *classe de perfectionnement* in the spring of 1830. Auguste Vestris, known as *Le Dieu de la Danse*, was an elderly man who had made his début as a dancer as far back as 1772. He understood what was needed to fill the auditorium. 'He was a sensualist,' explained the director. 'He demanded provocative smiles, poses and attitudes, almost without decency or modesty. I often heard him say to his pupils "be charming and coquettish; display the most captivating freedom in all your movements; you must inspire passion so that men in the audience want to go to bed with you".'[5]

In the summer of 1830, a revolution in Paris toppled the Bourbon monarchy and closed the opera house for nine days. The three-day uprising, known as *Les Trois Glorieuses*, began on 27 July. Six days later, the Bourbon king was replaced on the throne by Louis-Philippe d'Orléans.

Yolande ventured into the streets during the uprising to see the barricades and experience the sounds and smells of gunfire; when it was over, she walked to the School of Dance through the debris of the fighting. These three days would prove to be a major turning point in her life. The July Revolution removed the Paris Opéra from the control of the state. It became a subsidised private enterprise with an independent director – and Émile Lubbert was replaced by Dr Louis Véron.

Louis Véron was thirty-two years old, a doctor who was enriched by the launch of a patent medicine, Pâte Régnault, for the treatment of sore throats. A man of unprepossessing appearance, with thick features and a heavy frame, he was described by one contemporary as 'ruddy, with a pock-marked face, barely any nose ... pot-bellied ... lips thick, hair rare, eyebrows absent ... and with the affectations and mincing airs of the salon'. Another described him as 'a mould of Régnault paste in a setting of currant jelly', and a third as 'a bulky caricature-like figure, with a head entirely buried in an immense white cravat' which was believed to hide a skin condition.[6]

Véron applied for the post of director because he foresaw that the July Revolution would result in the rise of a bourgeoisie. After his appointment on 2 March 1831, he set out to indulge the tastes of this new fashionable class. He formalised the system of sexual assignation by opening the doors of the Foyer de la Danse, a room behind the stage with *barres* and mirrors where dancers gathered before a performance, to young men of society, most of whom were members of the Jockey Club. According to Albéric Second, another *habitué* of the opera, the Foyer provided these men 'with their amorous pleasures, just as the Pompadour stud-farm provides them with their equestrian pleasures; they use it as a storehouse for remounts, nothing more'.[7]

Véron also introduced the star system, presenting a sequence of 'young and beautiful dancers', each one dancing 'better and differently from those who have preceded her. If one is aiming neither at the intelligence nor at the heart, one must appeal to the senses and most particularly to the eyes.' He attended the *classes de perfectionnement* to select those pupils whose talent and charm would most appeal to his audience.

Yolande stood out in class for her beauty, her elegant figure and long legs, her lustrous dark hair and wide, sparkling eyes. She looked entrancing in her practice costume: a tight, low-cut bodice above a knee-length 'bouffant skirt of net or striped muslin'. Vestris could see that Véron found her attractive. On the rare occasions when she came to class alone, he would rush off to the opera house. 'He would run up all excited,' wrote Véron, 'his hair flying, his feet turned out, and say to me "she is there without her mother!"'

Véron was enchanted by Yolande, this 'ravishing young dancer'. It was easy for her mother to persuade him to take her to his bed. At the age of eighteen she became his mistress, as well as his first rising star. Just three weeks after he took over as director, he began to prepare her for leading roles, bypassing the normal route of the *corps de ballet* and the junior grades.

Taking the stage name of Pauline Duvernay, she was almost overcome by fright when she made her début in the opera house on 13 April, dancing a *pas de deux* from the ballet *Mars et Vénus* with Antoine Coulon. She was, wrote the critic of the *Courrier des Théâtres*, 'graceful, though a trifle weak. Poses particularly become her.'

Further performances increased her confidence and she danced her first leading role, Venus in *Mars et Vénus*, on 5 September. A few weeks later, when she was about to perform a *pas de deux* with Lise Noblet, Véron found her sobbing in the wings. He asked what the matter was, and when she remained silent, her mother took him aside.

'I will tell you,' she said. 'She is dancing this evening with Mademoiselle Noblet. Mademoiselle Noblet has the most beautiful jewels. My daughter has none.'

'Despite my long experience,' wrote Véron, 'a woman's tears always affect me and I sent at once to Madame Janisset [the jeweller] for the supreme remedy for such suffering and such poignant sorrow. It was one of my days of managerial weakness.'

Yolande had studied her 'pretty air of melancholy'. She had learned to be manipulative; she knew that tears were a powerful means of persuasion. She cried in class so frequently that, on one occasion, Vestris sprinkled the floor of his classroom with a watering can. 'Look,' he said to Véron, 'those are her tears.'

'This young dancer,' wrote Véron in his memoirs, 'lifted to prominence by a skilful mother, had above all studied the power of weeping.'[8]

2

THE FAIR *DANSEUSE*

*When I think of Duvernay prancing in as the Bayadère, I say it was
a vision of loveliness such as mortal eyes can't see nowadays ...
to the clash of cymbals and the thumping of my heart, in she
used to dance!*

William Makepeace Thackeray, 1863

At the end of the year, Yolande took over the role of the abbess
in a one-act *divertissement* performed during Meyerbeer's opera
Robert le Diable. The role had previously been danced by the star
of the Opéra, Marie Taglioni, who had trained with her father in
Vienna and never experienced life as a *petit rat*.

The curtain rose on an eerie scene of a ruined cloister with
overgrown tombs and glowing lanterns. The footlights were
extinguished; the effect of moonlight created by gas jets
suspended from the flies. Nuns who had been unfaithful to their
vows are summoned from their tombs by a young man. They
remove their habits to dance while the abbess encourages them
to give in to pleasure. She dances before the boy, luring him
towards the grave, but he escapes and the nuns sink back into
their tombs.

'One can vaguely see the coffin covers open up in the darkness,' wrote a young Théophile Gautier:

> then indistinct forms begin to emerge ... detaching themselves from each standing tomb and climbing each flag stone like smoky fumes. A ray of light from a gas-jet shoots forth across the church-like vaults, sketching in the bluish shadows the feminine forms which, under the whiteness of their shrouds, begin to move with a deathly sensuality.[1]

The seduction scene had proved difficult for Marie Taglioni, but it presented no problems for Yolande. She was, wrote the critic of the *Journal de Débats* on 14 February, 'very young and very pretty, dances to perfection, and her miming is full of fascination. This young virtuoso is making rapid progress and is following the traces of Mademoiselle Taglioni with a light foot.'

Meanwhile, Véron had commissioned a new ballet to exploit the talents of his young mistress. *La Tentation* was an opera-ballet in five acts and Yolande would dance the role of Miranda, a woman shaped by a demon to be more alluring than any woman on earth.

Rehearsals were underway by 26 March 1832 when four people died of cholera in Paris, the first deaths in an epidemic which would last for seven months and claim an estimated 20,000 lives. The disease marched through every arrondissement of the city; the ninth, where Yolande lived and worked, was one of the first to enter the records.

Véron kept the opera house open during the epidemic, so Yolande walked daily through the streets to rehearse the new ballet, avoiding the carts which carried away the dead. She did the same during the uprising of 5/6 June when republicans built barricades, fought battles and died in their hundreds, an insurrection immortalised by Victor Hugo in *Les Misérables*.

Two weeks after the uprising, she danced her first leading role in the opening performance of *La Tentation*. It was the evening of 20 June. The scenery was magnificent ('superb, staggering, prodigious'), the cast was huge, and her first appearance on stage was a *coup-de-théâtre*. A horde of demons cluster around a smoking cauldron. They throw ingredients into the mix; they recite magic incantations. As they cast the spell, a hideously misshapen green monster emerges from the smoke. The demons plunge it back into the cauldron. They throw further ingredients into the mix, they recite more magic incantations. When they cast the spell for a second time, the beautiful Miranda rises from the cauldron, 'fresh, timid and ravishing', dressed in white, her dark hair hanging loose around her shoulders.

The ballet was overlong and not a success, but Yolande's spirited dancing was received with enthusiasm. According to the journal *L'Entr'acte*, her performance was 'graceful and childlike in turn, and so modest, even when she accepts the mission which her creator and master, the demon, confides to her. Then, by degrees that are ably managed, she rises to the pathos, the devotion and the will of a martyr. She is a pretty woman and a talented one.'

She was the new star of the Opéra. 'Every evening,' wrote one of her admirers, 'the name of Duvernay was acclaimed by a thousand voices.' A stage painter, Charles Séchan, described her as 'one of the most ravishing women you could wish to see ... with charming eyes, an adorably turned leg, and a figure of perfect elegance. When she danced, she was full of grace and brio.' Another admirer, Paul Mahalin, wrote that she had 'the blood of a dancer and the heart of an artiste, but the spirit which Pauline Duvernay possessed above all else was the spirit of adventure'.[2]

One evening in the autumn of 1832, perhaps bored by long performances in *La Tentation*, perhaps weary of walking through disease-ridden streets, but more likely because she craved attention, she failed to appear at the opera house. Nor was she at home in the apartment which Véron had provided for her. Fearing that she might have drowned in the Seine, Véron and her mother made a visit to the morgue on the Île de la Cité. Unidentified corpses were exhibited here, displayed behind glass screens on tilted tables, their clothes hanging on pegs behind them.

Yolande was not in the morgue. Her disappearance became the talk of Paris and it was several days before Casimir Gide, the composer of *La Tentation*, received an anonymous note giving details of her whereabouts. He hurried through the streets and found her hiding behind the grille in a convent. She had, she told him, felt a sudden desire to become a nun.

She enjoyed the prank and reappeared on stage to the delight of her admirers. She was idolised for her 'beauty, wit and lightness of heart'; for the spontaneity of her conversation and repartee; and for 'the gaiety and sentiment, frankness and firm opinions' expressed in her letters, which Véron sometimes read aloud to his friends. She scorned an offer of 40,000 francs from the elderly Comte de Pourtalès and became renowned as a 'consummate mistress of sarcasm with would-be lovers'. Stories about her mischief with the men who tried to buy her favours did the rounds of newspapers and gossip sheets.[3]

'You say you love me,' she said one day to an elderly Russian aristocrat, 'but do you love me as much as 100,000 francs?'

The following day, she returned from class to find the Russian reclining on her sofa, his feet up on the cushions and a large cash box by his side. 'My dear,' he said, 'you asked me yesterday whether I loved you as much as 100,000 francs. Here is my answer.'

He opened the box to show that it was filled with gold coins. Yolande looked at them with disdain. 'Take your feet off my sofa,' she said, 'and take away that old iron. I was only joking.'

As news of this rebuff spread through society, a young diplomat made his way to her apartment. '*I* shall not offer you gold,' he said. 'It's my *life* I would sacrifice for you.'

Yolande laughed. 'If I wanted your head, you'd bring it to me, wouldn't you? You men are all the same. You offer things that are either impossible or of no use at all.'

After listening to the young man's protestations, she appeared to relent. 'Very well,' she said. 'Bring me one of your front teeth.'

An hour later, he returned with a handkerchief held to his mouth and a pill-box in his hand. As Yolande opened the box, he removed the handkerchief, opened his mouth and pointed to a bloody gap.

'Oh, you stupid man!' she said. 'I asked you for a lower tooth and you've brought me a top one.'

Such stories became legendary in Paris and soon reached London where two theatres, the Theatre Royal in Drury Lane and the King's Theatre in the Haymarket, functioned as opera houses on a seasonal basis, engaging members of the Paris Opéra on short-term contracts. In late 1832, Alfred Bunn, manager of the Theatre Royal, approached Louis Véron with a request that Yolande should appear there for the first six weeks of the 1833 season.

'Her mother does her more harm than good,' wrote Marie Taglioni. 'She was offered a London engagement, but her mother gave it out that it would be difficult for her to accept it, since she has had offers from all the foreign courts. I must tell you that I am not so difficult to please for I have just signed my London contract.'[4]

Despite her mother's intrigues, Yolande accepted the engagement at a salary of £750 (£80,000), plus a thousand francs for Véron. She and her parents crossed the Channel and took lodgings in Cecil Street near the Strand. Her first appearance in Drury Lane was on 13 February 1833 when she danced the role of Princess Iseult in a new production, *La Belle au Bois Dormant* (*The Sleeping Beauty*).

Princess Iseult was asleep for much of the ballet, so Bunn had inserted an additional scene in which Yolande danced a solo as a naiad, a water nymph. After the performance, as he led her to the front of the stage to acknowledge the applause, two bouquets – described dismissively by Marie Taglioni as 'garlands of artificial flowers' – were thrown from one of the side boxes, probably by her father. One fell into the orchestra pit, the other landed at the feet of Alfred Bunn who bent down, picked it up and handed it to Yolande with 'ineffable grace'.

The production was received with acclaim, 'a most gorgeous spectacle ... so beautiful that it called forth shouts of rapture', but the response to Yolande's performance was mixed:

Morning Post: To say that she proved herself equal to the undertaking would be but faint praise. Her beauty, grace, and skill were so conspicuous that everyone appeared anxious to join in acknowledging her merits, and we have never seen a foreigner meet with so flattering a reception.

The Times: She is handsome, of a good figure, and as far as could be judged from the slight exertions she made, not an ungraceful dancer ... The little which she did was of a fine quality, agile and graceful in a very eminent degree, and as good as to make us wish for more.

Morning Herald: Mademoiselle Duvernay belongs to the school of Taglioni and, and without being equal to her model, is remarkable for finished and unlaboured art, unfaltering precision in all the movements she attempts, and an easy and pervading gracefulness ... On the whole she is a star, but not one of the first brilliancy.

Theatrical Observer: We felt disappointed; very pretty she is certainly, and a graceful dancer, but not *la merveille* we were led to expect.

The future Queen Victoria watched a performance on 21 February. 'Mademoiselle Duvernay is a very nice person,' the thirteen-year-old princess wrote in her diary that night. 'She has a very fine figure and dances beautifully, so quietly and so gracefully, somewhat in the style of Taglioni.' Victoria saw the ballet again on 5 March: 'Mademoiselle Duvernay danced *beautifully* and she was encored in her *pas seul* in the dance of the Naiades. She looked likewise *uncommonly well*.'⁵

Yolande achieved greater success when she made her first appearance as Zelica in *The Maid of Cashmere (Le Dieu et la Bayadère)* on 13 March. The evening began badly:

> From some unexplained cause the overture was not commenced till a quarter past seven, which caused some slight disapprobation, but when it was finished and the curtain did not rise, the audience became very angry. After waiting a short time, the leader thought it best to recommence the overture, which he did, amidst loud cries of 'No! No!' and 'Off! Off!' ... In the midst of this confusion, up rose the curtain and the audience resumed their good humour.

This awkward start was forgotten as soon as Yolande appeared on stage:

> Duvernay infinitely surpassed the expectation her previous performance had led us to form; her dancing was graceful and elegant, and in the chastest style, her action simple and natural, and her dress was so becoming that she looked lovely ... In the Shawl Dance, she seemed like a spirit of air about to soar into brighter regions. She was greatly applauded throughout, and at the end of the ballet was obliged to come forward to receive the congratulations of the spectators.[6]

Four days later:

> Yesterday evening the *Maid of Cashmere* made her second appearance ... and was received with similar honours as on her début ... Mademoiselle Duvernay has risen wonderfully in the estimation of the public ... her gestures, in answers to the Grand Judge in the first scene, were given with so much expression that she did not require the aid of language to make herself understood, and her love for the unknown, her jealousy, and her affliction at the loss of his attentions, were depicted as vividly as mere action could do. We know not whether we were most charmed with her

pantomime or her dancing; her every movement was easy, graceful and unaffected.[7]

Princess Victoria, after watching a performance on 19 March, wrote that Yolande 'danced and acted *quite beautifully*, with *so much grace and feeling*; she looked likewise quite lovely ... It was in two acts, and I was *very much amused*.'[8]

A young William Makepeace Thackeray saw the production several times and fell deeply in love:

When I think of Duvernay prancing in as the Bayadère, I say it was a vision of loveliness such as mortal eyes can't see nowadays. How well I remember the tune to which she used to appear! Kaled [said] to the Sultan, 'My Lord, a troop of those dancing and singing girls called Bayadères approaches', and, to the clash of cymbals and the thumping of my heart, in she used to dance! There has never been anything like it – never. There never will be.[9]

Yolande's London season came to an end on 30 March, seventeen days after she first danced in *The Maid of Cashmere*. As a theatre critic wrote towards the end of the month:

Those who have not seen Mademoiselle Duvernay in the part have no idea of the extent of her talents. It is a great pity she did not make her first appearance in this piece, for then she would much earlier have done the trick. Now she is within a day or two of departure, the people are beginning to flock after her. Her benefit and last performance is next Saturday, 30 March, and we are led to understand that she posts off to Dover the moment the curtain falls, for she is under a heavy penalty to be in Paris on the evening of 1 April as she dances there the following night.

Meanwhile, the men-about-town had clustered around the new celebrity. Alfred Bunn 'declared his attachment by some tender but understood expression of the eye', while young Lord Ranelagh was so smitten that he followed Yolande to France where she flirted with him for a few weeks before sending him home to England. 'Although I play the sleeping beauty in public,' she told him, 'I cannot perform it in private without first passing through the ordeal of the church.'[10]

Back home in Paris, she starred in the ballet *Nathalie* in which, according to the *Courrier des Théâtres*, she was 'as pretty as an angel'. On 30 May, she danced the title role in *La Sylphide* with 'so graceful a timidity, so simple a modesty, and such touching expression, that she pleased everyone'.

In July, preparations began for a new ballet, *La Révolte au Sérail*, in which several dancers portrayed a group of female warriors. The production opened in early December and Yolande's pantomime stole the show. In one scene, the women formed a council of war, and while the other dancers simulated a few gestures of communication, 'Duvernay, by means of the wittiest miming and the most expressive and passionate gestures, managed to convey all the phases of an animated discussion and to give an idea of a council of war held by women. Universal laughter and applause greeted these gay and comical scenes.'[11]

In another scene, the dancers lifted their bows to shoot arrows into the wings. On the opening night, Yolande absent-mindedly aimed her bow in the wrong direction. Her arrow sped into the auditorium and embedded itself in a column to one side of the royal box, a few feet from the head of the Duc de Nemours, second son of King Louis-Philippe.

At the end of the year, Pierre-François Laporte, manager of the King's Theatre in the Haymarket, arrived in Paris to engage Yolande and Marie Taglioni to appear in London for the first ten weeks of the 1834 season. They opened the season in the King's Theatre on 1 March, with Taglioni dancing the title role in *La Sylphide*. The newspapers were quick to compare their talents:

Duvernay received more applause than Taglioni, we suppose because she is the greater stranger: the greater favourite she can never be of anybody who pretends to be a judge of grace and lightness. Duvernay cannot be placed in the first class of dancers at any time, but least of all when she is on the same boards as Taglioni.

We own, however, that Duvernay is a very charming creature: her face and person are both nearly faultless, and these, with certain admirers, go far to make her dancing seem faultless too. There seems to be a party disposed to set her on an equal footing, if not on a higher pedestal, than Taglioni; but the attempt must fail. The one is air, and the other earth; but still each is spring when it is clad in beauty.[12]

Yolande had many admirers in London and, as the *Morning Chronicle* explained, 'had Taglioni never been seen, Duvernay would have been considered one of the most charming dancers that ever exhibited'. Jealous of her allure, Taglioni felt the need to qualify her achievement. 'She has had here,' she wrote on 15 March, 'what we call a *succès d'estime* only, but as a beauty she has enjoyed enormous success.'[13]

Yolande had conquered the fashionable set in a way that the plainer Taglioni never could. The King's Theatre was the centre of high fashion and, just as the Paris Opéra had opened the Foyer de la Danse to men of society, the King's Theatre had opened a Green Room where performers mingled with their admirers. Men of the 'fast set' watched the ballet from omnibus boxes which abutted the stage, then strolled into the Green Room to make assignations with the dancer of their choice.

The men in the omnibus boxes included Lord Allen, a fifty-year-old Irish viscount described as 'a tall, stout, pompous-looking personage ... with an invariably new-looking hat and well-polished boots'; Lord Tullamore, another Irish peer and member of parliament; and Edward Ellice, twenty-three years old, son of the secretary of state for war. A gossip sheet, *The Satirist*, complained about 'the annoyance caused by these omnibus tadpoles, Tullamore, Allen and others, who ... keep up a continual clatter of approbation which reminds us of the unwelcome din of little children'.

Towards the end of her second London season, Yolande accepted a proposition from Edward Ellice (who, like his father, was nicknamed 'the Bear'). As the retired politician Thomas Creevey wrote on 3 May:

> [Ellice] being a very aspiring young man of fashion, has formed a connection with Duvernay the opera dancer, to whom he has paid £2000 down and contracted to pay her £800 a year. The dear young creatures were seen going down in a chaise and four to Richmond. Captain Gronow, the MP and duellist, negotiated the affair for the young Bear with the dancer's parents.[14]

The Star and Garter in Richmond, the haunt of 'dukes and dandies, pretty women of some repute and no repute, and bright young bucks', was the scene of many romantic assignations and Yolande's tryst with Edward Ellice gave rise to much jealousy. On 4 May, *The Satirist* reported that 'the ratification dinner given by Ned Ellice to his darling Duvernay at the Star and Garter has excited much remark amongst the admirers of that fascinating *danseuse*. Lord Allen is perfectly out of his wits and Lord Tullamore is stark staring mad with vexation and envy.'

Yolande's engagement at the King's Theatre ended on 8 May, when she danced 'with her accustomed grace and was rapturously applauded'. She intended to return to Paris two days later and, according to *The Satirist*, 'there was every reason to believe her ardent lover would accompany her or follow in the course of a few days. Papa Ellice protests strongly and firmly against anything bordering on a match with the Fair Brimstone as he styles her.'

A week later, Yolande was still in London. 'Duvernay was to have left for Paris on Saturday last,' explained *The Satirist* on 18 May:

> but at the pressing solicitation of the Duke of Devonshire, she was induced to prolong her stay and, on Monday, by special invitation,

she accompanied Ned Ellice to the Duke's villa at Chiswick where a splendid fork luncheon was prepared. The Duke enjoyed himself in unrestricted delight, and a jealous schism has arisen between the Duke and young Ned on the subject of the fair *danseuse*.

This was the 6th Duke of Devonshire, forty-four years old, unmarried and described as 'vain, dandyish and partially deaf'. Ellice watched Yolande flirt with the duke for the entire afternoon and, as soon as they set out on the return journey to London, he began to complain about her behaviour. She replied that she could do as she pleased – and resentful of any attempt to curb her freedom, she broke off their agreement.

'Young Ellice is inconsolable for the loss of Duvernay,' explained *The Satirist*, 'and what adds to his affliction is that his rival, the Duke of Devonshire, has made a proposition so liberal in its provisions that no doubt can arise as to its immediate acceptance.'

The duke had several mistresses; he was only playing with her affections, so Yolande returned to Paris and the arms of Louis Véron. 'Duvernay complains bitterly of the young Bear,' concluded *The Satirist*, 'and congratulates herself that she has escaped from his claws. Véron is quite delighted and gives it out that he is safe in the affection of the charming *danseuse*.'

3

THE IDOL OF ALL THE DANDIES

The most perfect managerial adept I ever met was my friend,
Monsieur Véron ... Véron knew his people; for many things can
be done with a foreign dancer if you commence operations with a
dinner and end them with a diamond.

Alfred Bunn, manager of the Theatre Royal, 1840

Yolande was fond of Véron, who had done so much to advance her career, but the behaviour of her mother was a constant threat. Madame Duvernay wanted power in the opera house and Véron was always on his guard. Soon after they returned from London in 1834, she tried to trap him into marrying her daughter. No details have survived but the plot was discovered by the *concierge*, Madame Crosnier, who had worked in the opera house for forty years.[1]

Then she set out to belittle Véron's influence over Yolande's career. 'My daughter's talent has no need of *anyone*'s protection,' she said to him one day when asking for a seat in the stalls for the evening performance.

Véron made no reply but he sent for Auguste Levasseur, leader of the *claque*, a group of sixty men who sat in the pit and led the applause in the opera house, cued by Auguste tapping his cane on the floor. Véron told Auguste to ensure that Yolande received no ovation that night, 'not even a single hand-clap'.

That evening, after finishing a pirouette, Yolande came to a halt and 'smiled graciously at the audience'. Auguste failed to tap his cane. The *claque* remained silent, the audience followed suit, and 'the theatre maintained the deepest silence'. Yolande fled from the stage and collapsed sobbing in the wings, while her mother demanded an interview with Véron.

'It's only happened once,' he told her, 'but now you must see that your daughter's talent *does* need some help.'[2]

By the autumn, an exasperated Véron could bear it no longer. More than three years into their affair, his ardour for Yolande had begun to cool. He had also found a new rising star, Fanny Elssler, an Austrian dancer who arrived in Paris in July. Yolande was rehearsing the lead role in a new ballet, *La Tempête* (based loosely on Shakespeare), when Véron decided to substitute Elssler in the role. She used all her power of weeping to persuade him to change his mind, so he had the scenario rewritten to include leading roles for both dancers.

Elssler was an immediate success when *La Tempête* was first performed on 15 September. A few weeks later, Véron openly displayed the change in his affections. Attending a performance at another theatre in October, he booked separate boxes for Yolande and Marie Taglioni, but sat close to Elssler in the most conspicuous box of all.

Yolande's response was to make a dramatic attempt to poison herself. Alone in her apartment, she swallowed a glass of vinegar in which she had soaked some copper coins. She then groaned loudly to ensure her neighbours could hear. On cue, they rushed into the apartment, found her 'writhing and gasping' on the sofa, and called for a doctor – who soon cured her of the effects of this curious concoction.[3]

Already a star of the Opéra, the loss of Véron in her bed did little damage to Yolande's career and her mother soon arranged for the self-styled Marquis de La Valette to take his place. The illegitimate son of an actress, Félix de La Valette was brought up by his mother in the theatre, took his father's surname, and added the spurious title of marquis. Twenty-eight years old, he was charming, elegant, good-looking, and 'richly endowed with audacity, loquacity and a talent for intrigue'. A familiar figure in the Foyer de la Danse – where he was known as 'very charming and very dangerous' – he enjoyed liaisons with several dancers who supported him financially. In the autumn of 1834, after deserting Pauline Guichard, a dancer who had recently borne him a child, his eye fell on the beautiful and spirited Yolande.

Her father had disappeared by this time and her mother was working her way through a series of venal and unscrupulous lovers. An English gossip sheet reported the rumour that Madame Duvernay and her lover of the moment had made a financial transaction:

Her mother was visited by an old French gentleman who, being very much embarrassed at the time, and knowing that La Valette had made many overtures to Mademoiselle Duvernay, proposed to the mother to raise money upon the prostitution of the young girl. The mother consented. La Valette was deeply enamoured of Duvernay, and she on her part was particularly attached to her admirer. Still the young girl entertained those notions of propriety which seemed to supersede any chance of success.

Her infamous mother, however, accomplished the aim desired. La Valette was invited to the house for supper; a potion was infused in the drink of the unsuspecting girl; and when she awoke in the morning she found herself in the arms of the handsome Frenchman. Being now ruined beyond redemption, and with truly French resignation, she abandoned herself to all the enjoyments and delights of illicit passion in the arms of La Valette. He behaved to her with the greatest kindness and affection; and she became devotedly attached to him.

The price that La Valette paid to the mother and her lover was 40,000 francs ... and with this sum the old lover absconded, leaving the lost girl's parent without a single *sou* of reward for the sale of her daughter's chastity.[4]

Whatever the truth of this story – and it seems unlikely that her affair with Véron was not common knowledge in Paris – Yolande was happy with her new lover. He was younger and better-looking than Véron and his adventurous personality was a match for her own. La Valette was happy too, but he still had his eye on the main chance. His title allowed him to mix easily in high society, and in May 1835 he agreed to marry Virginie de Méneval, a wealthy heiress.

This prompted another attempt at suicide, this time with an overdose of opium. As the *Courrier des Théâtres* explained on 23 May:

The breaking-off of an intimacy was denoted by the announcement of the marriage of one of the parties. The banns had been published and, so it is said, the contract signed. Upon hearing the news, our young artiste lost her reason, gave way to despair and, when she thought she had but little time to live, called on her former lover to whom she uttered these words: 'You are about to marry and I am about to die.'[5]

The news reached London where, on 8 June, *The Theatrical Observer* reported that Yolande's overdose had caused 'a great sensation in Paris'. It published a slightly different version of events:

It appears that her friend, the Marquis de La Valette, was about to marry a rich heiress. The night before the intended ceremony, *la danseuse* sent to request he would call on her. He went and she desired him to pour some soothing drops into her tisane, which she drank, and then saying it was poison refused to take any antidote ... Duvernay still continues very ill.

Yolande had taken too little opium to kill herself but the marriage was called off, mainly because of the scandal, but also because La Valette was genuinely fond of his mistress. She returned to the stage on 17 June and continued to dance during the summer and early autumn. On 9 October, she performed the leading role in *La Tempête*. Ten days later, she disappeared from public view. 'Pretty women,' explained the *Courrier des Théâtres*, 'are prone to more indispositions than others.'

This was Yolande's second pregnancy, a child conceived in April or May, shortly before she took the overdose of opium. This child too would form no part of her life. It was well known, even in the wilds of the Yorkshire moors, that opera-dancers tended to desert their children. In *Jane Eyre* by Charlotte Brontë (published in 1847), the child Adèle, for whom Jane was employed as a governess, was the result of Mr Rochester's youthful passion for a French opera-dancer who had given birth to a daughter:

And, Miss Eyre, so much was I flattered by this preference of the Gallic sylph for her British gnome, that I installed her in an hotel, gave her a complete establishment of servants, a carriage, cashmeres, diamonds, dentelles, etc. In short, I began the process of ruining myself in the received style ...

After I had broken with the mother, she abandoned her child ... I acknowledged no natural claim on Adèle's part to be supported by me ... but hearing that she was quite destitute, I ... transplanted it here, to grow up clean in the wholesome soil of an English country garden.[6]

On 19 February 1836, the *Courrier des Théâtres* reported that Yolande's health was recovering 'to the great satisfaction of her numerous admirers'. By 27 April, she was well enough to return to the stage, taking the leading role in *Le Dieu et la Bayadère*. During the spring and summer, she danced in several productions, including *La Tentation*, the ballet which had made her famous.

In August, Louis Véron resigned as director of the Opéra, to be replaced in November by the stage designer, Henri Duponchel. Yolande's affair with Véron was over, but she still found him a reassuring presence in the opera house. Her relationship with Duponchel, described as a 'lean, yellowish, pale man ... who looked as if he were in perpetual mourning', was not so comfortable.

In early September, Alfred Bunn arrived in Paris to negotiate for Marie Taglioni to appear at the Theatre Royal, Drury Lane, the following summer. At the same time, he 'concluded an engagement, for immediate purposes, with a lady whom some consider her rival ... Mademoiselle Duvernay, as genuine a specimen of a French dancer, both privately and publicly, as ever sandalled shoe ... It is impossible almost for a Frenchman, certainly for an Englishman, to be a match for a French dancer, who is a perfect mistress of *coquetterie* and has had the principles of *finesse* instilled into her mind from the earliest dawn of comprehension.'[7]

Three weeks later, the company of the Paris Opéra travelled to the Château de Compiègne where an army of 20,000 men was carrying out manoeuvres under the command of the king's two elder sons, the Duc d'Orléans and the Duc de Nemours. According to the Paris correspondent of *The Times*, the theatre at Compiègne:

is formed with exceeding elegance ... The seats are covered with rich crimson velvet and the fronts of the different tiers of boxes, as well as the ceiling of the theatre, are ornamented with gilt mouldings. Five glass chandeliers are suspended from the roof and shed a sparkling brilliancy over the whole of the place ... Much was added to the effect of this scene by the presence of many of the lovely ladies of Compiègne, by the gay colours of the uniforms of the military officers, and by the gorgeous dresses of the Royal party.

The performance on 29 September was *Le Dieu et la Bayadère*, in which Marie Taglioni danced the main role and Yolande danced a *pas de trois* in the first act. At a banquet after the performance, she 'received the most amiable attentions from senior officers' and was introduced to the Duc de Nemours, who teased her about her marksmanship three years before when she had almost impaled him with an arrow.[8]

In late October, Félix de La Valette, who had recently joined the diplomatic service, left for Stockholm on a short-term appointment as secretary to the French ambassador. At the same time, Yolande crossed the Channel for her six-week engagement at the Theatre Royal, Drury Lane, accompanied by her mother and her lover of the moment, one Monsieur Béliser (known as 'le Bélisaire'). Because of her popularity in 1834, she had used her *coquetterie* and *finesse* to persuade Alfred Bunn to pay her a salary of £150 (£15,000) a week.

The men of society awaited her arrival with anticipation. 'The competition for an opera-dancer of celebrity is immense,' wrote *Town* magazine:

> No sooner does she land and her address become known, than a regular bevy attend her dwelling, and envied indeed is the favoured one whom she first honours with her notice. But the nobs have singular ideas of mutual accommodation in this respect; they play a kind of 'follow my leader' game, and it is not at all an uncommon thing to see the lady driven to the theatre in the carriage of one swell, and back in another. She may take the air with a lord in the morning and with a duke in the afternoon.[9]

Yolande opened her third London season on 3 November, dancing in the second act of *The Maid of Cashmere*. The auditorium in the Theatre Royal was 'very full' and she was 'received with rapturous applause'. The critic of *The Times* was impressed:

> Duvernay acted the Bayadère very delightfully. The eloquence of her pantomime and the graceful finish of her dancing were

admirably displayed ... The shawl dance was remarkably well executed, and in particular that portion of it in which the draperies are so arranged as to embody the idea of a shell with Venus crouching in the centre of it. The arrival of this dancer is a subject of congratulation to the play-going public.

On 1 December, she danced the role of Florinda in the first London production of *The Devil on Two Sticks* (*Le Diable Boiteux*) in which she performed an unusual Spanish dance, the *Cachucha*. She stood on stage, castanets in her hands, wearing a pink satin dress trimmed with 'wide flounces' of black lace:

Her wasp-like figure is boldly arched back, making the diamond brooch on her bodice sparkle; her leg, smooth as marble, gleams through the fine mesh of her silk stocking; and her small foot, now still, only awaits the signal from the orchestra to burst into action. How charming she is, with her tall comb, the rose at her ear, the fire in her eyes and her sparkling smile. At the tips of her rosy fingers the ebony castanets are acquiver.

She springs forward and the resonant clatter of her castanets breaks out; she seems to shake down clusters of rhythm with her hands. How she twists! How she bends! What fire! What voluptuousness! What ardour! Her swooning arms flutter about her drooping head, her body curves back, her white shoulders almost brush the floor. What a charming moment! Would you not say that, in that hand as it skims over the dazzling barrier of the footlights, she is gathering up all the desires and all the enthusiasm of the audience?[10]

Yolande infused the dance with sexuality. She teased the men of society who sat in the omnibus boxes, well aware of the effect she was having on their libido. Alfred Bunn spoke of 'Mademoiselle Duvernay's lascivious *Cachucha* dance', while Charles de Boigne, one of her admirers, wrote breathlessly of 'those movements of the hips, those provocative gestures, those arms which seem to seek and embrace an absent lover, that mouth crying out for a kiss, that thrilling, quivering, twisting body ... that shortened skirt, that low-cut, half-open bodice'.[11]

The critic of *The Times* took a more academic view, commenting that Yolande's dancing belonged to 'the first style of the modern school':

Its chief excellence is that absence of all visible effort, which distinguishes truly good dancing from the more common style; the finish and precision with which everything she does is executed add great charms to the gracefulness of her movements and the intrinsic beauty of her form. In the *Cachucha* dance (which is nightly encored and is one of the most universally popular exhibitions of the kind that we have ever witnessed), she does something more; for the spirit and truth which she gives this singularly characteristic dance are as nearly akin to genius as anything in the way of dancing can be.

The *Cachucha* was a huge success and Yolande's sensual performance became the talk of London. A young Mr Simmons was so affected that he sent a poem to *The Times* for publication. It was titled 'To the Dancer Duvernay':

Song's fatal gift, they say, has long been mine
With all its love-fraught dreams, but until now
Never did Love, embodied love, divine,
Clothing the limbs and breathing from the brow,
Sparkle before my smitten sense! The air
Is burning with thy form, never to pass
From the deep mirror of my heart – but there
(While memory watches by the dazzled glass)
Belinked for ever with each lovely thing:
A flower breeze-swung, young morning's rosy cloud,

A blossom floating on the winds of spring.
Incarnate music, poetry endowed
With life, a visible bliss, a dancing thought,
A bounding silence, passion motion-wrought.

'This gentleman,' commented the newspaper when it printed the poem on 13 December, 'seems mightily smitten, and writes even more foolishly than is the privilege of people in his condition. However, the fair *danseuse* is entitled to all the praise she can receive, either from the wise or the silly.'

With the marvels of modern technology, we can see the dance as it was performed at the time, almost as if we are watching Yolande herself on stage. There are videos on YouTube of ballerinas dancing the *Cachucha* to the original choreography and music, and wearing the same pink satin dress trimmed with black lace. It is certainly very different from anything an audience in the 1830s would have seen before.[12]

Yolande was due to return to Paris in mid-December, but her success was so great that Alfred Bunn hoped to retain her services for a further six weeks. She, too, was eager to stay. Bunn negotiated with Henri Duponchel; he paid £80 for the extension and Yolande agreed to add six weeks to the length of her contract in Paris. On 7 December, Bunn announced that 'the enthusiastic reception given to the splendid ballet of *The Devil on Two Sticks* has induced him, notwithstanding the very great expense incurred, to perform it every night until Christmas'.

Princess Victoria was in the royal box on 22 December. The ballet was not to her taste:

It is a stupid subject ... long, heavy and tiresome, nay would not be bearable were it not for the charms of the delightful Mademoiselle Duvernay, who looked lovely, and danced ... and acted beautifully. She certainly is the best after the inimitable Taglioni, as she dances quite in the same quiet, graceful, light style. Duvernay ... has a beautiful figure ... and is so lady-like ... She is very much improved since I last saw her two years and a half ago.

Her two Spanish dresses are beautiful, particularly the one in the second act in which she dances the *Cachucha*, a very singular Spanish dance, all alone, with castanets, which she does *beautifully*, *quite*, so gracefully and with so much spirit. Her last dress, though not perhaps very *lady-like*, is very becoming; it is that of a Spanish officer of former times, and she looks *so* handsome.[13]

Four days later, the Christmas pantomime opened in the Theatre Royal. This included an 'obscene caricature' of Yolande's *Cachucha*, performed by a Mr Matthews, a parody received with 'roars of laughter and applause'. A weekly newspaper was not amused:

The best approved thing in the pantomime was a dance, or rather a series of disgusting postures called in the play-bills 'the popular cashew-nut dance', which was done by the Clown in a dress something like the one worn by Duvernay in the Spanish dance in the ballet recently produced at this theatre ... We cannot tell what are the feelings of Duvernay, but were we a performer of her distinction, and if so gross a parody of anything – universally accounted great – that we had done were given in the theatre that we assisted to support, we would certainly never enter its doors again.[14]

At the end of the article, the newspaper added a comment: 'Since the above was written, we have learnt that Miss Ballin appeared in the *Devil on Two Sticks* on Thursday night, as the substitute for Duvernay, who is reported *indisposed*.'

Yolande remained in a huff for almost two weeks. As the *Theatrical Observer* reported on 2 January:

On Saturday evening Miss Ballin was again the substitute for Duvernay who continues indisposed ... When Miss Ballin consented to undertake the part, her husband applied to Mr Bunn to know what was to be done about the dresses, as it was not to be expected that his wife could hire them; the lessee replied that she should have Duvernay's. On sending to the sick *danseuse* for them, she returned for an answer that if Miss Ballin wore any part of her dresses, she would never enter Drury Lane Theatre again.

Bunn was dismayed that Yolande had taken such exception to the parody. She was contracted to appear at the Theatre Royal until the end of January so he did his best to mollify her. When she finally returned to the stage on the 7th, she was 'received with great enthusiasm'. On the 24th, she gave her benefit performance and was 'overpowered by plaudits; overwhelmed by garlands and bouquets; at one time she was affected even to tears by the enthusiastic applause'.[15]

The additional six weeks at the Theatre Royal had ended but Yolande's popularity was still so great that Laporte, manager of the King's Theatre in the Haymarket, was now in negotiation with Duponchel to keep her in London for a further two months. At first Duponchel refused but, after Laporte offered to pay £200 and Yolande agreed to add a further two months to the length of her contract in Paris, he agreed that she could stay in London.

She opened in the King's Theatre on 25 February in a new ballet, *Le Brigand de Terracina*, which included a *pas seul* danced in a nightgown before a mirror. Her performance received glowing reviews. *The Times* wrote that 'the dancing was very good, particularly the *pas seul* of Duvernay in her nightdress before the looking-glass; her expression of perfect simplicity is exceedingly clever'. The *Morning Herald* considered the *pas seul* to be 'one of the most charming pieces of acting ever exhibited on any stage'. The critic of *The Satirist* was quite overcome:

The bedroom scene is rendered by her quite as warm – to say nothing further – as the frequenters even of the stalls can desire. The fashion in which she reclines on the bed we must not attempt to describe, but it inspired the bald-pated part of the audience (those whose brains are too ardent for the continued existence of hair above the ears) with intense delight.

On 16 March, the King's Theatre revived the ballet *Beniowsky*, which now included the famous *Cachucha*. Princess Victoria watched a performance on 1 April and wrote in her diary that Yolande performed a *pas de deux* 'delightfully and looked very pretty' and danced the *Cachucha* 'with great grace, spirit and character; she dances it delightfully. I am very fond of this dance, for it is so characteristic, peculiar and so truly Spanish; the actions are certainly somewhat bold, but Duvernay dances it in great perfection. She was compelled to repeat it.'[16]

Twelve days later, on 13 April, Yolande gave her benefit performance in the King's Theatre, dancing the *Cachucha* and the *pas seul* before the mirror. The occasion was 'a tremendous hit', according to the critic of *The Times*:

> The house seemed as full as it could be ... a brilliant as well as a crowded one, a larger number of the subscribers than usual retaining their boxes for this occasion ... Mademoiselle Duvernay's rise in general estimation has been rapidly accelerated in this and the past season, yet it rests evidently on the most secure basis – that of pleasing unaffected manners, in addition to real merit.

As Yolande acknowledged the applause from the audience, she may have seen, sitting alone in a private box close to the stage, a small man of unremarkable appearance leaning forward in his seat and gazing intently in her direction. He was the curiously named Stephens Lyne Stephens. He was thirty-five years old and heir to one of the largest non-aristocratic fortunes in the country.

4

A PRINCELY FORTUNE

Mr Stephens might make a vast deal more money by the factory than he does. He is already one of the richest men in Portugal and there is not, I suppose, a better man in any country.

Antony Gibbs, 10 December 1798

While Yolande remains on stage at her benefit performance, acknowledging the applause from the audience, this story goes back in time to the origins of the Lyne Stephens fortune and the circumstances which led the unassuming young man in the opera box to make the biggest decision of his life.

The story of the fortune began in 1778 when the young man's father, Charles Lyne, moved to Lisbon at the age of fourteen, invited there by his father's cousins, the Stephens brothers, who had made their home in Portugal. Charles worked as a merchant in Lisbon for twenty-five years and became rich in his own right from the lucrative business of Anglo-Portuguese trade.

English merchants in Portugal were laden with privileges. Under several treaties, they were exempt from domestic taxes, from the jurisdiction of Portuguese courts, and from most commercial regulations. Through their activities, the country had become reliant on imports, unable to feed or clothe its people from its own resources. It depended on imports of textiles, wheat, fish and other foodstuffs, which it paid for in gold and diamonds from the mines of Brazil – and because of the advantages conferred by treaty, it was the British merchants who handled the bulk of this highly profitable trade.

Nine years before Charles arrived in Portugal, his eldest cousin, William Stephens, had been given ownership of the royal glass factory in the village of Marinha Grande, ninety miles north of Lisbon. He was also granted a number of important privileges: exemption from all domestic taxes; a monopoly of glass supply in Portugal and its colonies; freedom to set his own prices; and free use of fuel from the royal pine forest, a valuable benefit because of the energy-intensive nature of glass production.

These privileges allowed William to build up an enormous fortune. They also allowed him to create a welfare state in Marinha Grande, decades ahead of similar developments in Britain. He paid good wages; opened a school where his apprentices received an education; provided a first-aid post where sick or injured workers were treated free of charge; organised a relief fund for illness; and set up a generous pension scheme. He employed teachers of music and dance, and built a theatre to one side of his private garden. Every Sunday, his glassworkers acted in theatrical productions, including plays translated from Shakespeare and Voltaire.

William's estates in the area totalled 15,000 acres of scrub and heath, which he used to extract sand for use in the factory. Having seen the poor harvests obtained by local farmers, and the backward methods used to cultivate the soil, he reclaimed some of his land and used it to teach more up-to-date methods of cultivation. He introduced the rotation of crops and imported mechanical seed drills and iron ploughs from England. He planted vegetable gardens and orchards, with fruit trees grown from imported seed.

The factory became so well known that it was visited twice by the reigning queen of Portugal, Maria I, together with the royal family and the entire court. The second visit, in July 1788, lasted for three days; Maria slept in William's private house and attended two performances in the factory theatre. As his sister Philadelphia wrote to a cousin in London:

> The performers acquitted themselves with honour and received universal applause, not only from the Royal Family but from all the audience who thought it impossible that a rude country place like this could have produced such good actors. Their surprise was greatly increased on finding that the greatest part of them had never been more than two or three leagues from this parish, and that they all worked in the Fabrick ...
>
> My brother has attained what nobody else in the Kingdom can boast of, which is the honour of entertaining the Royal Family and all the Court for two days, and given universal satisfaction to everybody from the Queen down to the scullions and stable boys. The first time of Her Majesty's coming here was not so surprising, as curiosity to see the Glass Fabrick was supposed to be the motive, but that she should come a second time and sleep two nights in the house of a private person, an Englishman and a Protestant, is a thing that never entered the idea of the Portuguese and has struck all people with amazement.[1]

'I never saw so excellent an establishment,' wrote the merchant Antony Gibbs when he visited the factory ten years later, 'where such strict discipline is observed to the hours of attendance or more diligence appears through the work of the day ... Mr Stephens might make a vast deal more money by the factory than he does. He is already one of the richest men in Portugal and there is not, I suppose, a better man in any country.'[2]

William Stephens died in 1803, leaving the factory and his fortune to his younger brother, John James. Twenty-three years later, John James left the factory to the Portuguese state, legacies totalling £64,000, and his entire residuary estate to his 'much loved and respected cousin Charles Lyne'. This consisted of John James's financial assets in Portugal, described by the British consul in Lisbon as 'a princely fortune of above £700,000', together with considerable financial securities in London.

Charles had left Portugal in 1803 to become leading partner in the merchant house of Lyne, Hathorn and Roberts in the City of London. He gained a reputation as a shrewd and able businessman, and in the spring of 1810 he was called to give evidence before the select committee investigating the high price of bullion. Against his advice, the committee concluded that over-issue of banknotes had led to the depreciation of paper money against the price of gold and recommended a return to the gold standard no less than two years in the future.[3]

A few months later, after the politician William Huskisson had written a pamphlet endorsing the committee's conclusion, Charles published a pamphlet of his own. Exasperated by what he perceived as ignorance, he explained that Huskisson's opinions were 'erroneous and dangerous in the extreme. Never was a doctrine more pregnant with evil nor, thank God, one founded upon more fallacious principles.'[4]

He then gave a complicated description of exchange rates between countries and shipments of bullion from one country to another to explain the high price of gold against paper money. 'Mr Lyne lays considerable stress upon the state of exchanges between the different countries of Europe,' wrote another merchant after reading his pamphlet, 'which I am persuaded hardly any man in this country can comprehend.'[5]

Parliament rejected the committee's recommendation. The price of gold continued to rise and, in need of bullion to cover the increasing costs of Wellington's campaigns in the Peninsular War, the government asked the Bank of England to buy gold to the value of £2 million. Impressed by Charles's trading experience with South America, the Bank employed Lyne, Hathorn and Roberts to import half this amount from Brazil.

After writing detailed instructions about the types of gold to be purchased, weighing and measuring techniques, insurance and shipping matters, Charles urged his agent in Brazil to strict secrecy:

> An operation of this nature may be viewed with no small degree of jealousy. It is therefore our most particular desire that you exert your utmost skill to do the transaction in that circumspect, careful, quiet manner, so that no person but yourself shall ever know the extent to which you are to carry out your operations. Nothing further should be known, even to your confidential clerks and assistants, than what may be absolutely necessary. The management and execution of the operation must be confined to as few of your clerks as possible and the greatest secrecy be enjoined, not only to them, but also to the captains and officers of the ships which take off the gold.[6]

Lyne, Hathorn and Roberts received a commission of 6 per cent on the transaction, of which a third was passed to the agent in Brazil. The bank covered all transport and insurance costs, so the profit on the deal was £40,000 (£3 million).

Charles had retired from business when he inherited John James's fortune in November 1826. 'In grateful and affectionate regard for the memory of his kinsman from whom he derives considerable property', he applied for royal licence to take the name Lyne Stephens. To his own assets of half a million pounds, he had added the Stephens wealth of more than a million, a total fortune estimated at over £150 million in today's values.

The heir to all this wealth was his only son, the unassuming young man in the opera box. Given a plural name in honour of both his cousins in Portugal, Stephens Lyne was born on 4 October 1801. The only son in a family of four daughters, he was brought up by nurses and maidservants in a narrow terraced house in Devonshire Place in London and was unaccustomed to the rough and tumble of normal boyhood.

During his childhood, his father spent long hours in his counting-house in the City and had firm opinions on how young men should conduct themselves in business. William Gibbs, twenty-one years old, received a taste of these when he visited Devonshire Place on 20 April 1812. As he wrote to his brother that night:

> It struck me that, having been ill and having no one to pour out his advice upon for some time, he thought it a good opportunity of relieving himself of it and giving it all to me. First I was to remove to his part of the town ... and ride into the City every morning with merchants of the first eminence who lived in the same neighbourhood and with whom I was instructed how to get acquainted.
>
> Then I was never to [attend] a gambling club, even though I had no intention to play – no, no, it must never be said that Mr William Gibbs was *even seen* at such a place. It was a bad custom too, which many young men had, of continually lounging away their evenings at playhouses, but there was a place at which I should now and then appear, as being a gentlemanlike and proper place, and that was the opera. It is well that I should be seen there now and then ...
>
> I dine there on Friday when I suppose I shall have an improved edition of my conversation with him this morning. He is certainly a very clever, sharp man, and though he carries his line of dictating to others to a disagreeable length, yet I believe he means well and a good deal of very useful information may be gained from him.[7]

On Friday evening, he was regaled with another 'interesting and instructive' lecture, during which Charles's wife fell asleep on the sofa. 'It is astonishing what a deal of information one gets out of the little man,' he wrote the following morning. Some of Charles's advice may have proved useful: in years to come, William Gibbs would make a fortune from the importation of guano from South

America and he built Tyntesfield, the Gothic Revival house in Somerset now owned by the National Trust.

At the time of William's visit to Devonshire Place, Stephens had spent two years as a boarding pupil at Fulham Park House, a 'respectable school' in Parson's Green run by the Reverend Joshua Ruddock and a widow, Mrs Bowen, 'a comely plump matron in a stone-coloured silk gown'. One of his near-contemporaries was Edward Bulwer-Lytton, who arrived at the school in 1812. In his memoirs, Bulwer-Lytton described his first day at what he called 'that horrible institution', an ordeal which Stephens had undergone two years earlier:

Mrs Bowen [who] had more especial charge of the younger children ... good-naturedly sent two boys, not much older than myself, to spend the evening with me in the parlour, and explain the nature of the place. These boys seemed to me like fiends ... their language was filthily obscene and my ignorance of its meaning excited their contempt, which they vented in vague threats and mocking jeers ...

Once in my little crib, I thought I was safe; but scarcely had I cried myself into an unquiet doze, when I was suddenly seized, dragged from bed, and carried away in the dark, gagged and bound ... I was borne into the open air, on a cold winter's night; and, two of my tormentors laying hold of my arms, and two of my legs, I was swung against the trunk of a tree in the playground, to undergo an operation termed bumping.[8]

After leaving the school, Stephens was admitted to Trinity College, Cambridge, where he took four and a half years to complete what was normally a three-year course of study. 'Cambridge is but a short distance from that place of sporting notoriety, Newmarket,' explained a writer of the time, 'so it is next to impossible but that a youth of an inspiring mind should be up to all the manoeuvres of a racecourse.'[9]

In 1825, at a cost of £840, his father bought him a commission in the Tenth Hussars. A year later, at even greater expense, he bought a promotion to the rank of lieutenant. The regiment was based in Leicestershire in December 1826 when Stephens received news of his father's inheritance. As he obtained leave and hurried home to London, the government was arranging to send troops to Portugal to help keep the peace in a country which was on the brink of civil war.

The Tenth Hussars formed the cavalry brigade; two squadrons sailed for Lisbon, a third was stationed in Ipswich as a depot. Overlooked for the service squadrons because of his absence in London, Stephens was the only lieutenant to remain in England. He travelled to Ipswich in January 1827 and remained there for thirteen months until the service squadrons returned from Portugal.

In January 1828, his father gave up the house in Devonshire Place and acquired a much grander property in Portman Square. This was a prestigious address comprising 'forty noble houses' occupied by two dukes, six earls, one viscount, four lords, and assorted knights, baronets, honourables and titled widows. Number 32, which Charles rented for £600 a year, had previously been the home of Lady Anne Hamilton, lady-in-waiting to Queen Caroline.

It was a much diminished family that moved into their new home. Stephens's eldest sister had died in 1817 (aged fourteen), followed by his mother in 1820 and his second sister in 1824 (aged nineteen). His two surviving sisters, Louisa and Sophia, were now in great demand by young men eager to marry into money. As Charles boasted to his elder brother in Cornwall:

Among the many offers of marriage made to my daughters, a number have been from young noblemen, one of them an earl for Louisa which, if she had fancied, she might have been a countess at this moment, and this besides other noblemen who have offered for her and also for her sister, among whom are some of the first families of rank.

Charles had hoped to be a peer himself by this time, hopes dashed when Lord Liverpool, the prime minister, suffered a massive stroke in April 1827 and was found paralysed and unconscious on the floor. Lord Liverpool had admired Charles's intellect and, as news of his inheritance spread through London society, he had offered him a peerage:

> Before Lord Liverpool was seized with the violent attack with which he lays so dangerously ill, I had the offer of being made a peer and Stephens a baronet. I refused the offer without hesitation and left it to my son to accept the baronetcy or not as he might like. He also refused the offer and my daughters appeared well pleased that we had declined, observing that ostentatious honours were of no good.

Charles was making the best of the situation. He would have loved a peerage but had declined in a show of humility, assuming that the prime minister would remain in power and make the offer for a second time. This was unwise for Lord Liverpool never regained his faculties. He was replaced by George Canning and then by the Duke of Wellington, men with whom Charles had little acquaintance.

Stephens sold his commission in the spring of 1828, preferring to spend his father's fortune in a life of leisure. Six months later, he and his family left London to spend several weeks in Brighton. They were staying in the Albion Hotel on the seafront when his youngest sister Sophia – who had been in the best of health and spirits – suffered a sudden brain haemorrhage and died on 1 November. She was nineteen years old.

Two days later, at five o'clock in the morning, a carriage-hearse left the Albion Hotel to carry Sophia's body home to London where she was buried with her mother and sisters in a private vault under St Marylebone church. 'The shock to the family,' wrote a newspaper in Brighton, 'has been enervatingly great.'

5

THE *PARVENU*

Lyne Stephens, hail! From Thames to Coaly Tyne,
Our land can boast no better soul than thine.
Poem quoted in *The Sporting Review*, September 1846

Five months after Sophia's death, Charles opened his London mansion to society, hosting the first of many grand dinners with food served on plates of solid silver. 'The Portman Square house soon had a name for good dinners,' wrote one of his nephews. 'The Duke of Cambridge considered the cook "not bad", Lord Eldon found no fault, and the newspapers would announce when the Lyne Stephens dinners for the London season had commenced.'[1]

While his father entertained high society in Portman Square, Stephens became a young man-about-town. He frequented the theatre, was a founder member of the Garrick Club, and was elected to Crockford's, the gambling house in St James's Street which opened in 1828. Captain Gronow – who would accompany Yolande and Edward Ellice to the Star and Garter in Richmond – described Crockford's in its early days:

A supper of the most exquisite kind ... accompanied by the best wines in the world, together with every luxury of the season, was furnished gratis. The members of the club included all the celebrities of England, from the Duke of Wellington to the youngest Ensign of the Guards. At the gay and festive board, which was constantly replenished from midnight to early dawn, the most brilliant sallies of wit, the most agreeable conversation, the most interesting anecdotes, interspersed with grave political discussions, and acute logical reasoning on every conceivable subject, proceeded from the soldiers, scholars, statesmen, poets, and men of pleasure, who, when the balls and parties were at an end, delighted to finish their evening with a little supper and a good deal of hazard at old Crockey's.[2]

During the first two seasons of the club, a total of £300,000 changed hands, much of it into the pockets of William Crockford, a man who had started life as a London fishmonger. Fortunes were won and lost, particularly on the hazard table where stakes of £1000 were placed on the fall of the dice. As Gronow described it:

Who that ever entered that dangerous little room can ever forget the large green table with the croupiers with their suave manners, sleek appearance, stiff white neckcloths, and the almost miraculous quickness and dexterity with which they swept away the money of the unfortunate punters.[3]

Stephens was an enthusiastic player at the hazard table, building up significant debts which had to be subsidised by his father. When *The Satirist* summed up the betting season at Crockford's in July 1832, he was listed as one of the main losers:

As the season for play is drawing to a close ... our readers may be curious to learn who have been winners and who losers. Among the successful winners of the season, we may instance Lord Queensberry ... Tom Duncombe and Count d'Orsay. In the list of losers are the Duke of Buccleugh, Lords Castlereagh, Ranelagh, Allen and Tullamore ... and Lyne Stephens.

He also took up country pursuits. He attended shooting parties. He bought a string of racehorses and appeared at all the important race meetings of the season. He spent the winter riding to hounds with the Quorn Hunt in Melton Mowbray, the most fashionable and expensive hunt in the country. According to Nimrod, a sporting journalist:

> A winter in Leicestershire is the *passe-partout* that leads to the best society in the world. When turned out of the hands of his valet, the Meltonian fox-hunter presents the very beau ideal of his caste. The exact fit of his coat, his superlatively well-cleaned leather breeches and boots, and the high breeding of the man can seldom be matched elsewhere.[4]

Stephens had learnt to enjoy hunting in 1826 when the Tenth Hussars was based in Leicestershire. 'The Tenth has placed fox-hunting above all sports,' wrote a fellow officer. 'It gives a quick eye, knowledge of terrain, the requisite dash and *going straight*.' During his first three seasons in Melton Mowbray, he stayed at the George Hotel which offered high standards of comfort and had an excellent cook; he also dined at the Old Club which held banquets several nights a week.

Before Stephens left London for his first winter in Melton Mowbray, his father signed an agreement with Sir John Osborn to rent Chicksands Priory in Bedfordshire. A religious house of the Gilbertine order, the Priory dated from the mid-twelfth century and was acquired by the Osborn family after the dissolution of the monasteries. During the autumn and winter of 1829, Charles made plans to redecorate the house and build a new stable block. In the spring, he made arrangements for the marriage of his only surviving daughter, Louisa, to Captain Charles Bulkeley of the Life Guards.

The marriage took place in St Mary's, Bryanston Square, on 1 June 1830. Bulkeley was already a rich young man and, as he departed on honeymoon, his wealth was increased by a dowry worth £20 million in today's money. 'Chicksands is let to Mr Lyne

Stephens, who is building stables and otherwise doing a great deal to the house,' wrote an elderly lady in Bedfordshire a few days after the wedding. 'He certainly has a million of money. Married his daughter last week and *only* gave her £200,000.'

Less than four weeks later, the death of George IV provided an opportunity for Stephens to become a member of parliament. It was a time of increasing demand for reform. Despite the changes of the Industrial Revolution, parliament remained in the hands of the land-owning classes. Charles's home county of Cornwall returned forty-four members, while the industrial towns of England had no members at all. In the boroughs of England, seats were bought and voters bribed, while the growing middle classes had no voice in electing their representatives.

The king's death increased the clamour for change. There were fears of revolution if parliament remained unreformed for much longer, fears fostered by the July Revolution in France which catapulted Yolande to fame and toppled the Bourbon monarchy. Although the prime minister, the Duke of Wellington, opposed reform of any kind, the mood of the people soon led to a general election.

Charles was eager that his son should stand for parliament, an aim encouraged by a neighbour in Portman Square, George Tudor, who was standing for Barnstaple in north Devon where the two sitting members had decided not to contest their seats. On 14 July, Stephens and his father drafted a letter to 'the worthy and independent freemen of the Borough of Barnstaple':

I hasten to offer myself as a candidate for the honour of representing your ancient and respectable Borough. Totally unconnected with any political party, I come forward with perfectly independent principles. A firm attachment to our excellent Constitution, and a steady and loyal devotion to the welfare and best interests of my country, are the grounds on which I venture to solicit your support. Should I be so fortunate as to succeed in the high object of my ambition ... I will most anxiously endeavour to prove myself worthy of your choice by a careful attention to your local interests, a strict regard to retrenchment and economy in the public expenditure, and a conscientious performance of my duties in Parliament.[5]

He visited Barnstaple a few days later, stopping at the almshouse to make a donation of £10 before canvassing the town and making 'a manly and eloquent speech' at the Castle Inn. At the election on 2 August, he topped the poll with 370 votes; George Tudor came second with 332.

It had cost Charles £5,130 (£530,000) for his son to enter parliament, £1,400 in today's money for every man who voted for him. Half of them lived outside Barnstaple, mostly in London. Their expenses amounted to £2,200; voters in the town were entertained at an additional £1,730; the election dinner cost £500; lodgings for Stephens and his valet were estimated at £200; and a further £500 was spent on agents and managers.

Three weeks after the election, Charles left London for his first autumn season in Chicksands, accompanied by Louisa and her husband who had returned from honeymoon to live with him in Portman Square. Stephens remained in London as parliament had been summoned to meet on 14 September; it was then prorogued and he joined his family at Chicksands to host a shooting party. At the end of the month, he returned to London, was sworn in as a member of parliament, and attended the House on 2 November when the Commons began to debate the King's Speech.

Stephens allied himself with the ultra-Tories, a right-wing faction which opposed Catholic emancipation and had split from the government in protest at the passing of the Catholic Relief Act in 1829. On 15 November, he was one of twenty-nine members who voted against the government in a division on the Civil List. This led to a government defeat. Wellington resigned, Lord Grey took the helm of a new Whig government, and during the winter of 1830/31, the Whigs worked in secret on plans to reform the representation of the country.

In late November, Stephens left London for Melton Mowbray and remained there for almost four months. As a result, he missed the dramatic sitting on 1 March 1831 when the paymaster-general, Lord John Russell, introduced the Reform Bill in the House of Commons.

It was six o'clock in the evening. The chamber was packed and the atmosphere electric. How widely would the bill extend the franchise? How many boroughs would be purged as land-owning peers lost their right to control seats in parliament? Soon the members learned that sixty boroughs would be abolished, while a further forty-six would lose one of their members. As Russell announced the names of the condemned boroughs, he was greeted by shouts of laughter from men unable to believe that such huge change was possible. 'More yet,' said Russell, smiling, before listing the boroughs which would have reduced representation.

Stephens also missed the first reading of the bill on 14 March, despite having been summoned to appear that day in the Commons. He arrived in London two days later and was present in the House when the bill was read for a second time during the evening of the 22nd.

The debate lasted for much of the night. The vote was taken shortly before three o'clock in the morning and, when the Speaker announced the numbers, it was learnt that the bill had been passed by just one vote: 302 votes to 301, the fullest House in parliamentary history. As an ultra-Tory, Stephens had voted against the bill, despite a petition from the voters of Barnstaple asking him to support it.

Five days later, he attended one of his father's grand dinners before returning to Melton Mowbray to enjoy the last few days of the hunting season. He was back in London when parliament reassembled on 18 April and the Reform Bill went into committee. The following day, after the government was defeated on a motion affecting the bill, Lord Grey asked William IV to dissolve parliament and allow him to obtain a larger majority in a general election.

At first the king refused but, on 21 April, he changed his mind. Next morning, he ordered the royal robes to be prepared and the crown sent over from the Tower of London. Appropriately dressed, he set out for Westminster in the early afternoon, cannons firing to signal his approach. Parliament had been forewarned of his intentions and the Commons was in uproar:

> The Speaker was agitated and several members were not collected enough to receive his decisions with the usual deference. Honourable members turned upon each other, growling contradictions. The spokesman of the opposition gained a hearing but, as soon as he was in full flow, boom! came the cannon which told that the King was on his way, and the roar drowned the conclusion of his sentence. Not a word more was heard for the cheers, cries and shouts of laughter, all put down at regular intervals by discharges of artillery.[6]

On entering the Lords, the king asked that the Commons be summoned and the members rushed in 'very tumultuously'. Flushed by the drama, his crown sitting awry on his head, the king read his speech and promptly returned to his carriage.

As the country prepared for a general election in May on the single issue of 'The Bill, the whole Bill, and nothing but the Bill', Stephens decided not to defend his seat. Opinion was overwhelmingly in favour of reform and he had no hope of re-election. As a flyer in Barnstaple put it:

> We will not lend our support to any individual who has opposed the progress of the Reform Bill, and we will frustrate all attempts to continue those infamous and fraudulent practices which have hitherto stigmatised this borough as the nest of fraud and corruption.[7]

Stephens's sister Louisa was now three months pregnant with her first child. To protect her from the jolting of a carriage journey to

Chicksands, the family remained in Portman Square until her baby was born in October. In a cruel twist of fate after the early deaths of her three sisters, Louisa was infected during the birth and she died a few weeks later. In despair at the loss of his fourth daughter, Charles asked his son-in-law to continue to live with him; with Stephens absent for several months every winter, he needed the company of Bulkeley and his infant granddaughter.

At the end of the month, Stephens returned to Melton Mowbray where he had recently teamed up with two brothers, William Massey Stanley and Rowland Errington, to form the New Club in premises opposite the George Hotel. Here the three men lived together and, as they employed one of the best chefs in the country (Francatelli, who later became chef at Crockford's), the club became renowned for its dinners.

In the spring of 1833, eighteen months after Louisa's death, Stephens persuaded his father to build him a stable block in Melton Mowbray, together with a coach-house and groom's accommodation, at a total cost of £2,000 (£215,000). There were 'summering yards and sheds, properly fenced off, and a large exercising yard, the whole comprising 2,769 yards of ground ... the most complete establishment of the kind in the Midland counties'.[8]

The buildings, which boasted the Lyne Stephens coat of arms in a prominent position above the hayloft, were completed in October. As his grooms and stable boys transferred his horses to their new accommodation, Stephens visited the dealers to increase his stock of thoroughbreds. Soon his stables contained eighteen horses and, with partitions of polished mahogany and a livery of green blankets embroidered in gold, they became renowned as the most luxurious in the town.

Later that winter he sat for the artist Francis Grant, who was working on a scene in the breakfast room of the Old Club. The painting, known as *The Melton Breakfast*, was commissioned by Rowland Errington, the newly appointed master of the Quorn hounds. It portrays a number of notable Meltonians. Stephens is depicted at the back of the group, sitting eagerly but unobtrusively on a sofa, while Errington, Massey Stanley and several men of title are engaged in various activities in the foreground. According to the *Morning Post*, 'the attitudes are all natural and easy, and the turn-out just what you might expect to see at Melton ... a spirited and gentlemanly representation of men about to engage in a spirited and gentlemanly amusement'.[9]

Meanwhile, Stephens's brother-in-law had married again the previous November and was continuing to live with Charles in Portman Square and Chicksands Priory. Stephens found this distressing; it seemed to him that the new wife had usurped Louisa's place in the family home. Unwilling to spend the summer with them in Portman Square, he suggested to Rowland Errington that they cross the Channel in March and spend the next six months together on the Continent.

They returned to England in September, a few weeks before the announcement of another general election. Once again, his father persuaded Stephens to stand for parliament, this time as a candidate for his home town of Liskeard in Cornwall. It was known that he had voted against the Reform Bill, so his election address had to be worded carefully. It was drafted on 25 November 1834 in Chicksands Priory:

My name is not altogether unknown to you, my family having long been connected with your town and neighbourhood. With regard to my principles, I am firmly attached to our unrivalled Constitution and therefore opposed to any sudden or incautious changes, while at the same time, I am not one of those who think that all improvement is impossible, or would resist the reformation of acknowledged evils. Such legislation would receive my most cordial support as would have for its object the protection of those great interests from which spring the prosperity of our country. I mean the agricultural and commercial, both of which ... appear to be endangered from the efforts of those who can see no safety but in perpetual change.

He concluded the address with the words 'it is my intention very shortly to pay my personal respects to you', but he never made the journey to Liskeard. Instead he withdrew from the contest and transferred his candidacy to Sudbury in Suffolk, where the existing member was retiring and where his father thought he had a greater chance of success. He spent a few days in Sudbury over Christmas:

> About four o'clock on the 22nd, Stephens Lyne Stephens entered the town and declared himself a candidate in the Conservative Interest. He commenced a spirited canvass, which he concluded on the 25th with every prospect of a triumphant result. After addressing the electors from the window of the Rose and Crown, Mr Lyne Stephens left the same evening for town.[10]

At the poll on 12 January, Stephens received the least number of votes. He then returned to Melton Mowbray for the last three months of the season. During the summer of 1835, he avoided the company of his brother-in-law and spent as little time as possible in Portman Square. In the early autumn, Charles and the Bulkeleys moved to Chicksands Priory where, on 20 September, Bulkeley's second wife gave birth to a daughter.

Two weeks later, Stephens arrived at Chicksands to host a shooting party. The two brothers-in-law were hardly on speaking terms and, one evening, when the house was full of guests, their feelings of bitterness and resentment erupted into an angry confrontation. According to Francis Lyne, one of Stephens's cousins:

> Captain Bulkeley quarrelled with my cousin Stephens and challenged him. Two officers of the Guards acted as seconds. As men of honour and gentlemen, they did the best they could and there was no fighting, but the commotion in the house was very great and, when it reached my uncle's ears, he said that a man who would seek to take the life of his son should not rest under his roof.

Early next morning, Charles Bulkeley, with his wife and children, left the house to know my uncle's face no more.[11]

Eight months later, Charles decided to give up Chicksands Priory. The ancient building had given him status, but it was remote and secluded and a solitary place for an elderly man to live alone. After Stephens hosted a final shooting party in October 1836, he and his father packed up their possessions and returned to Portman Square.

On 3 November, Stephens left London for Melton Mowbray. That same evening, Yolande opened her third London season, dancing in the second act of *The Maid of Cashmere* at the Theatre Royal, Drury Lane. On 6 November, Stephens and his friends enjoyed the opening dinner of the season and the Quorn hounds met for the first time the following morning.

During the winter, several sportsmen arrived in Melton Mowbray with stories of Yolande and her 'lascivious' *Cachucha*. Stephens had missed her previous London seasons (he was in Melton Mowbray in 1833; the following year he was travelling on the Continent). When news arrived in February of her further engagement at the King's Theatre, he wrote to his father asking him to buy a private box. On the 28th, Charles made a note in his account book: 'Payment to Laporte, opera box, £273.'

Every year, the hunting season ended with the Croxton Park Races which, in 1837, took place on 5/6 April. Three stewards were appointed – Lord Wilton, Lord Forester and Stephens Lyne Stephens – and the races attracted particularly large crowds. 'There were more strangers of rank and fashion than usual', reported the newspapers, 'and large dinner parties most evenings at the New Club.'

After the races, Stephens hurried home to London. On the evening of 13 April, he left Portman Square and made his way to the King's Theatre in the Haymarket. It was the evening of Yolande's benefit performance and he was eager to see what all the fuss was about.

6

THE LAST ADVENTURE

She danced like a fairy and died as a sylph should die; her tiny
wings dropping from their place, her gentle form bending like a
reed, and her whole frame not struggling but fainting into death.
Morning Post, on Yolande's performance in
La Sylphide, 26 April 1837

The auditorium was humming with anticipation, crowded with men and women of society eager to catch a glimpse of the celebrated Duvernay. 'Not only was every place which could command a view of the stage occupied,' wrote the critic of *The Times*, 'but many were content to traverse the lobbies for an occasional sight of it.'

As Stephens took a seat in his new private box near the stage, he was aware of a sense of dissatisfaction. In the ten years since his father inherited the fortune from Portugal, he had received monthly allowances totalling £80,000 (£8 million), more than enough for a life of indulgence, extravagance and pleasure, only briefly interrupted by a few sittings in a short-lived parliament. At the same time, he had failed to take advantage of many of the opportunities which had come his way.

He had missed a sojourn in Portugal, the source of his father's fortune, because of his absence from his regiment. He had turned down the offer of a baronetcy in deference to his father who was gambling on Lord Liverpool retaining his health. His parliamentary career was undistinguished: he never once spoke in the House and he missed debates on the Reform Bill, one of the most important bills in parliamentary history, because he preferred to be in Melton Mowbray with his horses.

He mixed with high society in Crockford's, on the racecourse and in the hunting field, but he was disadvantaged by the nature of his father's wealth. The Lyne Stephens fortune was made in trade and industry at a time when society treated all such work with disdain. He had inherited his father's lack of stature, but not his self-confident personality. He was acutely conscious that society looked down upon him as a *nouveau-riche*, a *parvenu*.

Living alone with his father in Portman Square, mixing only in male company in Melton Mowbray, he felt nostalgic for the female companionship that surrounded and comforted him when he was a child. He missed his mother, who died during his second year at Cambridge, as well as his four sisters, who had all died so young.

The noise in the auditorium quietened as the curtain rose to reveal Yolande standing on stage in her pink satin dress trimmed with black lace. As the orchestra played the first note, she snapped her castanets and began to dance. For the last two chapters she has been frozen in time, waiting for Stephens to take his seat in the opera box. Now, as she finishes the dance and comes forward to acknowledge the applause, an idea begins to take shape in his mind.

Not only might this beautiful young woman provide the female companionship that was so lacking in his life, but society might regard him more favourably if he could persuade such a celebrated ballerina to become his mistress. It was considered a 'great accomplishment', as Tom Duncombe, one of his gambling friends, described it:

> to cultivate intimate relations with the reigning *favorita*. It passed for admiration of genius. The 'protector' of the beautiful *danseuse* was certain of exciting the envy of his less fortunate associates, till

the lady left him for a more liberal admirer. This was so expensive a luxury that only an opera-goer with a handsome income could venture to indulge in it, but it was so fashionable that married men, even elderly men, were proud of the distinction.[1]

Yolande's contract was due to expire two days after her benefit performance, after which she would soon return to Paris. Stephens had little time to devise a plan of action, but events turned in his favour. On 24 April, the King's Theatre published an announcement in *The Times* and other newspapers:

> Mr Laporte has the honour to inform the supporters of the opera that, in compliance with the numerous wishes of the subscribers, he has with difficulty succeeded in effecting an arrangement with the director of the Paris Opéra, which has enabled him at considerable expense to make a further engagement of Mademoiselle Duvernay who will appear in the favourite ballet of *La Sylphide* tomorrow evening.

Yolande would remain in London until the season ended in August, a concession for which Laporte paid Henri Duponchel £300 and Yolande agreed to add a further four months to the length of her contract in Paris. She had also agreed to dance at the King's Theatre between April and July the following year, an arrangement which had not yet been confirmed with Duponchel.

During the previous nine days, Stephens had invited her to dinners and given her gifts of expensive jewellery. She had shown no interest. Now he had time to devise an alternative strategy. He approached Laporte at the King's Theatre, who advised him to target Madame Duvernay, a woman who was happy to be paid for her daughter's favours.

Hoping that a French aristocrat would be the right man to conduct negotiations with Yolande's mother, Stephens called on Count Alfred d'Orsay, a man he had known for several years. They were founder members of the Garrick Club, as well as fellow members of Crockford's, and d'Orsay hunted from time to time at Melton Mowbray.

Over 6 feet tall, strikingly handsome and always most exquisitely turned out, Count d'Orsay was known as the king of the dandies. He drove around London in a green coach, its white wheels striped with green and crimson. 'When I saw him driving in his tilbury,' wrote Captain Gronow, 'he looked like some gorgeous dragonfly skimming through the air.'

D'Orsay took on the task with pleasure. An *habitué* of the theatre, he already knew Yolande; he had entertained her to dinners during her London seasons and given her gifts of jewellery and fans. Stephens gave him some leeway in the negotiation – money was not an issue and he was flexible on the length of the arrangement – but he insisted that she should leave the stage and remain with him in England. Her celebrity was too great to risk the attentions she would receive from other men.

Yolande was staying with her mother and le Bélisaire in an apartment in the Haymarket. D'Orsay made several visits to talk privately to Madame Duvernay and her lover, and had no difficulty persuading them of the merits of Stephens's proposal. Persuading Yolande was another matter. Of all the men clamouring for her favours, he was 'the suitor she liked the least'. She was stubborn in her refusal and dissolved into tears whenever his name was mentioned.

On 25 April, she danced the title role in *La Sylphide* for the first time in London. 'She danced like a fairy,' wrote the critic of the *Morning Post*, 'and died as a sylph should die; her tiny wings dropping from their place, her gentle form bending like a reed, and her whole frame not struggling but fainting into death.' This is a poignant image. The sylph was dying, just as Yolande's life on the stage would soon be slipping away as Stephens, d'Orsay and her mother negotiated the price of her future.

On 29 April, the King's Theatre staged a performance of Mozart's *Don Giovanni*, in which Yolande and her *Cachucha* were inserted into the first act. *The Times* was unimpressed:

Don Giovanni, Duvernay and the *Cachucha* combined their influences last night to produce one of the most crowded and fashionable audiences of this or any other season. The house was literally crammed in every part ... Much as we admire and have praised Duvernay in the *Cachucha*, we hold it to be a sort of impertinence to introduce it in the middle of the first finale of *Don Giovanni*, where it forms an interruption to the design, and becomes a blot instead of a beauty; but the house was in too good humour to be severely critical and it obtained its invariable honour of an encore.

Princess Victoria was in the audience that night. She was 'very much delighted and amused', but noticed that Yolande was looking tired: 'Duvernay danced the *Cachucha* in the ball scene at the end of the first act of *Don Giovanni* with her usual grace and was encored; she looked wretchedly thin and pale.' Seven days later, Victoria watched a performance of *Le Brigand de Terracina*: 'Duvernay looked very pretty, only she is grown so dreadfully thin. She danced very quietly in a *pas de trois*.'[2]

Yolande was suffering from stress and conflicting emotions. She was twenty-four years old. She loved dancing. She loved the stage. She loved the applause from the auditorium and the attentions she received from men of society. She loved the jewels, the expensive dinners, the bouquets of flowers. She was still in love with Félix de La Valette who would soon return to Paris, his short-term contract in Stockholm having come to an end.

At the same time, she was uneasy about returning to the Paris Opéra under the new direction of Henri Duponchel. Even after their affair had ended, Véron continued to treat her with affection and favour; Duponchel would not be so easy to charm. She was the most beautiful, the most sensual of the opera-dancers but, as the critics noted in 1834, Marie Taglioni was more graceful and light on her feet.

She was also surpassed by Fanny Elssler who had created the *Cachucha* in Paris six months before Yolande danced the role in London. 'I had always admired Duvernay's ... *Cachucha*,' wrote the new Queen Victoria after watching Elssler perform the dance on 26 June 1838, 'but had never seen the original; and I really was quite charmed. Duvernay ought not to be mentioned on the same day after seeing Elssler.'[3]

Taglioni had recently departed to spend three years in St Petersburg but Elssler remained in Paris, a city to which Yolande must soon return after an absence of six months. She remembered the lukewarm reviews she received after returning from six weeks in London in 1833. 'Rarely does an artiste improve by touring,' wrote the critic of the *Courrier des Théâtres*. 'On her return, the public, which had grown accustomed to her defects, grew critical of her very talents ... and having little to lose, she was found to have made no improvement.'

By 6 May, when Princess Victoria commented that Yolande had grown 'so dreadfully thin', she had been withstanding her mother's pressure for eleven days. The prospect of leaving her home in Paris, of losing Félix de La Valette and spending three years with a man she found unattractive, was distinctly unappealing. On the other hand, she was at the height of her celebrity. She might never experience such adulation again, while Stephens's offer would make her rich for life. She held out for a few more weeks, but her spirit was failing. Even a revival of the vulgar 'cashew-nut dance' on 21 May – which this time was 'most heartily hissed by the audience' – failed to incur her displeasure.

She finally gave in at the end of the month. As a reward for persuading her daughter to accept the proposal and for consenting to have no further control or influence over her life, Madame Duvernay and le Bélisaire were paid £8,000 (£800,000). Yolande would receive an allowance of £2,000 a year, to convert into a life annuity from June 1840 on condition that she remained faithful in the meantime. The total cost of the transaction for the first three years was £14,000 (£1.5 million).

What happened next was told by Antoine Coulon, choreographer of *Le Brigand de Terracina*, who had partnered Yolande at her début performance in April 1831. The story was written down by Louis Gentil, *contrôleur* of materials at the Paris Opéra, in a notebook he kept to record anecdotes and gossip about life in the opera house. He titled the story 'The Last Adventure of Pauline Duvernay'.[4]

Soon after the agreement was signed, Félix de La Valette arrived in London on his way home to Paris. Eager to see Yolande after an absence of seven months, he made his way to her apartment where 'he was soon in her arms again. They passed a delicious night together and a rendezvous was made for the next evening at the theatre.'

The following morning, Madame Duvernay sent an urgent note to Portman Square to alert Stephens about La Valette's arrival. That evening, after watching the performance, La Valette made his way backstage to Yolande's dressing-room. He was stopped by a footman in livery standing guard outside the door.

'You may not enter, Monsieur le Marquis,' said the footman. 'You may not enter the dressing-room of Mademoiselle Duvernay.'

A puzzled La Valette sought out Antoine Coulon, who told him that Yolande was 'the idol of all the dandies' in London. 'The suitor she liked the least,' he said, 'is the son of a businessman, retired from commerce with an income of £140,000. After many coquettish but real refusals, he approached Monsieur Béliser who lives with her mother.' Coulon explained that Madame Duvernay had persuaded her daughter to accept 'such an advantageous proposal' and asked La Valette, on Yolande's behalf, 'to relinquish his hold on her affections and return to Paris'. She would, he said, 'always remember your love for her and the sacrifice she asks of you to ensure her happiness'.

La Valette had no money of his own and no wish to lose a mistress whose earning power was much greater than his. He asked two of his acquaintances to act as seconds and sent them to Portman Square to issue a challenge. This was the second time in two years that Stephens had been challenged to a duel. Alarmed at the prospect of having to fight for the woman he had worked so hard to win, he agreed that he would meet La Valette on Putney Heath but asked that La Valette should first talk to Yolande.

The meeting took place in her dressing-room at the theatre while Stephens waited outside, his seconds beside him armed with duelling pistols. Fifteen minutes passed before La Valette opened the door.

'Now, Sir,' said Stephens, standing to attention. 'Whenever you please, I am at your service.'

'The honours of a double triumph are yours,' replied La Valette. 'With your permission, I shall return to France.'

'The Last Adventure of Pauline Duvernay' includes three letters, supposedly written by Stephens and his father. These are clearly fictional, but they provide a flavour of the gossip circulating in Paris at the time. The first letter is from Charles:

My dear son. You have abandoned your hounds and your horses to the care of your servants and your friends. You are neglecting the excitement of the hunting field and the occupations of a gentleman for the pleasures of the opera. My dear son, what has happened to you? Tell me. It has been a long time since I have had to pay your gambling debts. I am worried about you.

The next letter, from Stephens, is a masterpiece of purple prose:

My dear father. Since I have seen a French lady dancer who jumps up and down so naturally in the Spanish manner in the King's Theatre, my dogs, my horses, steeplechases and the fox hunt bore me. I would happily exchange all my animals, snap my fingers at my horses and their harnesses of reindeer skin, for this Andalusian with her warm and moist eyes and flaring nostrils, whose long silky locks are black and lustrous, whose legs are so fine, whose calves are so firm, whose feet are so delicate, and who is called Duvernay. Laporte thinks she will cost me at least £3000 to be paid to the mother, of whom he thinks very little.

The third letter is again from Charles:

My dear son. I have received your good news with great satisfaction. Since you find advantage in the affair of the French dancer, it is important for there not to be too long an 'engagement' between you. I will pay for your hunting retinue and the price which you need to pay ... Thus, my dear Stephens, I enclose an order for £9000 on the House of Baring, which is the basic cost of the dogs, the horses and the servants ... Have attention to give the money to the French lady little by little and do not give it to her all at once.

Details of the arrangement soon became public knowledge. The June edition of *Bentley's Miscellany* published a long poem by Thomas Ingoldsby, which was reproduced in a local newspaper as early as 6 June. It included this stanza:

> My Lord Tomnoddy he raised his head
> And thus to Tiger Tim he said
> 'Malibran's dead, Duvernay's fled,
> Taglioni has not yet arrived in her stead;
> Tiger Tim, come tell me true,
> What may a Nobleman find to do?'[5]

Stephens had to bide his time while Yolande was wooed by other men during the final weeks of her contract. Although she had no intention of risking her life annuity, she enjoyed teasing him with stories about his rivals. On 11 June, *The Satirist* published a 'conversation' between them:

'Dat Lord Lowther,' observed Duvernay to Lyne Stephens, 'ver great – vat you call de leetle son of de dog?'

'Puppy.'

'Oui,' rejoined the *danseuse*, 'poppy, he ver great poppy, he make love to me every night.'

'Does he!' exclaimed the *parvenu*, 'then it is time for me to cease making love by day.'

7

MISTRESS LYNE STEPHENS

*Sad complaints are made respecting the kidnapping of the best
dancers by certain noted roués like Lyne Stephens.*

The Drama, 2 March 1839

Yolande danced for the last time on 19 August 1837, performing
the *Cachucha* and a *pas de deux* from *Le Corsair*. It must have
been a poignant moment as she came forward to acknowledge the
applause from the auditorium, knowing that she would never again
appear on stage. 'One cannot renounce this life of excitement and
triumph without pain,' wrote Charles de Boigne. 'It is a sacrifice
which only the heart can understand but which all the money in
England is not enough to repay.'[1]

Three days later, she and Stephens travelled to Paris where
they informed Henri Duponchel that she would not return to the
Opéra. She would not complete her original contract which had
another eight months to run, nor would she compensate him for
the additional thirty-two weeks she had spent in London. She
was too valuable a star to lose at such short notice. Duponchel
informed her that she was contractually obliged to him for the next
sixteen months, that her return to Paris would be announced to

the public and that if she failed to appear he would sue. Stephens replied that he was willing to pay any fine the court might impose.

On their return to London, he installed Yolande in a house in Kensington and provided a cook, housekeeper and lady's maid, as well as a carriage, coachman and two horses. Proud of his new acquisition, he entertained his hunting and gambling friends to show off the celebrated ballerina who was now his mistress. 'She had a fine mansion,' wrote a Paris journal (with some exaggeration), 'carriage, servants, etc., and entertained each week to dinner about a dozen of the wittiest and most distinguished men in town.'[2]

Stephens spent much of his time in Kensington but he continued to live with his father in Portman Square so Yolande was often alone. She occupied herself by giving dancing lessons to the children of the aristocracy and middle classes. 'She had a lovely foot,' remembered one pupil, the twelve-year-old Adeline de Horsey (future Countess of Cardigan), 'and was the embodiment of grace and charm.'[3]

During their first winter together, Stephens gave up his shooting parties and his hunting in Melton Mowbray. With Yolande's celebrity still fresh in men's minds, he felt it wiser to remain close to her in London. In the spring of 1838, they set out together on a tour of Europe. On 23 May, the *Morning Chronicle* published a complaint from Pierre-François Laporte:

Mr Laporte begs respectfully to submit to the impartial judgement of the subscribers the following statement of facts relative to the ballet department ... Mr Laporte had, as early as April 1837, engaged Mademoiselle Duvernay for three months of the present season (1838), calculating on her services from the 15th April to the 15th July ... In the early part of February, Mr Laporte received a communication from a person authorised to speak for Mademoiselle Duvernay, that she was at Milan, and was preparing to return to England *as soon as her health would allow*. On the very next day, Mr Laporte left London for Milan, and was there informed by a certificate of her medical adviser that Mademoiselle Duvernay's health would not admit of her dancing this season.

Yolande may have forgotten her agreement with Laporte, or perhaps she believed that the change in her circumstances had received such widespread publicity that he should have drawn his own conclusions. When it seemed that he would hold her to the agreement, she resorted to the time-honoured excuse of ill-health.

Laporte was angry that she had let him down 'at the eleventh hour'. Henri Duponchel was angry too. His suit for breach of contract was heard in the Tribunal de Commerce on 11 May, with damages set at 25,000 francs, a sum which Stephens could easily pay out of his monthly allowance from his father. By the time the case was heard, he and Yolande were back in England, making plans to spend the following winter in Paris.

On 24 October 1838, the *Morning Post* reported that 'Mr Lyne Stephens intends, in about a fortnight, to remove the whole of his splendid establishment to Paris for the winter'. This 'splendid establishment' included eighteen horses and a large number of stable boys and grooms. Yolande accompanied him and the change from Melton Mowbray proved a great success. 'Hunting is kept up in excellent style in the neighbourhood of Paris,' commented *The Era* on 20 January. 'Earls Pembroke and Yarmouth, Lords Leveson and Seymour, Count Demidoff, and Mr Stephens Lyne Stephens take the lead.'

During the summer of 1839, Stephens gave two grand dinners in Portman Square, one to 'a party of sporting gentlemen', the other to 'a party of fashionables'. In October, he and Yolande left again for Paris; the *Morning Post* reported on 16 November that 'Mr Lyne Stephens has been the leader in sporting circles in Paris since the commencement of the hunting season. Versailles is their headquarters.'

This was the last time that Stephens spent the winter riding to hounds. In April 1840, he sold his horses and let his stables and coach-house in Melton Mowbray to the Marquis of Waterford. Thirty-eight years old, with a taste for expensive food and wine, he was no longer fit enough for the hunting field. 'A rich repast with an abundance of wine or spirits occasions indigestion, headache and nervous debility,' wrote a sporting journalist, 'in which state no man is in a comfortable condition to ride over a country.'[4]

Yolande became entitled to her life annuity two months later. At first, she remained with Stephens, comfortable in the luxurious lifestyle he provided for her in Kensington, but in the summer of 1841, she travelled alone to Paris and remained there for several months. She had fulfilled the terms of the transaction negotiated with her mother; she was free to resume her affair with Félix de La Valette.

After their last meeting in the King's Theatre in 1837, La Valette had returned to Paris where, 'to punish himself for having loved the ungrateful Duvernay,' he threw himself into the skinny arms' of the opera singer Rosine Stoltz. A few months later, he began a relationship with Fanny Elssler, living with her in her apartment until she left Paris in the spring of 1840 for a two-year tour of the United States. He, too, was free to resume his affair with Yolande.

On 21 November, an English gossip sheet, the *New Satirist*, published a salacious report:

> Duvernay is now in Paris and, unknown to Lyne Stephens, constantly sees La Valette with whom her former intimacy is renewed. Again does he press that fair creature in his arms; again does her voluptuous bosom heave against his throbbing breast; again are her lips glued to his in all the tender dalliance of love's delights.

Rumours of the affair reached London several weeks before they were published in the *New Satirist* and may have led to a breakdown in Stephens's mental health. His illness was announced in the *Morning Post* on 9 October: 'Mr Lyne Stephens was taken suddenly ill on Thursday last, at his father's house in Portman Square.' Two weeks later, the newspaper reported that he remained 'in a very precarious state'.

Having enjoyed her affair for several months, and come to the conclusion that La Valette had little to offer in comparison with her English lover, Yolande returned to London in early December. Stephens was recovering by this time and felt well enough to confront her about the rumours. Dissolving into tears, she replied that she had been lonely in Kensington during the many days and evenings he spent with his father in Portman Square.

Her power of weeping softened his heart. Not only did Stephens forgive her, he also agreed that she should leave Kensington and come to live with him and his father. 'It is arranged,' reported *The Satirist* on 19 December, 'that Lyne Stephens Senior, and Lyne Stephens Junior, and *Mistress* Lyne Stephens are, after the present winter, to occupy one house – *the* one in Portman Square.'

Lyne Stephens Senior was unhappy with this arrangement. He had nothing in common with his son's mistress who insisted on conversing in French. He was also tiring of city life; he missed Chicksands Priory and the tranquillity of a house surrounded by woods and gardens. In June 1843, at a cost of £24,000 (£3 million), he acquired the freehold of the Roehampton Grove estate: a late eighteenth-century villa (Grove House), a smaller villa (Lower Grove House), and 144 acres of land.

A rural area adjoining Richmond Park, Roehampton boasted several grand villas where wealthy families came to enjoy the country air. Grove House was designed in neoclassical style by James Wyatt, the rooms were decorated in the style of Robert Adam, and the house was surrounded by formal gardens with a lake and a dummy bridge. Charles moved here in the autumn of 1843, leaving Stephens and Yolande alone in Portman Square.

Now Yolande could play the hostess as Stephens entertained his hunting and gambling friends, but these men never introduced her to their wives, nor was she invited into their homes. She was mistress of a grand house in London, but she was not a wife and attitudes were changing as Victorian morality tightened its grip on society. She was condemned for flaunting her relationship with Stephens, for living with him without his father's presence to provide a veneer of respectability.

In 1841, her tears had persuaded him to move her from Kensington to Portman Square. Two years later, after his father left for Roehampton, she began to think of ways of persuading him into marriage. Her chance arrived in January 1845, during a stay of several months in Paris, when the death of the ninety-year-old Lady Aldborough provided the perfect opportunity.

Lady Aldborough had employed a lady's maid, a middle-aged Englishwoman known for her religious views and strict morals, a lady's maid who was now in need of a new position. Yolande offered her employment as her own *femme de chambre*, failing to tell her that she and Stephens were not husband and wife. The maid accepted the position. A few weeks later, as English guests were arriving for dinner, she took Stephens aside and whispered in his ear that her mistress was unable to join the party. He made his way to the bedroom where he found Yolande weeping into the pillows.

'I can no longer live in such public contempt,' she sobbed. 'My *femme de chambre* has resigned from my service because we are not married. I cannot bear this insult. I shall leave the house tomorrow if you continue to think so little of me.'

Once again, her power of weeping served its purpose. Louis Véron wrote of her 'perseverance in achieving her goal', while Paul Mahalin commented dryly that the forthcoming marriage was 'proof that an English lady's maid can be useful for something'.[5]

Stephens, Yolande and a train of servants left Paris on 23 June and arrived in Dover two days later with 'a suite of two carriages and thirty-eight passengers from Boulogne'. They made their way to Roehampton, where Stephens asked for his father's blessing. On 3 July, the *Morning Chronicle* announced that:

> A notice is to be seen at the Mairie of the second arrondissement of Paris of the intended marriage of Mr Stephens Lyne Stephens with Mademoiselle Yolande Marie Louise Duvernay. Mademoiselle Duvernay is a native of Paris, where she made her first appearance as a *danseuse* at the Opéra in 1831 ... She retired from the stage in 1837, when, according to the *Le Constitutionnel*, 'she devoted her heart and life to the rich foreigner who is about to marry her'.

The owner and editor of *Le Constitutionnel* was none other than Louis Véron, who must have smiled to himself as he wrote this piece. Ten days later, another journal, *The Era*, went into greater detail:

> Do you recollect the opera-ballet called *La Tentation*? ... This fascinating nymph, this *Miranda*, was Mademoiselle Duvernay, then in her 20th year, with beaming eyes, a real Parisian foot, and elegant and light as a bird. All this took place at the Opéra, somewhat more than thirteen long years ago. Mademoiselle Duvernay, after six years of an eventful existence, quitted the theatre and consecrated ... her heart and future hopes to the rich foreigner whom she is now on the verge of marrying ...
>
> In Mademoiselle Duvernay's veins glowed in other days the true blood of a dancer and the passions of an artiste ... We have seen a whole generation of dancers pass away, and among that number not one who could boast of a romantic career. La Duvernay alone, a voluntary fugitive from the applause so dear to an artiste, resigns herself to live in opulence, to assume the air of a *grande dame* ... and well she may, for her father-in-law has £90,000 per annum – more than two millions of francs.

Charles would have preferred his son to marry into high society but he gave the marriage his blessing. He also provided a settlement of £10,000 (£1 million). The deed was signed on 5 July, with two of Stephens's friends acting as trustees: Rowland Errington and Errington's brother-in-law, Sir Richard Williams-Bulkeley.

On 14 July 1845, the wedding party left Grove House for St Mary's church in Putney, the parish church for Roehampton, where Yolande and Stephens were married in an Anglican ceremony. After the service, they were driven to the Catholic chapel in Cadogan Terrace, Chelsea, where Yolande attended mass when she lived in Kensington. Here they were married for a second time by a Catholic priest.

A few days later, they left England to spend several months on the Continent. During their stay in Florence, Yolande sat for a portrait bust in white marble by Lorenzo Bartolini, professor of sculpture at the Accademia di Belle Arti. Her left hand was also cast in bronze. Used today as a paperweight, this tiny sensitive hand has slender, slightly bent fingers and carefully manicured nails.

8

THE RICHEST COMMONER

*La Duvernay ... a voluntary fugitive from the applause so dear to
an artiste, resigns herself to live in opulence, to assume the air of a
grande dame.*

The Era, 13 July 1845

Yolande was thirty-two years old at the time of her marriage. She
had grown plump and well cushioned after eight years of luxurious
living and was 'now as remarkable for *embonpoint* as she used to
be for slenderness and agility'. She had hoped that marriage would
give her respectability. Instead it shocked society and did nothing
to improve her reputation. It was acceptable (if improper) for a
man to keep a mistress with a sexual history; to marry her was
social disaster.

When the tenant of Lower Grove House in Roehampton
left the property in 1844, Stephens commissioned an architect
to improve the house for use as a country villa. He added a
coach-house and stables and laid out formal gardens. Six months
after their marriage, he and Yolande decided to move away
from the censure of London society. They gave up the house in
Portman Square and, on 3 March 1846, the newspapers reported

that: 'Mr and Mrs Lyne Stephens have taken possession of their beautiful villa at Roehampton.' Yolande's notoriety followed her there. 'Because Mrs Lyne Stephens's character had not been spotless,' explained one of her neighbours, 'it was natural that the matrons of Roehampton refused to call upon her.'[1]

Two months later, they left England to spend the spring and summer in Paris. In the autumn, they stayed in the Bedford Hotel in Brighton, enjoying the sea air for six weeks before returning to Lower Grove House for the winter. They repeated this pattern the following year, but plans for an extended stay in Paris in 1848 were foiled by the revolution in February that year.

A reform movement had developed in France to expand the franchise, just as the Reform Act had expanded the franchise in Britain, but Louis-Philippe turned a deaf ear to the discontent. He abdicated two days after the uprising began, travelling in disguise to Dieppe where he boarded ship for England. The new republican government introduced liberal reforms, but Paris remained in a revolutionary frame of mind and there were further insurrections in May and June. In September, Louis-Napoleon Bonaparte, nephew and heir of Napoleon I, returned from exile. His illustrious name gave him great popularity, particularly with the army, and in December – helped in great measure by stirring editorials written by Louis Véron in *Le Constitutionnel* – he was elected president of the republic.

Yolande had lived through the July Revolution in 1830 when she was a ballet pupil in Paris. She remembered the barricades in the streets and the sounds and smells of gunfire. Now, living in luxury in Lower Grove House, she followed the news from her home city with concern. At the same time, her husband was paying attention to his ageing father who lived just a short distance away.

Charles was eighty-four years old. The days of his grand dinners were over. When a cousin was shown around Grove House by the butler, she saw the long table in the dining-room laid with a single place setting.

'Oh! What a melancholy sight,' she said.

'Ah, Madam, it *is*,' replied the butler.[2]

Towards the end of 1850, Stephens and Yolande moved into Grove House to keep him company. Father and son amalgamated their households and, when the 1851 census was taken on the night of 30 March, there were seventeen servants in Grove House: butler and under-butler, cook, housekeeper, valet, lady's maid, two footmen, five housemaids, three kitchen maids and a gamekeeper. The coachman and groom lived in the stables, and a cottage on the estate housed two gardeners.

In early May 1851, Stephens spent several days in London visiting the Great Exhibition in Hyde Park. During his absence, his father died of 'exhaustion from old age' with only his butler, George Fisher, at his bedside. Although interments were no longer permitted in London churches, exceptions were made for those with private vaults. On 15 May, the funeral cortège made its way from Roehampton to St Marylebone, where Charles was interred beneath his old parish church alongside his wife and four daughters.

Stephens was so grieved at the death of the father who had loved him and indulged him, so distressed that he had not been with him when he died, that Yolande took him away to the Bedford Hotel in Brighton. They left Roehampton three days after the funeral and stayed by the seafront for two weeks.

Ten days after returning to Grove House, Stephens proved his father's will in London. Written in his own handwriting, and signed on 14 November 1842, Charles had left £50,000 (£6.5 million) in trust for the granddaughter he had not seen since his son-in-law stormed out of Chicksands Priory in October 1835. He left legacies and annuities to a large number of his Lyne relatives, a year's wages to his household servants, and £1000 to 'my old, faithful, and very excellent servant, George Fisher'.

Finally, he left the residue of his estate 'to my very dear and much beloved and most excellent son, Stephens Lyne Stephens, who is my only son and the only child of mine now living'. Having come to the conclusion that Stephens might never marry, he had added a proviso:

> The property I leave to him will be his absolutely and he, of course, may do with it whatever he may think proper, but should he die unmarried, it is my wish and most earnest desire that he should leave the bulk of the property to his and my near relations, the Lynes, that is to say to such of them as he may think proper and in such proportions as he may think proper.

The *Royal Cornwall Gazette* reported that Charles 'was a man of great benevolence to whomsoever he found needing his assistance'. According to his niece, Mary Chudleigh, 'he distributed his wealth by thousands every year, to relatives, friends and depressed merchants'. Stephens continued his generosity, 'spreading his money by thousands, literally so. He was one of the noblest-minded and kindest of men.'[3]

He helped many members of the Lyne family, paying for the education of some, giving money to others. He gave generously to charity and, because marriage to Yolande had mellowed the anti-Catholic opinions of an ultra-Tory, he also gave to Catholic institutions. 'On looking over our annals and reports, we find many notes referring to the goodness of this worthy gentleman,' wrote the mother superior of a convent in Hammersmith:

> He gave £500 towards the building of Nazareth House and on many occasions when driving by, he would stop the carriage and hand the sister who opened the door a five or ten pound note for coal or something else needful for the aged poor or orphan children, always with the injunction, 'Mind, you are not to say anything of this to Mrs Lyne Stephens. She has her charities, I have mine'. Twice or three times a week, he would leave at the door bouquets of the choicest flowers from the hot-house, with the request that they be put on the altar for him.

On one occasion, when two sisters were returning from Roehampton laden with cans of milk, Mr Lyne Stephens overtook them, stopped the carriage, and insisted on the sisters getting in with their cans, much to their discomfiture for the milk spilled over the carriage. Mr Lyne Stephens possessed that rare quality which makes the giving of charity so pleasing to those who give as well as those who receive, he never had to be asked.[4]

Stephens had now inherited the entire Lyne Stephens fortune. With an annual income of £52,000 a year (£6.5 million), he set out to become a man of culture. He had already bought a few paintings from salerooms in Paris: a Claude Lorrain in December 1840; a coastal scene by Backhuysen three months later. Now he would acquire one of the most celebrated art collections in Europe. He and Yolande attended auction houses and sales of great European collections and bid successfully for old master paintings, French and Italian sculpture, Gobelins tapestries, French antique furniture, Sèvres porcelain, and a wide range of *objets d'art*, including Chinese dragons from the Summer Palace in Peking.

He also set out to become a man of property. In the summer of 1851, he employed the architect William Burn to design alterations to the back of Grove House, remodelling the elevation and adding a new wing and an Italian-style terrace which he adorned with statuary and an intricately carved Viennese well-head.

Three years later, he made improvements to the estate, employing the architect William Wardell to design a new lodge and gardener's cottage. Wardell sailed for Australia soon after completing the work, taking with him a reference from Stephens. This is the only letter written by him to have survived the years:

I was entirely satisfied and much pleased with your services as an architect in erecting some buildings here. You evinced talent, judgement and taste, combined with a conscientious and diligent discharge of your duties in superintending the works in progress. I consider you to be a finished architect possessed of much talent, having sedulously studied your art, and that you are thoroughly acquainted with it theoretically and practically.

I am fully convinced that you are a man of scrupulous integrity and untiring industry. I much regret that you are leaving the country, because we cannot afford to lose men of talent and probity, and with a feeling for a conception of high art. I wish you success in the country to which you are proceeding. I think it cannot fail to attend you, and I only desire for you that it may be commensurate with your merit.

On 10 May 1856, Stephens bought the Hôtel Molé, a *hôtel particulier* in the Rue du Faubourg Saint-Honoré in Paris. 'One of the historic mansions of the Faubourg Saint-Honoré has just been sold,' wrote the French journal *L'Entr'acte* five days later:

It conjures up memories of Comte Molé, minister of King Louis-Philippe, but the new owner will be a celebrity of quite a different sort. She made her début as a dancer at the Opéra in 1831. She had an adorable figure, slim, supple, elegant, magnificent eyes and perfect legs. The ballet was called *La Tentation*. Into a witch's cauldron diamonds, flowers and pearls were thrown, while the ballet danced around it to diabolical music. Out of it arose the beautiful Miranda.

Albéric Second wrote a letter published in the same journal:

The Hôtel Molé has recently been sold to an Englishman who has an income of two millions. His wife ... created the role of Miranda in *La Tentation* as a remarkably beautiful dancer who was also very witty, something not so usual in the Paris Opéra. This dancer's story is a legend and the Alexandre Dumas of the future will write long novels in many volumes about it.

The Hôtel Molé occupied a corner plot between the Rue du Faubourg Saint-Honoré, the Avenue Matignon and the Rue Rabelais. It was originally built for the Marquis de La Vaupalière in 1769 and was described as 'the most delightful house in Paris'. In 1844, it was acquired by Comte Molé, who had served as minister under several administrations from Napoleon I to Louis-Philippe. He occupied the property from 1844 until his death in November 1855 and he was, according to Benjamin Disraeli, 'a rich and cultivated man, a grand seigneur of the highest breeding'.[5]

By the time Stephens acquired the Hôtel Molé, the Second Empire of Louis-Napoleon Bonaparte had been underway for almost five years. Having taken power in a *coup d'état* in December 1851, Louis-Napoleon was no longer president of the republic. He was Emperor Napoleon III. His ambition was to restore the grandeur of France, to make his Second Empire as magnificent and powerful as the First Empire of his uncle Napoleon I.

The style of decoration in the Second Empire was hugely ornate and grandiose. Yolande and Stephens redecorated the Hôtel Molé with painted ceilings, richly-carved and gilded woodwork, and heavy velvet furnishings. The decoration of one of the rooms on the ground floor was inspired by the *Oeil-de-boeuf* salon in the palace of Versailles, the royal 'double-L' on the cornice transformed into the letters 'LS'.

Every year, Yolande and her husband spent the spring and early summer in the Hôtel Molé, enjoying the glamour and the opulence of Second Empire Paris. 'The salon or drawing room of a lady of fortune,' wrote an Englishman who visited the city at about this time:

exceeds everything in splendour that one can venture to imagine, the furniture being of the richest kind, the walls covered with mahogany relieved with gold borders, and now and then with glass, and in various parts of the drawing room are figures of exquisite workmanship, with couches covered with red velvet, ornamented on each side with artificial flowers.[6]

In the autumn and winter, they led a very different life in the British countryside as Stephens hosted shooting parties in East Anglia and the Highlands of Scotland. In 1850, he rented the Glevering Hall estate in Suffolk from a fellow member of the Garrick Club. The property included an eighteenth-century mansion, a shooting lodge and 330 acres of land. He planned to turn his hand to farming and animal husbandry, and employed a farm manager to raise cattle and pigs.

Two years later, he took the lease of Pitmain, a sporting estate near Kingussie in upper Strathspey in Scotland. The estate included a stretch of the River Spey, a loch stocked with trout, a grand hunting lodge adorned with stags' heads and antlers, and 12,000 acres of grouse moor and farmland, together with a farmhouse and several cottages. Stephens enjoyed the shooting in Kingussie and Yolande was popular in the village. According to the *Inverness Courier* on 29 September 1853:

> Stephens Lyne Stephens and his Lady left Kingussie for the south on the 21st inst. This is their second season in this part of the Highlands. The charities of Mrs Lyne Stephens have been on the same liberal scale as last year, and she has not spared trouble or expense in supplying the wants of the needy in both clothing and in money.

Stephens held the Pitmain estate for four years until he acquired a shooting estate of his own. About the time he bought Hôtel Molé, his lawyer, Meaburn Tatham, told him about an estate in the Breckland of Norfolk which his legal firm was handling and which was due to be auctioned in the summer.

The Lynford Hall estate was one of the finest sporting estates in East Anglia, 'a very valuable and important freehold estate ... presenting an opportunity of investment rarely to be met with'. The eighteenth-century mansion was surrounded by 'a beautiful park through which flows a branch of the River Wissey, intersecting the pleasure grounds and plantations and terminating in an extensive lake'. The estate included:

> ornamental pleasure grounds, shrubberies and fishponds, ice-house, stabling, kennels, carpenter's dwelling, yard and workshops ... ten substantial farmsteads, with all convenient agricultural buildings, nine game-keepers lodges, eighty houses, tenements, shops and cottages, a well-accustomed inn, and a corn windmill ... upwards of 7700 acres of arable, meadow, pasture and woodland in a ring fence, comprising the entire parish of Lynford, and nearly the whole of the parishes of West Tofts, Mundford and Cranwich. The estate is abundantly stocked with game and wildfowl.[7]

The auction was held on 2 July 1856 at Garraway's Coffee House in Cornhill. Stephens had instructed Meaburn Tatham to bid on his behalf and Tatham bought the estate for £133,500 (£13 million).

The existing house was not sufficiently grand for his purposes, so Stephens planned to demolish it and build a larger, more opulent mansion on slightly higher ground on the far side of the river. He re-employed William Burn and asked him to study Hatfield House in Hertfordshire before working on his plans. He had passed this Jacobean mansion many times on his journeys to and from Melton Mowbray and was impressed by its domes and towers and magnificent windows.

William Burn had the largest country-house practice in Britain and the new Lynford Hall would be one of his biggest houses. The plans included a grand entrance hall and staircase, six large reception rooms, several smaller rooms for family use, and a total of fifty bedrooms and dressing rooms. The house would be plumbed with running water and lit by gas from a private gasworks. The ancillary accommodation included a servants' wing, an extensive stable block and three entrance lodges.

In the winter of 1856, Stephens and Yolande moved into the existing Lynford Hall where they planned to live during the shooting season until William Burn's new house was ready for occupation. Work on the new house began the following autumn. It took five years to complete and cost £60,000 (£6.5 million). The project was so large that, in 1861, it swelled the census figures for the area by an additional 500 men, all employed on the building works at Lynford.

In February 1858, because of the money he was spending in the county, Stephens was appointed high sheriff of Norfolk. The term of office lasted for one year and the role was largely ceremonial. Duties involved formal occasions and official dinners at which he appeared in the livery of his office, 'olive green with scarlet braid and facings', and arrived at functions in a 'carriage drawn by four horses with two outriders'.

At a dinner in his honour, he 'expressed the deep interest he would henceforth take in the county from the hearty welcome with which he, a comparative stranger, had been received by gentlemen of all ranks'. To celebrate his appointment, he commissioned a life-size portrait of himself, an unflattering likeness for he was now grossly overweight and had chosen to be depicted with a wad of banknotes in his hand, a symbol of his status as the richest commoner in England, an unofficial title he had inherited after the recent death of a merchant banker.

Stephens was not only overweight, he was also in very poor health. He smoked constantly, drank too much, enjoyed the rich food prepared by his French chef, and took little exercise. He began to feel unwell in the summer of 1859, suffering from faintness, sickness and headaches. His symptoms worsened in November during a shooting party in Lynford and, when he and Yolande returned to Roehampton in January, he retired to bed, no longer able to lift his heavy body on to his feet. Unaware of the danger, he was astonished when the doctor told him that he had only a short time to live.

'Are you not surprised?' Stephens asked him.

'No,' replied the doctor, 'but I am very sorry.'[8]

Stephens died on 28 February 1860. He was fifty-eight years old and may have suffered from a variety of conditions: diabetes, heart failure, high blood pressure. The doctor certified that he had died of albuminuria (protein in the urine) and 'cerebral effusion', fluid in the intracranial cavity which had caused most of his symptoms.

The funeral service was held on 6 March in the Anglican church in Roehampton, after which a long cortège made its way across London to the cemetery in Kensal Green. Following the custom, Yolande remained at home during the funeral, the blinds of Grove House drawn against the winter light.

She had grown fond of Stephens. He was the only person who had ever been kind to her. Her mother had controlled her, Louis Véron had used her to fill his theatre, Félix de La Valette had lived off her earnings. Stephens had bought her favours for his own reasons, forcing her to leave the stage, but since then they had shared a comfortable companionship for almost twenty-three years.

She ordered elaborate mourning dresses of rich, jet-black silk, and during the next three weeks, the servants watched her small black-clad figure as she took slow, solitary walks around the lake at the back of the house. Now Stephens was gone, she was alone in a society which had little respect for her, which looked down upon her, not only as a woman with a sexual history, but also as a Frenchwoman and a Catholic.

9

THE BILL OF COMPLAINT

Yolande Marie Louise Lyne Stephens ... is not entitled to receive such large benefits, and it is doubtful what amount of income she ought to receive.

Bill of Complaint, Court of Chancery, July 1860

At the time of his death, Stephens's financial assets, excluding real estate, were valued at over a million pounds. In his will, dated 5 December 1851 and drafted by Meaburn Tatham seven months after Charles's death, he named Yolande as sole executor and appointed three trustees: his friend Sir Richard Williams-Bulkeley; the banker Sir John Lubbock; and Lubbock's eldest son, a partner in his father's bank.

He left legacies totalling £30,000 and bequeathed £300,000 (£33 million) to Yolande in trust. He left Grove House and his art collection to Yolande absolutely, and Lynford Hall to Yolande for her lifetime, after which it would fall into his residuary estate. This also was left to Yolande in trust. Only after her death would the fortune pass, following his father's wishes, to the descendants of his four Lyne uncles, most of whom had little or no money of their own.

Yolande and Meaburn Tatham proved the will in London on 29 March. A few days later, she crossed the Channel to find solace in the Hôtel Molé. Stephens had added a codicil to his will in October 1859, adding Lynford Hall to his residuary estate, but the codicil made no mention of the property in Paris which he bought in 1856. According to Yolande, she searched his papers in the Hôtel Molé and found a handwritten note in French:

> I give and bequeath to Madame Lyne Stephens, my wife, my house and messuage situate at Paris, Rue du Faubourg Saint-Honoré, 85, together with the household furniture, horses and carriages found there at the time of my decease for her own absolute use and benefit, and to dispose of the whole as being her personal property from the day aforesaid. Paris, 17 April 1857.

After her return to England in June, Yolande produced this note which was, she told the trustees, a valid will under French law, so the Hôtel Molé was hers absolutely and not part of Stephens's residuary estate in which she only had a life interest. The feminine-looking handwriting was not Yolande's, but it did not appear to be Stephens's either. The trustees sought legal advice and were advised that, even if the note was valid in France, Stephens was domiciled in England so his 'immoveable property' in Paris would in any event fall under his English will.

At the same time, the trustees were daunted by the size and complexity of the administration. To relieve themselves of responsibility, they applied to have the will administered as a friendly suit in the Court of Chancery, the court renowned for its inefficiency, the court known to swallow up whole fortunes in legal charges. Even friendly suits could drag on for decades and lawyers took their costs from the funds year by year until, in some cases, little or nothing was left for the beneficiaries. 'At the present moment,' wrote Charles Dickens in August 1853:

> there is a suit before the Court which was commenced nearly twenty years ago; in which from thirty to forty counsel have been

known to appear at one time; in which costs have been incurred to the amount of seventy thousand pounds; which is a *friendly suit*; and which is (I am assured) no nearer to its termination now than when it was begun. There is another well-known suit in Chancery, not yet decided, which was commenced before the close of the last century, and in which more than double the amount of seventy thousand pounds has been swallowed up in costs.[1]

The trustees (the plaintiffs) approached the court in July 1860 with a bill of complaint filed by Meaburn Tatham: 'The plaintiffs are advised that they ought to convert the testator's residuary estate and invest the proceeds according to the trusts of his Will ... and that owing to its extent and magnitude such conversion is attended with difficulty and risk.' Because of this 'difficulty and risk', they asked that the 'residuary real and personal estate may be administered under the directions of this honourable Court, and that the rights of all parties therein may be ascertained and declared'.[2]

Other issues mentioned in the bill of complaint were the legal situation regarding the Hôtel Molé ('a residence at Paris of large value, with handsome and valuable furniture and horses and carriages there') and the amount of interest and dividends that should be paid to Yolande from the residuary estate. Stephens's will was clear on this point: the income from his residuary estate was to be paid 'into the hands of my dear wife, to the intent that such interest, dividends and annual produce may be for the sole and separate use of my wife, independent of any future husband'. The trustees asked the court to vary this provision:

> The defendant, Yolande Marie Louise Lyne Stephens, claims to be entitled to the actual income of the testator's residuary personal estate as from the day of the testator's death, but the plaintiffs are advised that, having regard to the nature of such estate ... the defendant is not entitled to receive such large benefits, and it is doubtful what amount of income she ought to receive.

Several motives were involved in this attempt to pay Yolande less than her due, motives in which jealousy, bigotry and snobbery all played a part. Her command of English was poor and she found it difficult to communicate with the lawyers and trustees who were treating her with disrespect. They thought it inappropriate that such a large fortune should have fallen into the hands of a woman who was not only foreign but also a Catholic. They hoped the court would restrict her inheritance to the £300,000 which Stephens had left her in trust, so that income from the residuary estate could be reinvested, increasing its value during her lifetime and providing a larger payout to the English beneficiaries.

In early 1862, the court ordered the sale of Stephens's stables and coach-house in Melton Mowbray. The auction took place on 29 May, the lot described as 'extensive and unequalled freehold stables, coach-house and premises, now unoccupied'. The trustees had also been trying to sell Lynford Hall, despite Stephens having left it to Yolande 'for her own use and benefit' during her lifetime. When Queen Victoria was looking for a country estate for the nineteen-year-old Prince of Wales, they suggested that Lynford might be suitable. The queen considered the offer but, in February 1862, she chose the larger Sandringham estate instead.

Eight months later, the trustees gave permission for Yolande to take possession of Lynford Hall which was now ready for occupation, although work was still in progress on the stable block and other ancillary buildings. 'There is always something melancholy,' wrote *Country Life* magazine, 'in contemplating the building of a house by one who has looked forward to dwelling therein, and to find him cut off before his hope is realised.'[3]

Stephens had longed to occupy Lynford Hall. He had looked forward to playing the man of substance in Norfolk, to hosting shooting parties and showing off his great wealth. Instead, in September 1862, Yolande moved without him into the mansion on which he had lavished so much money, hope and expectation.

The following year, the Court of Chancery met to consider the sums which had been spent on completion of the house. Nineteen barristers attended the session in November 1863 when the judge ruled that all claims should be paid from the residuary estate, except the claim for furniture which Yolande should settle on her own account.

Finally, in a decision typical of the Court of Chancery, the judge 'directed a reference to Chambers to inquire whether the pulling down of the old house at Lynford was for the benefit of the testator's estate and what had been done with the materials'. Although the value of these materials might have added a tiny proportion to the value of Stephens's estate, this would have been more than offset by the cost of lawyers investigating the matter.

The trustees failed in their attempt to reduce Yolande's income: the Court of Chancery upheld the wording of the will and granted her sole benefit from the Lyne Stephens fortune. The financial assets in the estate – 'principally invested in consols, bank stock, Russian, Brazilian, and Royal Exchange stocks and annuities' – were valued at £800,000 (£88 million). The value of the real estate in Paris, Roehampton, Norfolk and Melton Mowbray was in addition to this.

Yolande's name became famous throughout the English-speaking world as newspaper articles about her husband's will were printed and reprinted around the globe. One example was the *Moreton Bay Courier* in Australia which, on 28 July 1860, reprinted an article originally published in the Liverpool *Albion*:

By far the most fortunate, so far as sterling fortune goes and a great many other things too, of all enriched stage favourites is the long-time belle of all ballets, unparagoned tripper on the lightest of all fantastic toes, the once superb and still sumptuous Yolande Marie Louise Duvernay, wife and now widow of the late millionaire Lyne Stephens, who has just left her the trifle of £300,000, besides making her sole executrix to twice as much ready money, as well as uncontrolled mistress of castles in the country, cottages *ornées* in the suburbs, *chateaux en* France (her native land), shooting boxes here, fishing ditto there, and hunting ibid. everywhere else. Duvernay was a divinity of dance ... and it is easy to understand that she should have walked off with the heart of a captivated capitalist.

A number of men began to cast hopeful eyes on her fortune. One of these was the Duc de Richelieu, whom Stephens had met several times at race meetings and in Melton Mowbray. On 28 June 1861, after Yolande had returned to Roehampton after a few months in Paris, *The Times* and other newspapers published a report titled 'Mademoiselle Duvernay':

> A lady much and justly admired as Taglioni's only rival twenty-five years ago, since then the wife and now the widow of Mr Lyne Stephens, is to be promoted to the rank of Duchess. The once brilliant ... Duvernay is about to give her hand to the Duc de Richelieu.

Yolande may have flirted with Richelieu, but she was still in mourning and had no intention of marriage. She acted quickly to prevent the rumour spreading. The following day, *The Times* published a correction: 'We are authorised to state that there is no foundation for the report ... of the approaching marriage of the Duc de Richelieu and Mademoiselle Duvernay, now Mrs Lyne Stephens.'

During the summer, she commissioned a stained-glass window 'in memory of her late husband' for the parish church in Mundford, the local village to Lynford Hall. She also applied for permission to consecrate a small area of land on the Grove House estate, close to the main entrance on Roehampton Lane. She explained in her application that she wanted to bring her husband's body home from Kensal Green and 'to erect a tomb of some importance to his memory'.

Permission to consecrate the land was granted in March 1862 and she employed William Burn to design a mausoleum in Romanesque Revival style. In December, she put the land into trust with an endowment of £150, so that it 'may henceforth ... be used for a place of burial' for Stephens and herself, 'to remain there for ever undisturbed'.

Completed in 1864 and built at a cost of 'several thousand pounds', the mausoleum forms the shape of a Greek cross almost 30 feet square. Inside, the walls are decorated with blind arcading, the floor is covered with patterned tiles, and four small windows high on the walls provide a gloomy light. In the centre stands an enormous white-stone sarcophagus, intricately carved with interleaving arches, heads of angels, and the Lyne Stephens coat of arms.

The building was consecrated on 16 August 1864 by Archibald Tait, Anglican Bishop of London, after which a 'limited number of relatives and intimate friends' were entertained to refreshments in Grove House. Twelve days later, Stephens's coffin was disinterred from Kensal Green cemetery and brought home by carriage-hearse.

The Anglican clergy of Roehampton officiated at the reinterment. Followed by Yolande, they accompanied the coffin as it was carried through the rose garden, up the steps of the mausoleum, through the double doors, and into the gloom of the interior. The lid of the sarcophagus was lifted and, as the clergy intoned the prayers for the dead, Stephens's remains were lowered into one side of the tomb to await the day when Yolande would join him.

A LAWYER'S WILL

The lawyers must make more than they ought out of this will and
the Lyne family must very largely suffer. Elaborate wills from a
lawyer do sometimes more confuse than explain.

Francis Lyne, 1883

The news of Stephens's death – and the details of his will – spread
quickly through the extended Lyne family, giving rise to a great
deal of excitement. A large number of potential beneficiaries
attended the funeral on 6 March 1860 and followed the cortège as
it made its way from Roehampton to Kensal Green.

Two weeks later, a newspaper report, titled 'Unexpected Legacies,
Plymouth', was published in *The Times*:

The gossips of this neighbourhood have been discussing the will of
a rich Englishman who has recently died on the Continent. More
than a quarter of a century since, there was landed at Plymouth the
body of a gentleman in a rough ship coffin covered most closely
with tarred stuff. Deceased was a native of Cornwall who had
made a princely fortune in Portugal and, when returning home in a
sailing vessel, died on board. His will required that the two millions

which he left should become the property of a poor nephew, provided he took his name, Lyne Stephens.

These terms the nephew accepted and, for some unexpected reason, he quitted England and went to Italy where, like his uncle, he became prosperous in trade, dealing chiefly in wines. His fortune was doubled and, having died recently childless, the entire of his property, said to be four millions, falls (after the death of his wife) in equal proportions to the blood relations, most of whom are called Lyne and Stephens. They reside chiefly in this vicinity and are in number about eighty; each receives at the present time £1000 and it is estimated that, hereafter, every one of them will obtain £50,000 in addition.

This extraordinary report was taken up by several local newspapers, prompting one of the beneficiaries, Mary Chudleigh, to write to the editor of the *Royal Cornwall Gazette*:

Having heard of the many absurd stories now circulating in different newspapers respecting the family of Stephens, I beg the favour of you to insert, firstly, what I know to be true and, secondly, what I believe to be the origin of the mysterious stories which have spread about, as such marvellous tales are wont to do.

Having told the story of the fortune (somewhat inaccurately), Mary explained that Stephens:

had no children, but leaving his wife more than handsomely provided for, he willed, at her decease, the whole of his residuary property to the issue of his four uncles, thereby blessing about eighty claimants who will not fail to bless him for the largeness of his heart in this great outspread of benevolence, giving a joyous independence which may extend downwards through generations.[1]

Stephens's motives were not as altruistic as Mary supposed. He had signed his will seven months after his father's death, having instructed Meaburn Tatham to draft a clause that followed Charles's expressed desire that his son should 'leave the bulk of the property to his and my near relations, the Lynes'.

Tatham had worked for Charles and Stephens for many years but, whereas Charles had written his will in his own clear and unequivocal language, Stephens had relied on the lawyer to draft it for him. With no business or legal experience, he simply signed the will that Tatham placed in front of him. This stated that his residuary estate, after the death of his widow, should be divided between 'such issue' of his four uncles 'as shall be living at my decease, share and share alike'. The four uncles were Richard Lyne, a clergyman in Cornwall, and his merchant brothers, Joseph, Edward and William, all three of whom had been declared bankrupt.

In December 1860, *The Times* and the *Royal Cornwall Gazette* published a notice titled 'The Estate of Stephens Lyne Stephens, deceased':

The descendants of the late William Lyne, Reverend Richard Lyne, Edward Lyne, and Joseph Lyne (uncles of the late Stephens Lyne Stephens of Roehampton), who were living at his decease or born since, are requested to furnish evidence thereof on or before Saturday 22 December next, to Albert H. Elworthy, solicitor, 14 Southampton Buildings, Chancery Lane, London.

This was a good try by Albert H. Elworthy, who appears to have been a lawyer acting for one of the beneficiaries. On the same day, another firm of solicitors published a different notice. This was titled 'In Chancery':

As solicitors engaged in the suit filed for the administration of the estate of the late Stephens Lyne Stephens of Roehampton, we hereby inform the residuary legatees entitled under the Will ... that no person is at present authorised by the Court to receive their claims, and that due notice will be given to the legatees of any order that may be made by the Court relative thereto.

Two months later, Meaburn Tatham wrote personally to the potential beneficiaries about the evidence required by the court:

> The Court of Chancery has made a decree directing the administration of the estate of the late Mr Stephens Lyne Stephens, and amongst other enquiries which are to be made, the first is as to who were the Issue at the time of the testator's death of the former uncles named in his Will. When the proper time arrives, I am directed to take in the claims of a great number of those who represent themselves as such Issue, and I shall be glad to hear from you if it is your wish that I should carry in your claim also.

Writing to the beneficiaries was a smarter move than advertising in newspapers and most of them did instruct him to act on their behalf. Tatham was already employed by the trustees of Stephens's estate; now he would also work for the beneficiaries, preparing family trees and drafting documents which had to be signed and witnessed. He would make a fortune from the will he drafted in 1851; when he died twenty-four years later, he was worth more than £18 million in today's money. As Francis Lyne, one of the beneficiaries, explained:

> My cousin was not equal to his father in knowing the value of a word. The lawyer who made his will left out some words, which my cousin did not notice, hence it became what is called a lawyer's will and very materially frustrated the intention of my uncle and, of course, my cousin. The lawyer did much injury to the Lyne family and, not long after my cousin's death, he told me that he already had sixty of my relations as clients. The lawyers must make more than they ought out of this will and the Lyne family must very largely suffer.[2]

One problem was that Tatham failed to define the word 'issue'. Stephens had intended it to mean the children and grandchildren of his four uncles but, because the word was not defined, the court gave it the widest possible interpretation. Every beneficiary had to prove his or her pedigree. This took time and it was not until 1863 that a definitive list was drawn up with ninety-three names.

The term 'living at my decease' was taken to include infants still in the womb at the time of Stephens's death. There were four such infants, born between June and November 1860. The last of these may not have been conceived in time, but this was a difficult matter to prove. There were rumours of lawyers attending the birth of at least one of these children to certify the safe arrival of a beneficiary.

The person who did most to help Tatham prepare the claims was the elderly Virgil Stephens Lyne, who provided information for a family tree several yards long. 'It was at Mr Tatham's special request,' he wrote to his brother in December 1863, 'that I undertook to procure the necessary information as to births, marriages, deaths, christenings, etc. I did so at a time when I was a great invalid and scarcely able to go through with it. It not only occasioned me much trouble but also subjected me to much expense and, notwithstanding Mr Tatham's repeated request, I refused all remuneration.'

The beneficiaries on Tatham's pedigree were a diverse bunch, ranging in age when Stephens died from a (maybe) not-yet-conceived foetus to a geriatric widow in Liskeard. Many of them were clergymen and lawyers, stockbrokers and shipowners, typical of the professional middle classes of the time. Several had moved to the colonies, spreading the Lyne Stephens net into many corners of the globe.

They varied from establishment figures, such as General Sir Frederick Glubb, to the eccentric, one of the oddest of whom was Joseph Leycester Lyne, the self-styled Father Ignatius who tried to re-establish monasticism in the Anglican Church. A sanctimonious man of astonishing hypocrisy, he built a 'monastery' in the Black Mountains of Wales, where he subjected his band of followers to a regime of austerity and discipline while he lived more comfortably in what he called the 'superior's quarters'. He would have preferred to restore one of the great ruined abbeys of England. As he wrote to the *London Standard* on 20 October 1865:

> We are most anxious to restore an old ruined priory to its original purpose. Would any gentleman who owns such a thing kindly give it to me? By my late cousin Lyne Stephens's will, I am to have some few thousands of pounds myself. I would give every penny towards the building up of an old desecrated monastery ... I should very much like to have Bolton Abbey, or Fountains, or Kirkstall in Yorkshire, or Llantony Abbey in Monmouthshire, or Vale Crucis Abbey near Chester, or Furness in Lancashire, or Tintern on the Wye ... As for Westminster Abbey, at present I am almost afraid we cannot obtain that.

His self-professed 'monks' and 'nuns' were adult volunteers, unlike the two-year-old boy he adopted as an 'infant oblate'. This was a medieval custom, 'whereby mere babies could be dedicated to the service of God by being adopted by a religious House, clothed in its habit, and in time ... professed as a vowed son of its cloister'. Ignatius took 'the Infant Samuel' from his impoverished mother and brought him up as a miniature monk. It was, he explained, 'a pleasure and solace to have the patter of tiny feet about him, and a spotless soul which from the very dawn of its infant perceptions he might train and fashion from bud to blossom as an oblate of unsullied purity'.[3]

Pope Pius IX thought differently when Ignatius visited Rome in February 1865. 'Remember,' he told him, 'a habit does not make a monk.' The writer Augustus Hare was in St Peter's when Ignatius, leading the Infant Samuel by the hand, emerged from his interview with the pope:

> He has come to Rome for his health, and has brought with him a sister (Sister Ambrogia) and a lay brother to wash and look after the Infant Samuel ... He vowed him to the service of the

Temple, dressed him in a little habit, and determined that he should never speak to a woman as long as he lived. The last is extremely hard upon Sister Ambrogia, who does not go sight-seeing with her companions, and having a very dull time of it, would be exceedingly glad to play with the little rosy-cheeked creature.

The Infant is now four years old, and is dressed in a white frock and cowl like a little Carthusian, and went pattering along the church … by the side of the stately Brother Ignatius … exciting great attention and amusement amongst the canons and priests of the church. A lady acquaintance of ours went to see Brother Ignatius and begged to talk to the Infant. This was declared to be impossible, the Infant was never to be allowed to speak to a woman, but she might be in the same room with the Infant if she pleased, and Brother Ignatius would then himself put any questions she wished.[4]

Another oddball among the beneficiaries was the stone-deaf Lewis Jedediah Lyne who lived on a goldfield in South Australia. He had sailed for Australia as a young man and thereafter avoided all contact with his family. He found employment in various merchant companies, but 'was very obstinate and determined and would not work one minute (literally) after the clock struck the appointed hour'. By the mid-1850s, he was working as a stable-hand in the Burra mine at Kooringa.

He fell ill at the time of Stephens's death and, for the first time in thirty years, wrote to one of his brothers, Richard Benjamin Lyne, who replied with news of the death of his wealthy cousin and explained that, under the terms of the will, he was entitled to a share in the Lyne Stephens fortune. Lying in the makeshift hospital at the mine, Lewis Jedediah was befriended by the medical officer and, after his death in January 1861, the doctor wrote to Richard Benjamin in London:

When your late brother came under my care, he was put on the benefit club and received fourteen shillings a week sick pay.

When he became worse, I made enquiries as to his comforts but he always replied that he required none. One could get nothing out of him. He associated with no one ... He was very deaf indeed and this may have had a great deal to do with his almost misanthropic disposition. I became interested in him and treated him as a friend. I felt so distressed at his miserable existence that I proposed he should enter the hospital here, but he was so proud that it was difficult to get him to consent. He died very quietly and was kept up for a long time before his dissolution by brandy alone. I must mention that he believed in brandy and took more than was good for him.

He left no will. He drew a sketch of a will which I sent to a lawyer to be properly drawn, but I could never get him to sign it. I can tell you what his intentions were. He informed me that, on the death of a lady, a cousin of his named Mrs Lyne Stephens, he would become possessed of several thousand pounds and he wished it to be divided equally between his brothers and sister.

It was too late for Lewis Jedediah, but Stephens's will changed the lives of hundreds of members of the Lyne family, even if they did not live to receive their inheritance. Ninety-three beneficiaries (and their heirs) were waiting for Yolande to die, after which they would be enriched by the equivalent of £1.3 million in today's money. The will also split families, the difference of a few days in the presumed date of conception or a few hours in the time of death determining whether an individual became a beneficiary or was excluded from all interest in the Lyne Stephens estate.

Several beneficiaries sold their reversionary interest in the will, although shares sold in the 1860s, when Yolande was relatively young, achieved less than a third of their full value. 'As soon as the contents of the will were known,' wrote Francis Lyne, 'every son and every daughter throughout the Lyne family were set free of their parents' control, and thousands upon thousands of pounds have been lost to the family by the sale of reversions.'[5]

Over the years, thirty-nine beneficiaries sold their interest, sometimes to relatives but mostly to assurance companies. The first share was advertised for auction in *The Times* on 24 December 1860, just ten months after Stephens's death:

> The absolute reversion to a share, supposed to be one ninety-third part of the residue of the estate of Stephens Lyne Stephens ... the estimated value of which is £972,800. 13s. 7d., or thereabouts, receivable on the decease of a widow lady, now in her 48th year, to be sold by auction at the Mart, Bartholomew Lane, opposite the Bank of England, on Thursday 3 January 1861, at 12 o'clock.

Many beneficiaries who retained their interest would die during Yolande's lifetime, their shares falling into their own estates, to be passed on to further beneficiaries. Lewis Jedediah was the first to die. Meaburn Tatham divided his share between his brothers and sister, and advised on the matter of death duties. In a letter written in May 1865, he recommended immediate payment:

> The present value of a share may be roughly taken at £3000. The duty thereon payable by (say) a brother succeeding to such share in right of a deceased brother or sister would be at 3 per cent. In other words, if paid now, £90. This share when it falls into possession will be (say) £9000. The duty payable at 3 per cent would be £270, supposing it *not* to have been already paid ... If the course I have suggested be adopted, there will be a saving of much trouble by and by, and of some expense. I am of the opinion that, in order to keep matters clear, the duty should be cleared whenever a share devolves by death on others.

Each time a reversionary interest changed hands, lawyers were employed to draw up the documents. An example of this absurdity was the short life of Frances Nicholas, one of the beneficiaries still in the womb at the time of Stephens's death. The court accepted her claim on the grounds that she was born eight months and three weeks later, although she lived for less than a year. When she died in August 1861, her one ninety-third share passed to her father as next of kin; and when he died two years later, it was bequeathed to his wife, herself a beneficiary, who then became entitled to two ninety-third shares.

It was not only beneficiaries who became involved in complicated genealogy. Because the money was placed in Chancery, fraudsters had taken up the matter and were persuading large numbers of people to make erroneous claims to the fortune. Normally, when estates were put into Chancery, it was because the heirs could not be found. Lists of estates held by the court were published in the *London Gazette,* allowing fraudsters to circulate local newspapers with exaggerated reports of fortunes waiting for heirs to claim them. Most editors believed these stories to be true and published the details, whereupon the fraudsters advertised in the same newspapers, offering to claim the fortunes on a fee basis. Whole families were deceived in this way.

'No public office causes more heartbreak among the ignorant public, or raises more unfounded hopes, than this branch of the Supreme Court,' said a member of parliament when the matter was raised in the House of Commons:

> It is believed by many persons that the amount of unclaimed funds in Chancery reaches something like £100 million. There exist, not only in London but also in the provinces, flourishing agencies which lay themselves out to deceive the public. One adventurer has been spending as much as £350 a week in advertisements, suggesting that people apply to him for information which will lead them to realise fortunes in reference to those funds.[6]

While genuine beneficiaries employed lawyers to prove their claims, families in Cornwall were defrauded by the conmen, a widespread deceit which continued throughout the period the

Lyne Stephens fortune remained in Chancery, a total of forty-eight years. Families with the name of Stephens invented ancestors who had gone to Portugal and built glass factories; even today, there are puzzled family historians whose pedigrees contain the names of the Stephens brothers, dropped fraudulently but hopefully into unconnected family trees.

Letters from a William Philp of Liskeard to a family in St German's are just one example of how people in Cornwall were led to believe they had a claim to the fortune. His first letter was written on 23 January 1862:

> As a Christian, I feel it my duty to inform you that there has been a meeting held at Liskeard concerning the money which was supposed the late Stephens Lyne, by some unlawful means, had defrauded the Stephens family of. Their family connections are now making their claims and, since your late husband's mother was called Nanny Stephens previous to her marriage, you will do the same by getting your husband's register and his mother's. From what I can hear, there is every probability that you will get the money and their counsel informs them that it will be settled in March.

On 3 February, he wrote again:

> From making further enquiry into your business, I am informed that this gentleman who accumulated such amount of money was called Stephens and died at Lisbon some thirty years since, leaving Stephens Lyne a certain amount of his property and the sum of £700,000 to the nearest relation he had. Where this money has been during this time, I do not know but, at present, it is in Chancery for the nearest in kin who will make claim for it.
>
> I have not the least doubt that you and your family connections are the nearest in kin to that Mr Stephens. I hope you will lose no time in making it known to your family, and also that the Lord will incline the heart of some gentleman to take up your case by putting

it in some wonderful counsellor's hands on condition that you make amends for their trouble. I believe an influential gentleman would be a strong tower to you and delight at the idea of doing good to the poor.

And again on 1 April:

All my spare time since I saw you last has been taken up in making a diligent search concerning your affairs. They now find from the Will that John James Stephens left his grandfather's descendants £30,000. Granny Tucker's mother must have been his aunt and therefore Granny Tucker and John James Stephens, the last brother that died at Lisbon, must have been first cousins. I trust that you will be able to work up Granny's claim and send it in before the fifteenth of this month as the Chancery business will then again commence. Bless the Lord, there is hope for all of you now.

Nine days later, he learnt that the family was becoming disheartened by the lack of progress:

I am sorry to find you are getting discouraged about the Will. If I was my own master and could afford it, I would search all the churches that was necessary and send in your claims in a fortnight. A poor man by the name of Stephens at a place called Burnt House about five miles from here has sent in his claim. He came in through one of the grandfather's sons who had a daughter called Jane Stephens after his mother. If so, this Jane Stephens ... must have been a sister to him whose daughter you come in by.

For almost fifty years, this poor and ill-educated family would live in hope. 'My father died twenty-two years ago,' wrote a Margaret Dymond to one of her cousins in 1887:

and I have been trying to find out the mystery ever since ... I understand that you have a lawyer working for you. What I know might be of service to some branches of the family if they would only try to link the family and make a claim ... The Court knows who the family is that the money belongs to. So if we could not find everything, the Court might make up the deficiency and the right parties would have the money.

These letters relate to just one family but the conmen persuaded most Cornish families with the name of Stephens to consider a claim on the fortune, money to which they were not entitled. There was never any doubt that the three wills in the case, those of John James, Charles and Stephens, were all valid and clear in their intentions.

THE STILL SUMPTUOUS DUVERNAY

Mrs Lyne Stephens ... has asked me to manage a good many of her
affairs ... It is an object to me not to disappoint her.
Colonel Edward Claremont, 23 September 1862

While members of the Lyne family set about proving their entitlement to the Lyne Stephens fortune, they took little interest in the woman whose life expectancy would determine when they received their share. At the same time, the men who had stayed on friendly terms with the richest commoner in England felt less inclined to maintain relations with his French Catholic widow. The matrons of Roehampton continued to ignore her and the gentry in Norfolk made no attempt to befriend the lonely woman who would soon take possession of Lynford Hall.

Yolande had no access to the capital in her husband's estate but the income on his wealth, about £6.5 million a year in today's values, was more than she could possibly spend. As a result, the money in her own name began to accumulate and she would soon amass a fortune of her own. She was ill-equipped to handle her financial affairs or deal with the lawyers and trustees who were treating her with so little respect. She had neither the skills nor the aptitude for the management of three grand houses, thousands of acres of land, and a large complement of servants and ground staff. She needed someone to look after her affairs – and she found him in Paris in the spring of 1861.

Colonel Edward Stopford Claremont was the British military attaché in Paris. Forty-two years old, slim, fit and with a military bearing, he was very different from the overweight and ageing Stephens of the last years of her marriage. Six years younger than Yolande, he was the illegitimate son of Anaïs Aubert, an actress in the Comédie-Française, and General Sir Edward Stopford who had served on Wellington's staff during the Peninsular War. Conceived during the three-year occupation of Paris after the Battle of Waterloo, he was born in the city on 24 January 1819 and baptised in the British Embassy, the Hôtel de Charost in the Rue du Faubourg Saint-Honoré.

Yolande perceived Edward as a kindred spirit. He had lived with his mother for the first thirteen years of his life, so they shared memories of theatrical Paris; he may even have seen her dance in the Salle le Peletier. They could also speak together in French, a huge pleasure for Yolande who had never learnt to be fluent in English.

The relationship had its tentative beginnings when she spent a few months in the Hôtel Molé during the spring of 1861 when she was still in mourning. It became a love affair soon after she returned to Paris the following year.

The Hôtel Molé was five minutes' walk from the British Embassy, along the Rue du Faubourg Saint-Honoré, past the Élysée Palace to the corner of the Avenue Matignon. It was easy for Edward to slip away from the embassy to spend time with the lonely widow who had retained her beauty: the fine bone structure of her face, her large, wide-apart grey eyes, her smooth skin. In a carte-de-visite photograph taken in 1864, she is wearing an off-the-shoulder gown, her dark hair is swept back into a chignon, and she looks much younger than her fifty-one years.

During his visits to the Hôtel Molé, she told him about the bill of complaint drawn up by the trustees in England, how they tried to amend her husband's will to reduce her income, how they refused to accept that Stephens had given her the Hôtel Molé in her own name. She was unable to handle any of this, she told him, using her power of weeping to emphasise her distress. She was in need of someone to help her – and at this early stage in their relationship, it seemed a simple matter for Edward to offer 'to manage a good many of her affairs'.

Edward Claremont was living beyond his means in Paris. His salary of £1,100 a year was insufficient for a senior attaché, particularly one with a wife and six children. Unlike most army officers and diplomats of the time, he had little or no private income. At the same time, it was necessary to put on a show of uniform and equipage to impress Louis-Napoleon and senior officers in the French army.

His lodgings were unusually modest for a man of his standing: a narrow, three-storey terraced house in the Rue Lord Byron, a small street behind the Champs-Élysées. When asked to entertain senior officers in the French navy, he complained that 'my dining room is so small that it will be difficult to have more than two at a time'.

He had been protesting about his salary for several years. In December 1859, the British ambassador in Paris, Lord Cowley, had written a private letter to Lord John Russell, the foreign secretary:

> Claremont has written me a very piteous letter with the desire that I should endeavour to obtain for him an increase of salary … I am afraid that he has little or nothing else … If he had been an unmarried man, his present allowances should have been more than ample. As it is, he must I apprehend be in great difficulties.[1]

On 30 April 1862, about the time he began his love affair with Yolande, Edward also wrote to the foreign secretary:

> I find myself in such a difficult position here … I was not given anything as an outfit, and the expense of establishing myself here not only ran away with the little money I had put by … but got me into debt besides … [and] I am sorry to say that I have never been able to

bring up my arrears. My debts have gone on increasing and are so pressing now as to cause me the greatest uneasiness and anxiety.

The expenses of living in Paris are enormous for a man like myself with a large family and with but very small private means. I cannot accuse myself of any extravagance and I can safely say that my difficulties have arisen from the wish to carry on the duties entrusted to me in the most efficient manner. I have not been so foolish as to do anything for show, but to obtain information I have been obliged to mix a good deal in society and to a certain extent to return the civilities I received from French officers who have entertained me ... with whom it is indispensable that I should keep up my relations ...

I feel that I can do more good in this country than anywhere else. Therefore I do not ask for any change. I do not either ask for any increase in salary as this might in some way interfere with the diplomatic service ... but I throw myself on your Lordship's favourable consideration in the hope that you will see fit to allow me a certain sum in lieu of the outfit which I did not receive, and which may enable me to get over my present difficulties.[2]

Yolande returned to Roehampton two months after Edward wrote this letter. He crossed the Channel a few weeks later, accompanying Lord Cowley on a visit to the Foreign Office in London. He took the opportunity to stay with Yolande and, on 31 July, he wrote to Cowley on Grove House headed notepaper:

I was sorry on all accounts to miss you yesterday but I should have liked to have shown you a letter from Lord Russell who says he is sorry to have kept me waiting so long for an answer; he was in hopes that he could have acceded to my wishes but on reflection he cannot increase my pay and allowances ... His Lordship had not my letter either before him or present in his mind for, if you recollect, I did not ask for an increase of pay and allowances, but merely for a sum equivalent to what I should have received had I been given an outfit ... Of course I am very anxious to bring this to a settlement and may be detained for a few days which I hope you will not mind.[3]

Edward was more than happy to be detained for a few days in Grove House, and he and Yolande returned to Paris together in early August. Five weeks later, they were back in England, the newspapers reporting on 13 September that 'Mrs Lyne Stephens and Colonel Claremont' were among the 'fashionable arrivals' at the West Cliff Hotel in Folkestone. Yolande was about to take possession of Lynford Hall. She was nervous about moving into the new house alone, so Edward had agreed to accompany her.

They travelled by train to Brandon, five miles from Lynford, where a carriage was waiting. After driving through the park and through the elaborate wrought-iron gates decorated with the Lyne Stephens coat of arms, the carriage came to a halt outside the front door where the servants were lined up to welcome her. The red-brick mansion was adorned with mullioned windows, stone balustrading, shaped gables, dormer windows, turrets, and leaded cupolas, 'forming a very imposing and picturesque pile of the Tudor style of domestic architecture'.

The house had been designed to Stephens's specifications, for hosting shooting parties and grand dinners, for showing off his wealth and prestige. The huge reception rooms were neither comfortable nor congenial for a woman living alone. Yolande was hoping that Edward would stay with her for at least a week, but even her tears could not persuade him to stay longer than three days. He was needed at the embassy and his wife may have been fretting at his absence.

He returned to Paris on 18 September, but was almost immediately recalled to Norfolk. On the 23rd, he took Lord Cowley into his confidence:

Mrs Lyne Stephens, who has asked me to manage a good many of her affairs, wishes me very much if possible to go over to England for three or four days to talk over some important matters. It is an object to me not to disappoint her and my absence would not extend beyond the middle of next week ... I would go right through London and not near anybody, nor would I tell anyone here except Atlee who might telegraph if I was wanted. Of course I would take it all on my own shoulder in case of an accident, and naturally not move if you disapprove in any way.[4]

Cowley wrote a brief note of acquiescence and Edward left again on 26 September. Despite his protestations of an early return, he was away for almost two weeks. On 3 October, he wrote to Cowley from Lynford Hall:

> I meant to have gone back to Paris tomorrow but a business has just occurred at the new house which Mrs Lyne Stephens is building. The clerk of works who has been here for five years has had a fit and I have telegraphed to the architect to come over tomorrow as it is feared drinking and confusion in the accounts may be at the bottom of the whole thing. Mrs Lyne Stephens would feel so very much at a loss what to do that I venture to remain to investigate the circumstances and, Sunday then intervening, I shall not be able to be in Paris till Tuesday morning. I hope you will not think I have abused your indulgence. You know it is not often that I neglect my duty.[5]

There is no evidence that the clerk of works had created such a mess; William Burn was too efficient an architect to allow this to happen. It was an excuse for Edward to remain longer in Lynford Hall, as Yolande had no doubt begged him to do. He wrote a note to Cowley as soon as he returned to Paris on 7 October: 'I am in great hopes you did not want me during my absence. I am very sorry it should have been so prolonged and I assure you it was very much against my will but I could not help it.'

Two months later, he returned to Lynford to spend a few more days in her company. She had prepared an indenture to put the land for the mausoleum at Roehampton into trust and on 9 December, he signed the deed of conveyance as a trustee. Now he was legally, as well as emotionally, involved in her life.

12

THE FIRST MILITARY ATTACHÉ

The expenses of living in Paris are enormous for a man like myself
with a large family and with but very small private means.
Colonel Edward Claremont, 30 April 1862

Edward was not only finding it difficult to resist Yolande's demands, he was also increasingly concerned about money. This was an old story: even as a boy, he had lived beyond his means. At the age of fourteen, General Stopford placed him in a boarding school in Paris and wrote affectionate letters to his 'dear little scamp' and 'dearest rascal' and advised him not to go to the Comédie-Française because of the people he might encounter there.

'So you little rascal,' his father wrote in March 1834, 'you have spent all your money and want more – was there ever such a fellow ... I have sent you an order for some to go on with ... As you know I am always happy to contribute to your pleasures, though it deprives me of the *shirt on my back*.'

'You are now flush in money again,' he wrote in April, 'and will not deserve I hope the name you give yourself, *spendthrift*.' Seven days later, he gave his son some financial advice:

As far as it can be done and without being *niggardly*, I should prefer your being a *sparethrift* to a *spendthrift*. The latter ... spends his money on trifles and orders things from the caprice of the moment without being really in want of them, and that is the advantage of always paying ready money; you think a moment before you go in to buy or *perhaps*, which may *sometimes* be the case, you have not in pocket the wherewithal to pay and, after a moment's reflection, you say what a *goose* I was very near being, to buy a waistcoat merely from caprice ... I don't say that this has *ever* happened to you, but it has to me in my younger days.

When Edward was sixteen, his father brought him to England to join his boyhood friend, Frederick Leveson-Gower (son of Lord Granville, the British ambassador in Paris) at a school near Nottingham. As Leveson-Gower wrote in his memoirs: 'I was fond of some of my companions, amongst whom was Edward Claremont, the best friend man ever had.'[1]

His father also arranged for Edward's naturalisation as a British citizen, which at the time could only be done by private act of parliament. The head of the Stopford family, Edward's cousin, the Irish peer Lord Courtown, refused permission for an illegitimate son to take the Stopford surname, so instead he was given the invented name of Claremont. The 'Act for Naturalising Edward Stopford Claremont' passed through both houses of parliament in May 1836 and received royal assent in June.

General Stopford died in September 1837. Five months later, Edward joined the army as a cornet. He was posted to Montreal in 1840, assigned to the newly formed Royal Canadian Rifle Regiment which had been raised to police the Canadian frontier and prevent British soldiers deserting across the border into the United States. Detachments of the regiment, wearing uniforms of 'rifle-green', manned a series of frontier posts spread along the Canadian border.

Promoted to lieutenant in July 1841, Edward was appointed aide-de-camp to Colonel George Augustus Wetherall, commander of the garrisons in west Canada. Two years later, he accompanied Wetherall on leave to England where, in October 1843, he married the colonel's daughter Frances. On their return to Montreal, he was promoted to captain and given the appointment of deputy assistant adjutant-general.

When the regiment trimmed the number of its staff officers in March 1851, Edward was one of three who became surplus to requirements. He returned to England where he became available for other duties. In June 1852, he acted as aide-de-camp to 'His Highness Said Pasha, Hereditary Prince of Egypt' on a state visit to England; he accompanied the prince to a dinner at Buckingham Palace and a 'grand reception' given by Benjamin Disraeli.

Five months later, after the death of the Duke of Wellington, he was employed as aide-de-camp to 'the Russian, Prussian, Spanish and Portuguese officers who have arrived in England to be present at the Duke's funeral'. This took place in St Paul's Cathedral on 18 November and was attended by large numbers of senior military men from overseas. Edward made their arrangements and accompanied them to functions held in their honour, including a state dinner in Windsor Castle.

Eight days after the funeral, the foreign officers made a visit to Woolwich Arsenal, accompanied by Lord Raglan, master-general of the ordnance, and Queen Victoria's cousin the Duke of Cambridge. They arrived in a fleet of eight carriages, 'all in their respective uniforms, the distinguished foreigners attended by Captain Claremont in a rifle-green uniform'. Having inspected the weaponry in the arsenal, they mounted on regimental horses to ride up to Woolwich Common for the displays. The *Morning Post* described the scene:

> Although the rain was falling in torrents, and a strong south-west gale blowing all the time, and the ground was in as bad a state as it could well be, His Royal Highness the Duke of Cambridge and the distinguished visitors remained on the bleak common and witnessed the troops of the Royal Horse Artillery go through the

entire evolutions of a field-day, firing twenty-five rounds from each gun in the various positions they took up.

The scene on the common today will not be readily forgotten. The constant heavy rain was drifted by the wind in great force, sufficient to pass it through any clothing in a short time, and the bright flashing and the booming of the guns made a good representation of a thunder-storm, with the difference that the wind was bitterly cold and piercing, and all who were out for five minutes were completely wet through. The royal and distinguished visitors entered the carriages in their wet uniforms and left for town at four p.m.

In January 1853, Edward was appointed to 'the senior department of the Royal Military College, Sandhurst'. Fourteen months later, England and France declared war on Russia, allied with Turkey in the conflict in the Crimea. Because of his fluency in the language, Edward was appointed assistant military commissioner at the headquarters of the French army. He sailed for Turkey in April 1854, accompanied by three horses, two servants and a luggage mule.

Later that year, he was present at the battles of Alma, Balaclava and Inkerman, as well as several other engagements during the siege of Sevastopol. It is a tradition in the Claremont family that, during the Battle of Balaclava, he overheard General Bosquet utter the famous words when watching the Charge of the Light Brigade: '*c'est magnifique mais ce n'est pas la guerre.*'

Promoted to the rank of major, Edward was twice mentioned in despatches. In October 1854, Lord Raglan, the British commander-in-chief, forwarded a letter from General Canrobert, the French commander-in-chief, acknowledging 'the high esteem in which Major Claremont is held by the French army for his courage, the uprightness of his character, and the services which he has rendered'. In the second despatch, forwarded to the Foreign Office in February 1855 by the British ambassador in Paris, Edward was commended for his 'constant bravery when deployed in the face of the enemy in the battles of Alma and Inkerman, and also in operations during the siege of Sevastopol during which he served with distinction during the most difficult missions and displayed a perfect understanding of all the details of war'. 'This officer,' wrote General Canrobert, 'has gained great esteem in our army ... both in a military capacity and as an intermediary in the cordial and perfect relations which exist between our two armies.'[2]

Edward returned from the Crimea in June 1855. He was awarded the Légion d'Honneur (fourth class), the Crimean medal with four clasps, and the Turkish Order of Medjidie (second class). Queen Victoria also made the specific request that he be awarded the CB (Companion of the Order of the Bath).

On 2 September, the foreign secretary recommended that he take the place of General Torrens, the British military commissioner in Paris who had died nine days earlier. Louis-Napoleon had requested that Edward be given the appointment, stating publicly that he wished no other British officer to be military commissioner at his court. The request was endorsed by Queen Victoria:

> The Queen writes ... to enquire whether Major Claremont has gone to Paris. If not, she thinks he should do so with as little delay as possible, as it is very important to have some military man on the spot to be able to communicate freely with the French Government.[3]

On the 11th, Edward wrote to the foreign secretary asking for funds to equip himself with an outfit:

> I suppose my appointment may be considered as partly of a diplomatic nature. I believe that what is called an outfit or sum of money to assist in defraying the expenses of a first establishment is sometimes granted to diplomatic agents, and I would beg your Lordship to have the kindness to consider whether such a boon could not be extended to me.

I am not a rich man and shall have to buy a great number of things, I shall have to pay in advance for an apartment in Paris, all of which will make a great hole in my first quarter's pay. Were there any army sources from which I could have procured them, I would not have called upon your Lordship, but the Regulations only apply to an officer taking the field. I am waiting for my final instructions ... after which I am to report myself at the Foreign Office and start for my post, which I am ready to do at any moment.

He was promoted to lieutenant-colonel on the 22nd. The following day, accompanied by Lord Cowley, he was officially introduced to Louis-Napoleon as the new British military commissioner in Paris. Five months later, when peace was declared in the Crimea, his wartime appointment as military commissioner came to an end. However, 'as it was considered that I might still be of some service here, I was asked whether I would remain in Paris as Military Attaché ... to which I immediately acceded'.

The post of military attaché was specifically created for Edward Claremont. He could no longer act as military commissioner because the war in the Crimea had ended, but his friendship with General Canrobert and other officers in the French army was useful to the Foreign Office.

The change in title also involved a reduction in pay. From a salary of £1,500 a year as military commissioner, he was offered the greatly reduced sum of £555 as military attaché. Military commissioners served only in wartime; they were not accompanied by their wives and children, and there was no need to put on a show of uniform and equipage. As the first peacetime military attaché in history, Edward was breaking new ground.

In 1857, he suggested that a salary of £800 a year might be more suitable. This was granted and, when he was promoted to full colonel the following year, he received a further £100. In 1859, his lodging allowance was increased by £200, bringing his total income to £1,100. This was still insufficient for his purposes, particularly in the opulent Second Empire of Louis-Napoleon.

Since peace was declared in the Crimea, the French emperor had been making a concerted effort to build up his military muscle. This soon led to fears of invasion in England. Was Louis-Napoleon planning to do what his uncle had failed to achieve more than fifty years earlier? Edward submitted long, thoughtful and detailed reports on military and naval developments in France and came to the conclusion that there was no danger.

'You have no idea how the public are frightened about this French invasion,' he wrote to Lord Cowley on 15 June 1858 while on a fact-finding visit to London, 'and how implicitly they believe it all. It is quite marvellous ... can anything be more untrue ... and yet people swallow it.' Ten days later, he wrote again:

> Everyone seems so much alarmed that it is quite enough to shake the best-rooted convictions and I sometimes ask myself whether after all I may not be mistaken, yet I feel I am not ... The completion of the railway to Cherbourg makes [men] see everything *en noir*, but what answer can one make to military men who tell one gravely that an army could be sent to the said Cherbourg and embarked there without our knowing anything about it ... I dine at the Palace on Monday and I hope the Queen will give me an opportunity of also telling her the plain truth.[4]

The dinner at Buckingham Palace on 28 June was a banquet for Leopold I of Belgium who was making a state visit to London. The following day, Edward wrote again to Lord Cowley:

> Last night I dined at the Palace and had an opportunity of telling Her Majesty that there was no actual ground for all the alarm that has been felt here with regard to France ... her answer was rather a clue to me of the apparent exaggeration of the whole thing. She begged me not to say too much about the want of preparation on the other side and not to let people feel too secure here; she coughed when I said I would take the hint. It is evident that it is done in great measure to get up our own establishments.[5]

Edward had another reason to talk to the queen. Cowley had instructed him to report on the invasion scare in England, but he was also working for Louis-Napoleon who had asked him to arrange a meeting with Victoria and Prince Albert. As the newspapers reported in mid-July:

> Colonel Claremont was the special envoy of the Emperor of the French for the purpose of inviting Her Majesty and the Prince Consort to Cherbourg, which accounts for the distinction with which he has been received, so different to what would be accorded to an ordinary officer of his rank. The Colonel has not only been most graciously received at Court, but has had an audience of the Earl of Derby, to see if he could prevail on the Premier to give that advice to Her Majesty which would bring the mission with which he was charged to a successful issue.
>
> Failing a visit to the Emperor himself, we believe there was an alternative suggested, of the Queen's taking an excursion in the Royal yacht, with a numerous escort of British men-of-war, and just 'dropping in' at the port of Cherbourg while the Emperor was there, in order that there might be an exchange of courtesies between the two fleets.[6]

His meeting with the prime minister took place in Downing Street on 5 July. The following day, he travelled to Aldershot where the queen and members of the royal family were attending a military review. He dined with them in the Royal Pavilion, the party including the Duke of Cambridge who had commanded a division during the Crimean War and was now commander-in-chief of the army.

Edward's negotiations were successful. The meeting of the monarchs took place in Cherbourg in early August. It was not a success and Victoria returned to England incandescent at the size and strength of the French navy. Eight months later, France did declare war, not on Britain but on Austria, a brief engagement known as the Italian Campaign.

In July 1858, Louis-Napoleon signed a treaty of alliance with Sardinia-Piedmont. In exchange for the territories of Nice and Savoy, France would ally itself with Sardinia-Piedmont in the event of Austrian aggression. Sardinia-Piedmont then provoked Austria with a series of military manoeuvres close to the border. Austria issued an ultimatum on 23 April 1859 and, when there was no reply, declared war six days later.

Edward was ordered to accompany the French army into the field. 'As far as I am concerned,' he wrote to Lord Cowley on 5 May, 'a campaign in Italy will be only too interesting ... I shall naturally be put to a great expense fitting myself out.' He estimated that it would cost £600 to provide himself with horses, equipment and weaponry. 'What compensation shall I receive?'[7]

In mid-May, Louis-Napoleon took personal command of his army. On the 22nd, *The Times* correspondent in Marseilles sent a report to London:

> Colonel Claremont, who was with the French staff in the Crimea, arrived here last night and leaves today for Genoa, where he will proceed to join the headquarters of the French army ... His arrival has been expected for some days past by many officers who had the pleasure of making his acquaintance in the Crimea, and who express the greatest delight at the prospect of renewing that acquaintance.

During the campaign, Edward sent 'most valuable reports' to the Foreign Office in London, as well as several personal letters to Lord Cowley in Paris. 'It is very hot already in the middle of the day,' he wrote on 17 June, 'and one is eaten up with vermin at night in the miserable villages where we put up. I would a thousand times rather be under canvas.'[8]

Often riding at Louis-Napoleon's side, Edward advised the emperor on military strategy during the battles of Magenta (4 June) and Solferino (24 June). The battle on the plain of Solferino was particularly bloody. More than 250,000 men took part and the battle lasted for more than nine hours. Edward wrote to Lord Cowley the following day:

> When I saw that all was well, I was obliged to ride back to Castiglione, for I felt so sick from the effects of the sun that I could hardly sit my horse ... The heat is becoming almost insufferable and the villages we come to now are perfectly denuded of everything, the water hereabouts also scarce which adds to the men's sufferings; the cries of the wounded for it yesterday were heart-breaking. It was really enough to make one look upon the whole thing with detestation ... the Emperor looks vastly well, though a little tired.[9]

On 30 June, the foreign secretary wrote about Solferino in his journal:

> Colonel Claremont ... with the French army writes that it has lost 15,000 killed and wounded, among whom are two generals ... He says also that the Austrians retreated in perfect order, and at that moment a tremendous storm came on; the sky was perfectly black, and the constant flash of the lightning, the hurricane, and deluge of rain and hail, all mingled with the roar of cannon, made the most awful scene that can be imagined. When the sun again shone forth, the Austrian columns were just visible in the distance.[10]

The Italian Campaign lasted for less than three months. The armistice was signed on 11 July. At the end of the month, Edward travelled to London for debriefing by the Foreign Office and, on 7 August, he visited Queen Victoria in Osborne House. Ten days later, he received a letter from the foreign secretary congratulating him on 'the manner in which you performed your duties at the headquarters of the French Army'.

Almost as soon as the armistice was signed, Louis-Napoleon announced further measures to reform the army. This led to renewed invasion fears in England. When Edward joined him at a shooting party in Compiègne, the emperor complained 'about the alarm which he understood was prevalent in England with regard to his intentions towards us. He said he was quite at a loss to think why.'[11]

During the next two years, Edward wrote a number of despatches on the strength of the French army. He remained convinced that there was no danger. On 30 January 1861, he handed a despatch to Lord Cowley for onward transmission to the Foreign Office:

> Public opinion both in this country and abroad seems decidedly under the impression that the French government are making great preparations for war, and to a certain extent I can understand it, but I can say only that all the military men with whom I have made it a point to converse on the subject do not seriously think so ... It is undeniable that the military resources of France are very great, and when such resources are in the hands and at the disposal of one man, it is quite natural that other countries ... should feel uneasy.
>
> One must have followed up the matter very closely to see through the sort of halo and prestige which is purposely made to surround everything connected with the army ... There is no doubt that France is able at any moment to make a brilliant dash, but I doubt very much whether she would be able to keep up long sustained efforts ... That the French will always be an extremely awkward and dangerous enemy I do not attempt to deny, but cool stewardship will, I think, always get the better of them in the end.[12]

Edward met Yolande for the first time a few weeks after writing this despatch. He was riding high in his career, both as an army officer and as a diplomat. He was well respected by the military and the Foreign Office, by the commander-in-chief of the army, and by Queen Victoria. In October 1862, when his relationship with Yolande had matured into a love affair and he was helping her settle into Lynford Hall, he was appointed groom of the privy chamber to the recently-widowed queen, an appointment-in-waiting which required him to attend functions at court.

Victoria enjoyed Edward's company. 'When is Major Claremont expected here?' she wrote after he returned from the Crimea. 'The Queen would wish much to see him when he comes.'[13]

13

THE *GRANDE DAME*

The salon ... of a lady of fortune exceeds everything in splendour
that one can venture to imagine.

John Diprose, *Life in Paris*, 1871

When Edward left Lynford Hall in December 1862, Yolande was left alone in the great Jacobean-style mansion. From the windows at the back of the house, she looked over the wide expanse of formal gardens laid out to the designs of William Andrews Nesfield, one of the finest garden designers in England. Beyond the gardens lay the park, its glades and woods receding into the distance as far as the eye could see.

When spring came, she was eager to return to the Hôtel Molé and the arms of her lover. She arrived in Paris in early April, in time to attend a grand reception in the British Embassy to celebrate the marriage of the Prince of Wales. 'The *toilettes* of the ladies were magnificent,' wrote the correspondent of the *London Evening Standard*, 'and the gentlemen were either in uniform or court-dress. No fewer than 1500 invitations had been issued and the whole of the state apartments were thrown open to receive the guests.'

The Times described Paris in the early 1860s as 'the glittering days when the Second Empire was in meridian splendour, when Paris was a name for all that was gay and pleasurable and luxurious'. It was a city where almost all men of society indulged in love affairs, from the emperor downwards; where Yolande's sexual past was nothing to be ashamed of; where she encountered none of the ostracism she experienced in England.

Edward's friendship with Louis-Napoleon, forged during the Italian Campaign, brought her into court circles. She was introduced to the imperial couple and became one of the *grandes dames* of Paris. She was known for the richness of her furniture and furnishings in the Hôtel Molé; for the elegance of her barouche, drawn by two gleaming bay horses, in which she was seen every afternoon in the Bois de Boulogne; for her expensive jewellery and her elaborate dresses from Worth, the English couturier, the high priest of fashion in Second Empire Paris.

Worth dressed the Empress Eugénie, as well as royal and aristocratic ladies from every country in Europe. His dresses were immensely expensive but their materials were rich, their designs intricate and their workmanship exquisite. His workforce of more than a thousand seamstresses was kept busy, for Louis-Napoleon had made it clear that any lady who appeared at the palace in the same dress twice would incur his 'utmost displeasure'.

The couturier employed a number of elegantly-dressed young men who pampered and flattered the customers in his showrooms in the Rue de la Paix. On the first floor, beyond the rooms displaying swathes of rich silks and velvets, was the *Salon de Lumière*, a room lined with mirrors. Thick drapes over the windows removed all natural light and the room was lit only by gas lights with modelling shades. When Yolande tried on her dresses here, she could see herself as she would appear at a candle-lit ball in the Tuileries.

Edward introduced her to three of his English friends in the city: the banker Edward Blount, the Marquis of Hertford, and Hertford's illegitimate son, Richard Wallace, who would inherit his father's fortune as well as one of the finest private art collections in Europe. As Blount explained in his memoirs:

> Claremont ... was a great friend of the Marquis and used to accompany him and Richard Wallace in their expeditions to the heights of Montmartre, or the Latin Quarter, in search of artistic treasures. It was possible in those days, during the latter days of the Empire, when ... art dealers generally were not so well educated as to the merits and value of painters and sculptors ... to pick up, in the most unlooked-for quarters, works of the greatest value for a mere nothing. The three friends were men of taste and connoisseurs, but Wallace was undoubtedly the best and safest of them and his opinion invariably used to prevail. In fact, the Marquis would never buy a picture without taking Wallace to see it and asking his opinion.
>
> The art auctions at the Rue Drouot Public Sale-rooms were ... attended by them, and not a few of the gems of the Wallace Collection were purchased there. But Lord Hertford did not trust only to chance to put together his collection. He used to visit the dealers of the Rue Taitbout and the Rue Laffitte, and when he came across something which he considered worth having, he did not mind paying a good price for it.[1]

In need of paintings to hang in the huge rooms of Lynford Hall, Yolande accompanied them to the auction rooms in the Hôtel Drouot and to private sales of great collections. With their advice, she bid successfully at several auctions during the latter half of the 1860s. Her purchases included three paintings by Velasquez, two by Murillo, a Rubens-Brueghel collaboration, and a full-length portrait of Cardinal Richelieu by Philippe de Champaigne.

In 1867, she arrived in Paris in time to attend the grand opening of the Exposition Universelle on 1 April. The exhibition on the Champ-de-Mars covered almost 200 acres, with 50,000 exhibitors from around the world displaying their wares. Prussia flaunted a variety of military hardware, including a 50-ton steel cannon from the Krupp ironworks capable of firing 1,000-pound shells, the largest cannon ever seen.

During the seven months of the exhibition, Paris was filled with dignitaries from all corners of the globe, many of whom were taken aloft by the photographer Nadar in his hydrogen-filled balloon. Balls were held several nights a week and Yolande was a guest at the Tuileries when Louis-Napoleon entertained the royalty of Europe, including the Prince of Wales, Tsar Alexander II of Russia and Kaiser Wilhelm I of Prussia, accompanied by his chancellor, Otto von Bismarck.

Processions of imperial carriages were seen almost every day on the new wide boulevards of which Louis-Napoleon was so proud. The centre of Paris had been a construction site during much of the Second Empire as Baron Haussmann, the city prefect, swept away a warren of narrow streets through which the cholera epidemic had spread so rapidly in 1832 and replaced them with long, straight, tree-lined streets of impressive width.

Five weeks before the end of the exhibition, Louis Véron died in the Rue de Rivoli. He had sold his newspaper, *Le Constitutionnel*, in 1862, after which, crippled with arthritis and suffering from gout, he withdrew from society and lived quietly with the housekeeper he had inherited from Fanny Elssler more than twenty years before.

While the public profile of one of Yolande's lovers was sinking, another was rising in prominence. A year after their renewed love affair in 1841, Félix de La Valette had married Adeline Welles, a rich American widow. The marriage was, according to her family:

Without doubt the occasion of some surprise and much solicitude to many of her friends, but in making this choice, Mrs Welles displayed her usual discernment, for while others beheld in the Marquis only a brilliant man of fashion, she recognised in him those commanding traits which raised him to the highest posts in the land.[2]

With Adeline's help, La Valette made a name for himself as a diplomat and politician. In 1842, he acted as consul-general in Egypt. After the revolution of 1848, he became friendly with Louis-Napoleon. In May 1851, he was appointed ambassador to Constantinople. His brief was to persuade Turkey to accept France as the sovereign authority over its Christian population, a policy which was a contributing factor in the outbreak of the Crimean War.

Back in Paris ten years later, he was appointed minister of the interior in March 1865 and minister for foreign affairs in December 1868. He and Edward Claremont often spoke together on official occasions, and Yolande would have seen him at balls and other functions. Maybe they exchanged pleasantries about the change in both their fortunes; maybe they just eyed each other across the room.

By the end of the decade, Louis-Napoleon was sixty-one years old. He was tired and had become reliant on his ministers, particularly La Valette and Pierre Baroche, his minister of justice. 'The Emperor and his government are wearing out,' Edward wrote in January 1869. 'People say France is now ruled by a trio consisting of the Empress, Baroche and La Valette. I am not sure that this last does not come number two, so well has he played his cards with His Majesty.'[3]

Despite his friendship with the emperor, La Valette was unpopular in many quarters. The heir to the throne called him a *canaille* – a scoundrel – and according to an anonymous reporter in 1870:

Justice demands that one should give La Valette the benefit of the doubt. Unfortunately, those who know La Valette best are not disposed to give him that benefit ... There is the constant preoccupation to appear *le très grand seigneur* ... He has only conceit, impudence and cunning ... and is irritating beyond endurance.[4]

Louis-Napoleon took the waters at Vichy several times during the 1860s. Members of society followed suit, including his ministers and senior diplomatic staff, as well as Edward Claremont and his family. A photograph of Yolande was taken in Vichy in the summer of 1866. She is standing under a tree in one of Worth's elaborate dresses, her arm around one of Edward's young daughters.

She had been introduced to the Claremont family as a friend. A story would circulate among Edward's descendants that they first met after she had seen his children at play in the garden of his house in the Rue Lord Byron, a garden which was visible from the windows of her apartment in the Champs-Élysées. This story was invented later as a smokescreen, for not only did Yolande not move to the Champs-Élysées until 1875, but the frontage of Edward's house faced the street some distance from her apartment: the garden would have been out of sight.

His wife must have had her suspicions, not least because Edward spent several weeks in Lynford Hall every winter, ostensibly for the shooting but also for the pleasures of Yolande's company and to hang the old master paintings she bought at auction in Paris. She rarely associated with the aristocracy and gentry in Norfolk, although she and Edward sometimes attended the annual 'grand ball' in Thetford Town Hall. They were treated as a couple at these events, the local newspapers referring to 'Colonel Claremont and Mrs Lyne Stephens' – without the customary comma between their names.

Edward's love of shooting at Lynford soon led to feuds with neighbouring farmers who complained about their land being overrun with hares bred for sport. He was present – as 'the manager of her estates' – at the Mundford Petty Sessions on 2 January 1866:

> The Court House in Mundford was crowded throughout the sitting, with a more than ordinarily respectable audience, doubtless attracted by the *cause célèbre* arising out of the unfortunate state of things between Mrs Lyne Stephens and

the Reverend Augustus Sutton, one of the magistrates who has for the last sixteen years acted on this bench ... Mr Sutton owns land at West Tofts over which Mrs Lyne Stephens has the exclusive right of shooting. So destructive is the game to the cropping of his land as to render it almost worthless ... He has therefore adopted ways of reducing the head of game by means of trapping, and a very unpleasant state of feeling has been engendered, not only between the Reverend Mr Sutton and Mrs Lyne Stephens, but also between their servants.[5]

Edward testified on Yolande's behalf as two of her keepers were charged with assaulting a labourer who was laying traps on Sutton's land. One had threatened the labourer with a weapon 'which had a large knob on it and was about a foot in length'; the other had 'assaulted and beaten him'. The Reverend Sutton was also charged with assault, having delivered 'a good kicking' to one of Yolande's keepers as he was manhandled back over the fence.

The following winter, Edward left Paris on 15 December after writing a cryptic note to Lord Cowley: 'I have asked for no extension of leave as I would not do so without your previous sanction, so what can I do?'[6] He stayed in Lynford over Christmas and was still with Yolande during an extremely cold spell during the first week of January. As her head gardener wrote to Messrs Sanders, Frewer and Co., manufacturers of patent glasshouses:

I have had a good trial of your Patent Houses this week ... They resisted thirty-seven degrees of frost without breaking one square or losing one plant; and I like them better and better every day. I certainly thought on Wednesday morning at half-past two o'clock ... that something must give way, but all went off as if nothing had been the matter. I was interrogated by Mrs Lyne Stephens and Colonel Claremont the same day as to the frost and the Houses, and they appeared *very satisfied*.[7]

Edward's plans to return to Paris the following week were thwarted by massive falls of snow which began on the 11th and increased in intensity for several days. According to the *Norfolk News*:

> The appearance of the roads in the country districts was such as has not been witnessed for many years past ... The most serious consequence of the storm was the stoppage of railway traffic ... The blocking up of the railways in all parts of the district is described as beyond anything which has been experienced during the past twenty years.

With snow drifts up to 9 feet high, Edward was detained in Norfolk until the weather cleared towards the end of the month. He was back in Paris in February, attending several functions at court and making preparations to welcome the Prince of Wales to the Exposition Universelle.

14

A MERE POINT OF ETIQUETTE

*Colonel Claremont is doing his best to look after the interests of
my fellow-countrymen. He is a man of energy and good common
sense, with very little of the pipeclay about him.*

Henry Labouchere, Paris, 8 October 1870

Every year, Louis-Napoleon conducted a grand review of his army
at which Edward Claremont, 'whose scarlet tunic always produces
the most striking effect at a French review', represented the British
nation. During the Exposition Universelle in 1867, the review was
held on 6 June on the racecourse at Longchamp. Louis-Napoleon
watched the proceedings from horseback, accompanied by Tsar
Alexander and Kaiser Wilhelm, while the massed ranks of soldiers
shouted '*Vive l'Empereur!*' as they marched and rode past, their
weapons gleaming.

The final grand review of the Second Empire took place in
the Bois de Boulogne on 7 May 1869. This time, the emperor
was accompanied by Archduke Franz Joseph of Austria and the
Prince of Wales, who looked 'very striking' in his uniform as
colonel-in-chief of Stephens's old regiment, the Tenth Hussars.
During the summer, Edward was awarded the Légion d'Honneur

(third class), an honour bestowed personally by Louis-Napoleon. He needed royal assent before he could wear the insignia, an assent granted by Queen Victoria in November when he was making his annual visit to Yolande in Lynford Hall.

He returned to Paris in December. Seven months later, the outbreak of the Franco-Prussian War would not only change the face of Europe, it would also have far-reaching consequences for Edward and Yolande. Once again, she will be absent from most of the next two chapters as events unfold to create a major change in both their lives.

In 1867, as part of his plan to extend German unification, Bismarck had annexed adjoining German states to form the North German Confederation. Three years later, he set out to provoke France in an attempt to draw southern German states into alliance with the northern confederation. As he explained in his memoirs:

> I was convinced that the gulf ... between the north and the south of Germany could not be better overcome than by a national war against the neighbouring people ... I did not doubt that it was necessary to make a French-German war before the general reorganisation of Germany could be realised.[1]

Bismarck provoked Louis-Napoleon by creating a diplomatic crisis over the succession to the Spanish throne. After a meeting on 13 July 1870 between Kaiser Wilhelm and the French ambassador to Prussia, he sent a carefully edited despatch to France which made it appear that the French emperor had been insulted. There was outrage in Paris when the despatch was published in the newspapers. People marched through the streets with flags and banners, singing the *Marseillaise* and shouting '*Vive la guerre!*'

Louis-Napoleon took the bait. On 19 July, he declared war on Prussia. 'The Second Empire,' commented the *Illustrated London News*, 'goes to war on a mere point of etiquette.' People were confident of a quick victory and the public was assured that the army was 'ready down to the last gaiter button'. Only a few voices, Edward Claremont's among them, made the point that – despite the glittering displays at his grand reviews – Louis-Napoleon's army was ill-equipped and badly organised.

The emperor's health was failing. He had chronic pain in his legs and feet. He found it difficult to ride a horse and he walked slowly, often with a cane. He suffered from urinary problems which were treated with opium. In February, Edward wrote that he looked 'fat and heavy'. In April, an English visitor found him 'terribly changed and very ill'. In June, he was diagnosed with gallstones. On the outbreak of war, he told one of his generals that he felt too old for a military campaign.

Edward sent his wife and children to safety in London; as soon as they left, he moved out of the Rue Lord Byron and into the Hôtel Molé. A few days later, he persuaded Yolande to leave the city with her servants and return to England. She left him installed in a wing of the Hôtel Molé (85 *bis*, Rue du Faubourg Saint-Honoré). The French government denied his request to accompany the army into the field, so he asked the Foreign Office for permission to return to England for the duration of the war. This too was refused.

The mobilisation of the army was chaotic, with 200,000 soldiers converging on the long German border, choking the roads and the railways, without proper orders and finding it difficult to regroup in their regiments. On 28 July, Louis-Napoleon travelled by train to the front, leaving the Empress Eugénie to act as regent in Paris. On 2 August, he accompanied his troops across the border and won a minor skirmish; unable to ride, he supported himself during the engagement by leaning against a tree.

There was dismay in Paris when news arrived on 7 August that the French had been defeated three times in battle. The prime minister resigned and the empress took charge of the government. There was a further setback in mid-August, followed by a major defeat at Sedan, near the Belgian border, on 1 September. Some

17,000 French soldiers were killed and 21,000 taken prisoner – including their commander, Louis-Napoleon.

The following day, an English army surgeon, Charles Gordon, arrived in Paris with instructions to serve as a medical commissioner with the French army and report to the War Office in London. 'An impression was in the air that all was not well,' he wrote in his memoirs, 'but beyond rumours more or less vague, nothing seemed to indicate knowledge of actual events.' Next morning:

> Colonel Claremont ... conducted me to the several offices, from one or other of which he expected that the necessary orders would be issued to enable me to carry out the mission assigned to me. Failing to obtain those orders ... he made direct application to the Minister for War, but with no other result ... It was evident that something very unusual had taken place or was in progress; the demeanour of the officials ... indicated the fact with sufficient clearness. Colonel Claremont was in all probability made acquainted with the nature of the events in questions, for as we separated ... his parting remark was, 'I don't expect now that you will go much beyond Paris.'[2]

Edward was a few hours ahead of the crowd. When news of the surrender at Sedan became public at midnight, 'the rage, excitement and indignation were indescribable'. 'All through the night,' wrote Charles Gordon, 'there were sounds of movement in the streets: the tread of troops on the march, the heavy roll of guns, tumbrils, and wagons.' Shortly after midnight, the Chamber of Deputies announced that the imperial regime had fallen. In the morning:

> A dense and tumultuous crowd filled the Place de la Concorde. In the Rue Royale and Faubourg Saint-Honoré, workmen were hauling down the imperial eagles by which public buildings were distinguished ... the mob cheering them as they proceeded ... The gates of the Tuileries were open, the gardens of the palace filled

with people. Down the Rue de Rivoli and upwards towards the Arc de Triomphe and the Champs-Élysées, streams of people were in motion.[3]

The Tuileries was surrounded and Eugénie, peering out of a window, heard 'the menacing roar of the crowds' and shouts of '*Vive la République!*' She slipped out of a back door wearing a long cloak and a veil, and made her way to the house of Dr Thomas Evans, an American dentist who looked after the imperial teeth. Next morning, she and Evans set out on a two-day journey to Deauville, travelling in disguise as an Englishwoman in the care of her physician. In the harbour, Dr Evans found Sir John Burgoyne, owner of the yacht *Gazelle*, who agreed to take Eugénie across the Channel to safety.

Prussian troops led by Wilhelm I were marching on Paris. Versailles was taken on 18 September and became the Prussian headquarters. On the same day, the provisional government left the city to relocate in Bordeaux, leaving one of Edward's friends, General Trochu, in charge of the defence of Paris. On the 20th, the city was surrounded and the siege began.

Lord Lyons, who had replaced Lord Cowley as British ambassador, had left Paris on the 17th, together with most of the embassy staff. In his opinion:

> The protection of our countrymen who might still remain could not be transferred to better hands than those of Colonel Claremont who, from … his large acquaintance among French military men and well-known influence with them, would have peculiar means of befriending and assisting British subjects if actual danger from military operations should be imminent.[4]

On the 23rd, he wrote a personal letter to Edward, who had again asked to be relieved from duty in Paris: 'Whether this letter will ever get to you, and if so when, I am unable to divine …

I miss your morning visits very much ... and have not the satisfaction of thinking that you are in a better place and that my loss is your gain.' He had received a letter from the Foreign Office confirming that Edward should stay in Paris. If there was a bombardment, 'that would be precisely the time that a military man could obtain most valuable information'.

Communication with the outside world was erratic. Letters out of the city were despatched by hot-air balloons which flew over Prussian lines into the safety of unoccupied France. Incoming letters arrived by carrier pigeon. On 5 October, fifteen days after Paris was surrounded, Edward sent a despatch to Lord Lyons by balloon post:

> The feelings of the people here are getting so excited that it is almost unsafe to walk about the streets, and certainly to go on the line of the fortifications ... The Red or Republican party are almost the only advocates for a serious resistance ... The government is obliged in a great measure to yield to them for fear of having either to make way for them or to have civil war raging in the streets at the same time as they have to face the enemy outside. Altogether it is a most painful and unprecedented position and I am afraid we shall have to witness dreadful scenes.

He continued with news of the availability of supplies: 'Provisions that will not keep, such as fresh butter, eggs, fruit and vegetables, have already disappeared from the market. Poultry is getting scarce. I am afraid that the supply of meat will not hold out very long ... Prices, of course, are on the rise.'[5]

Towards the end of the month, he received a letter from Lord Lyons by pigeon post, enclosing a note from his wife and further news from the Foreign Office. The letter was dated 21 October:

> You will see what the Foreign Office says about your leaving Paris. They offered me some time ago an extra-mural Military Attaché,

which I accepted, having no hope of your being able to come away so soon ... I have given no opinion, my only preference among military men is for you – and that is a very decided preference indeed.

'Colonel Claremont is doing his best to look after the interests of my fellow-countrymen,' wrote Henry Labouchere, an English resident, on 8 October. 'He is a man of energy and good common sense, with very little of the pipeclay about him.'

By the end of the month, it was agreed that British residents who wished to leave, together with the few remaining embassy staff, would be given *laissez-passer* through the opposing lines. Only Edward Claremont and the naval attaché, Captain Hore, would remain at their posts. 'The English at last are about to leave,' wrote Labouchere on 7 November:

> They are very indignant at having been, as they say, humbugged so long, and loud in their complaints against the Embassy. I do not think, however, that the delay has been the fault ... of Colonel Claremont [who] did his best, but he was unable to get the Prussian and French authorities to agree upon a day of the exodus. On the one hand, to send to Versailles to receive an answer took forty-eight hours; on the other, from the fact that Britain had not recognised the Republic, General Trochu could not be approached officially. Colonel Claremont happens to be a personal friend of his, and it is thanks to his exertions ... that the matter has at length been satisfactorily arranged.[6]

Edward accompanied the first contingent, 'two or three English gentlemen', in the early morning of 8 November. Snow had fallen overnight and their carriage travelled along roads 'deep in slush'. After they had passed safely through the lines, Edward returned to Paris, while a further seventy-five British residents made their way to Versailles, the wealthy in carriages, the poor on foot. Perhaps surprisingly, about 4,000 chose to remain in the city.

On 19 November, Edward sent a despatch in cypher to Lord Lyons by balloon post: 'There must be fighting soon. I have no great confidence in the army. I think that it will bring matters to a crisis which can hardly be done now without more bloodshed. We have food for nearly two months more.'[7]

His instruction from the Foreign Office, included in Lord Lyons's letter of 21 October, was brief: 'As regards Colonel Claremont, he should follow the course adopted by the Military Attachés of other countries who may have remained in Paris.' On 23 November, the military attaché at the Russian embassy, Prince Wittgenstein, received orders to leave the city, so Edward decided to join him. 'Colonel Claremont and a porter now represent the British nation,' wrote Labouchere:

> The former, in obedience to orders from the Foreign Office, is only waiting for a reply from Count Bismarck to his letter asking for a pass to leave us. Whether the numerous English who remain here are then to look to ... the porter for protection, I have been unable to discover.[8]

Edward sent another despatch in cypher on 6 December, after French troops had attempted a five-day sortie which ended in disaster: 'Ten thousand men altogether killed and wounded. I am afraid the morale is low.' He and Wittgenstein had put off their departure to follow the sortie; according to Labouchere, Edward 'was nearly killed several times by bombs from La Faisanderie, which was behind him, falling short'.

Having obtained his pass through the American ambassador, Elihu B. Washburn (who commented that Edward was 'slightly disgusted at Paris life at present'), he left the city at dawn on 12 December, accompanied by Wittgenstein and Captain Hore. They had difficulty passing through the lines and it was 'a tedious and distressing journey' to Versailles involving an overnight stop in the village of Villeneuve-Saint-Georges. 'Sleeping in one's clothes in an omnibus,' explained the special correspondent of the *London Evening Standard*, 'with the thermometer below freezing point is not pleasant.'

When they reached Prussian headquarters on 13 December, Edward learned that he had been promoted to the rank of major-general, a promotion back-dated to March 1868 'to give him greater importance during the progress of the military operations'. He had an interview with the director of the siege, General von Blumenthal, during which he maintained 'a proper silence on military matters ... without concealing his opinion that the city is not at all disposed to surrender'. In the evening, he dined with Wilhelm I and 'was graciously received. If his reports had been diligently studied, there would have been no great surprise felt in official circles at the catastrophe which befell the French armies.'[9]

Edward left Versailles four days later, arriving in London on the 21st. Reunited with his family in their rented lodgings, he drafted a despatch for Lord Lyons in Bordeaux and for Lord Granville, the foreign secretary, which he sent to the Foreign Office on 30 December with a covering letter:

I have the honour to forward herewith the draft of a despatch for Lord Lyons which I would request you to send to Bordeaux by the first messenger. I was anxious to get it off as soon as possible and have not had time to copy it, which I hope you will excuse – my wish being that Lord Granville should in this way have cognizance of it and no unnecessary time be lost ...

The best ally that the Germans have is hunger, for it is quite clear that a large town like Paris, with over two million inhabitants, cannot hold out forever if not revictualled; there will be nothing brilliant in such a success and it will be very much sullied by the acts of open theft and pillage which are now perpetrated in every direction.[10]

On 12 January, Lord Lyons wrote to the Foreign Office. He had been asked for his opinion on:

> the necessity or advisableness of Major-General Claremont coming to Bordeaux and to state also in what way I consider, if his services are required, they can be turned to best account. I do not think that there is any great necessity under present circumstances that a Military Attaché should reside with the Embassy in Bordeaux, as no active operations are going on in the immediate neighbourhood of this place and very little information on military matters is to be obtained here.

However, he continued, if a 'competent military officer' could accompany the French Army of the East commanded by General Bourbaki, this would provide 'important and interesting information'. He had already obtained French approval for this. Six days later, in a despatch dated 19 January, the Foreign Office instructed Edward to travel to Bordeaux 'without delay' and to act as observer in the French Army of the East.[11]

By this time, Edward was no longer in London. He was with Yolande in Lynford Hall, having travelled to Norfolk in early January. He did not reply to the order from the Foreign Office for fifteen days – by which time Bourbaki's army had been defeated, an armistice had been signed in Paris, and the war was effectively over. His letter to the Foreign Office, dated 3 February and written in Lynford Hall, was brusque:

> I hope you will excuse my not answering your despatch of the 19th ultimo sooner, as the delay is owing to a circumstance over which I had no control. I suppose the fate which has befallen the army of General Bourbaki precludes the necessity of my complying with the instructions you conveyed to me in the said despatch and I shall therefore await Lord Granville's further orders.[12]

The seven weeks between Edward's departure for Versailles on 12 December and the armistice on 28 January had been appallingly grim in Paris. By early January, there was almost no food left in the city. People were eating cats, dogs, horses, and rats. The taste of rat was described as 'something between frog and rabbit', and a Paris journal offered tips on how to 'fish for sewer rats with a hook and line baited with tallow'. Animals in the zoo at Vincennes were slaughtered for food, and restaurants and street vendors sold meat and offal from bears, buffaloes, camels, elephants, monkeys, and zebras.

It was a cold winter too. The Seine was frozen, gas supplies were exhausted, trees in the parks had been cut down and burnt, and there was little coal or wood remaining for warmth or for cooking the meagre amounts of food available. Crowds attacked the homes of the wealthy to obtain fuel, felling garden trees and pulling down fences.

Before his departure, Edward had arranged with General Trochu to leave the embassy in the care of his friend, the banker Edward Blount. 'The Embassy is now gone,' Blount wrote to his wife by balloon post on 22 December, 'and I have all the English miseries on my back.' In early January, the Prussians began a bombardment, firing shells into the city every night for several hours. 'I am terribly tormented by the English,' Blount wrote on 23 January. 'They are frightened out of their wits, have no money, and are watched as spies. My whole day is occupied with them. The ministers treat me as if I had official powers, but I have none.'[13]

Two days later, Bismarck intensified the bombardment by firing 1,000-pound shells from Krupp's 50-ton steel cannons, one of which had been proudly displayed at the Exposition Universelle. On the same day, Blount received a despatch from the foreign secretary in London giving him the temporary appointment of consul. Lord Granville thanked him 'for the kind attention which you are showing the interests of British subjects shut up in Paris, and I have thought it might aid you in doing so if you were provided with some official authority'. Lord Lyons wrote on the 27th: 'I cannot tell you what a relief it is to me that you should have official authority to take care of our countrymen in Paris in these terrible times.'

In his capacity as temporary consul, Blount officiated at the marriage of his friend Richard Wallace to Julie Castelnau, the former *parfumerie* assistant with whom Wallace had been living for many years. There was a thirty-year-old son of the liaison but they were only free to marry after the death of Wallace's father, Lord Hertford, a few weeks before the city was surrounded.

Wallace, too, remained in Paris during the siege. He was untiring in his efforts to help the people, providing two field hospitals and donating an estimated £100,000 to charity. He became a popular and recognisable figure as he walked through the city to distribute money to the mairies: 'a tall gentleman with a grizzled moustache, accompanied by a black-and-tan retriever dog'.

15

LA SEMAINE SANGLANTE

The state of Paris is heart-breaking ... Fires in all directions, the air
oppressive with smoke and unpleasant odours, the incessant roar of
cannon and musketry, and all kinds of strange sounds.

Lord Lyons, 26 May 1871

Edward returned to the Hôtel Molé on 27 February to be reunited with
his friends who were exhausted and demoralised after four months of
fear, cold and hunger. His orders from the Foreign Office, received
three days earlier, were to 'proceed at once to Paris' to prepare 'a full
and professional report' and 'furnish much valuable information on a
variety of subjects'. The despatch concluded with the words, 'Unless
Lord Lyons should summon you to Bordeaux, it is his desire that you
should, whatever events may arise, remain in Paris.'[1]

On 1 March, the Prussian army made a triumphal entry into the
city for an occupation of three days. Edward chose to remain out of
sight in the embassy: 'I was afraid I might be recognised and accosted
by some of their officers and anyone seen talking to them was roughly
handled by the bystanders.' Edward Blount had no such qualms:

I saw them come in yesterday and they were very splendid in
appearance and conduct. The mob surrounded them and called

them all sorts of names, but they took it all quietly and with disdain ... The shops are all shut, the people all idle and talking dreadful words.[2]

Meanwhile, the provisional government had disbanded after the armistice and elections held on 8 February had brought a conservative, royalist government to power. This led to unrest among republicans in the city. 'One of the worst features of the situation,' Edward explained on 6 March, 'is that even good people are so exasperated by the way in which their affairs have been mismanaged ... that they now trust and respect no one, and this I am afraid will constitute a dangerous state of things for some time to come.'[3]

Seven days later, during a debate in the House of Commons, a member of parliament raised a question for Lord Enfield, under-secretary of state for foreign affairs. He asked whether 'General Claremont, to whom Lord Lyons transferred the protection of English subjects in Paris ... was subsequently authorised by Lord Lyons to leave Paris several weeks before the conclusion of the siege'. He also asked whether 'Her Majesty's Government approved the withdrawal of General Claremont under the circumstances which then existed'.

Enfield replied by referring to the instructions which Lord Granville had sent Lord Lyons in October, 'under which General Claremont deemed himself at liberty to act'. He read out the words: 'As regards Colonel Claremont, he should follow the course adopted by the Military Attachés of other countries who may have remained in Paris.'

At this point, Sir Robert Peel (who had described the behaviour of the embassy as 'slinking away with ignominy and disgrace during a season of great trial and difficulty') rose to his feet and spoke 'in severe terms' about Edward's departure during the siege. It was, he said, 'a gross dereliction of duty', with 'deplorable' effects on British residents in the city.

The debate was reported in *The Times* on 11 March, copies of which arrived in Paris two days later. On the 14th, Lord Lyons and his staff returned to the city to find the embassy 'quite uninjured, no trace of the siege in the neighbourhood, and the town merely looking a little duller than usual'. The following day, Edward handed the ambassador a long letter of justification which he had been drafting for the last two days:

Owing to the questions which have been asked in the House of Commons on the subject of my leaving this place on 12th December last, I am anxious to lay before your Excellency the circumstances under which I considered myself justified in doing so ...

On 21 October, we received by pigeon a despatch from you saying from Lord Granville that the Prussian Government was ready to pass the *personnel* of the British Embassy and such British subjects as would join them. As far as I can recollect, a telegram to the same effect came in the next day from Lord Granville, through Versailles, the last sentence of which was 'Claremont will know what the other Military Attachés do'.

He pointed out that the Italian military attaché had already gone and, apart from Prince Wittgenstein who left with him in December, there remained in the city 'only Count Uxkull for Austria, for I hardly counted a Turk whom I never heard of before ... Captain Leontiew, a Russian, a kind of aide-de-camp to Prince Wittgenstein, and Colonel de Capellen, a Dutchman who has been settled here for years and who had been driven in by the occupation of his country-house by the Germans.' These men, he suggested, could hardly be considered competent military attachés with the ability to represent their countries at a time of war.

On 23rd November Prince Wittgenstein received orders to leave and asked me to accompany him. Knowing that a sortie on a large scale was contemplated, I suggested that we had better wait to see the result, as it might be very important; to this he most readily assented. I have reported the result of this sortie ... which made it very evident that all efforts on the part of the garrison to break through the German lines would be unavailing.

After waiting a few days, Prince Wittgenstein and I agreed that we might then leave and I called on General Trochu for the purpose; I did not consider myself in any way attached to his headquarters, but from the terms I was on with him I declared to him that, if in any way he thought I could be of any use by remaining, nothing would induce me to go. He answered that, on the contrary, he was of opinion I could be of more service by going, as I could tell people outside the exact state of the case inside; indeed, other official persons entertained and expressed to me the same opinion.

The news of Edward's arrival at the Prussian headquarters on 13 December was 'immediately telegraphed' to the Foreign Office, after which:

I remained four days at Versailles, and had any desire to that effect been intimated to me, I do not suppose any difficulty would have been made to my returning to Paris ... Not hearing anything, I proceeded to England on the 17th, and on my arrival there, I did not appear to be unexpected, nor had I then any reason to suppose I had acted contrary to any instructions; and I can safely and conscientiously say that it was far from my wish to do so ...

My position differed very materially from that of an officer attached to a regular army; the foolish and absurd suspicions of the National Guards and irregular corps made it more than disagreeable to go about amongst them; still I should have gone on bearing with it had I received no communication whatever from either the Foreign Office or from your Excellency. As it was, I really and sincerely thought that it was not contemplated that I should remain here.

Edward had always been prickly and impulsive, traits commented on by the previous ambassador, Lord Cowley. On the morning of 16 March, after spending another sleepless night in the Hôtel Molé, he wrote a second letter to Lord Lyons:

> As I explained to your Excellency in my despatch of yesterday's date, I acted from the best motives when I left Paris in December last. It is only from what has taken place lately that I have been led to suppose that I made a mistake in so doing; and the only way in which I can atone for such a mistake is to beg you to place my resignation at Lord Granville's disposal. I have had the honour of being connected with this Embassy now for a long time; it is not without some degree of pain that I shall cease to belong to it, but it would be altogether foreign to my nature to remain in any position, whatever may be the personal consequences to myself, without the full approval of those under whom I serve.

This hastily written letter, which he handed personally to Lord Lyons, was intended as a gesture which he assumed would not be taken at face value. The Foreign Office did not have to accept his resignation. Indeed, when forwarding the letter to the Foreign Office that afternoon, Lord Lyons made the specific recommendation that it should not be accepted:

> It will be a great misfortune for this Embassy if his official connection with it be allowed to terminate ... I might cite many instances in which the information furnished by General Claremont has been of very remarkable value during the time he has been under my orders; and certainly your Lordship cannot have failed to be struck ... with the sagacity and foresight respecting military and also political matters which are manifest in the despatches which General Claremont has written from the time when the war became imminent in July last up to the present day.

The assistance which I have derived from my personal intercourse with General Claremont has been very great; and I am sure that my predecessor ... would speak with equal satisfaction of his own intercourse with him ... Supposing that an officer could be found with the same natural aptitude for the work, and supposing, which is far from probable, that such an officer should have equal opportunities of becoming intimate with French military men, it would still necessarily require many years for him to attain the position here which General Claremont has made for himself. I therefore consider that it will on public grounds be deeply to be regretted if this Embassy be deprived of General Claremont's services.

The Foreign Office thought differently. Lord Granville replied to Lord Lyons, asking him to inform Edward 'that his resignation is accepted and that he is consequently, as far as this office is concerned, free to leave Paris as soon as his successor, who will be immediately appointed, shall arrive to relieve him'.[4]

Here the plot thickens a little. Lord Granville, the foreign secretary, was the elder brother of Edward's boyhood friend Frederick Leveson-Gower, who was also in parliament as the member for Bodmin. Leveson-Gower wrote to Edward on 17 March:

I am much annoyed at the persistent and unjust way in which you are attacked. If an opportunity occurs, I should like to remind the House of your long and valuable services. It certainly would have been better if you had remained in Paris till the end. It is a pity that you did not have more definite instructions ... It would be a great folly on your part to resign at the present moment. Do not be angry with me for saying to you what I think. You know how warmly I have at heart your real interests.

On the 18th, two days after Edward's resignation, republican sympathisers overthrew the government in Paris and took control of the city. 'The Reds are the complete masters of the town,' wrote Edward the following day. 'I called at the War Department this morning ... The confusion seemed complete.'

The government moved to safety in Versailles and, on 21 March, Lord Lyons and most of the embassy staff followed suit. Only Edward Claremont and three other men remained in Paris. 'I have desired General Claremont to stay at Paris,' Lord Lyons explained to the Foreign Office, 'as I consider that his assistance in providing, in case of need, for the safety of Her Majesty's subjects would be extremely important and valuable.'

On 26 March, the Reds won a majority in municipal elections and, as the Commune of Paris installed itself in the Hôtel de Ville, Parisians gathered in their thousands, wearing red scarves and shouting '*Vive la Commune!*' while cannons were fired in salute and massed bands played the *Marseillaise*.

Lord Lyons changed his mind on 6 April and instructed Edward to join him in Versailles: 'Your knowledge of French military affairs, and in particular your large acquaintance with French military men, would be better turned to account during operations now in progress by making Versailles your headquarters for the present.'[5]

Edward left the Hôtel Molé and, during the next three weeks, wrote despatches about the organisation of the army and the difficulty of attacking the Reds in Paris. 'All military men of any standing with whom I have conversed here,' he wrote on the 15th, 'seem more and more convinced of the difficulty of entering Paris, and indeed it does not require much military experience to see this ... It is altogether the most extraordinary state of things; for five months the French army tried to get out of Paris and could not; now it is just as difficult for them to enter it, and no professional man who knows anything seems to see the end.'[6]

He spent a few hours in Paris on the 22nd and reported that the Reds were 'putting up enormous barricades in different parts of the town, very superior to those they made at first'. His replacement as military attaché, Colonel James Conolly, arrived in Versailles on the 27th and Edward wrote his final despatch the following day:

> The formidable barricades ... continue to rise up in every direction ... I may be thought to be taking too gloomy a view of the affair, but I try to see things as they are, not as I should wish them to be, which people are too apt to do here. I only hope that Colonel Conolly, who arrived here yesterday to relieve me, will be able to give your Excellency a brighter account in future.[7]

Soon there were skirmishes in the suburbs. The army began to bombard the city centre, as the Prussians had done four months earlier, and a number of shells fell on the Champs-Élysées. 'This is not intended,' explained Colonel Conolly on 4 May, 'but as most of the artillery men of the old school are still prisoners in Germany, the gunners are now for the most part very young, and their fire is often wild.'[8]

Civil war was declared on 14 May. Seven days later, government forces entered the city, the people of Paris were called to the barricades and the streets became a battlefield. The Reds set fire to buildings in the city centre, fires which – fanned by hot weather and strong winds – consumed entire streets. 'The state of Paris is heart-breaking,' wrote Lord Lyons, who returned from Versailles for just one night:

> Fires in all directions, the air oppressive with smoke and unpleasant odours, the incessant roar of cannon and musketry, and all kinds of strange sounds ... a fire raging in the next street but one, shells falling on the roof which might set fire to the house at any moment, and shot flying so fast on both sides that escape in case of fire would have hardly been possible.[9]

Soldiers executed all the Reds they could find, as well as those suspected of harbouring them, and when there were no more barricades to defend, surviving Reds were lined up against walls and shot, their corpses burnt on funeral pyres or thrown into mass graves. There was fighting in the Rue du Faubourg Saint-Honoré, followed by soldiers dragging Reds from their hiding places and killing them in the street. More than 10,000 people died during what became known as *La Semaine Sanglante* – Bloody Week.

It was all over by the end of the month. The government took control of the city on 28 May, order returned to the streets, and an Englishman emerged from hiding. 'What a sight met my eyes,' he wrote in his diary, 'destruction everywhere. From the Châtelet to the Hôtel de Ville, all was destroyed, not a room left.'[10] The palace of the Tuileries, the scene of so many glittering occasions during Louis-Napoleon's Second Empire, was reduced to a burnt-out shell. A few weeks later, Thomas Cook was advertising special excursions to see 'the ruins of Paris'.

Five days after the defeat of the Commune, news arrived in Versailles that Sir Robert Peel had attacked Edward for a second time in the House of Commons. In a debate on the salaries and expenses of the Foreign Office, he complained that 'General Claremont ... has received £500 per annum for many years out of the Secret Service money for what were called his services, in addition to his fixed stipend'. He also complained that, 'to use a common expression', Edward had 'levanted from his post as soon as the condition of things round Paris became precarious'. Peel's speech was followed by another member saying that it was 'monstrous' that Edward should have received £500 a year from 'Secret Service money'.

Edward had lost his position in the embassy, he was being vilified in parliament, and his mother, Anaïs Aubert, was dying in the village of Louveciennes near Versailles from an illness which caused her 'much suffering'. He looked after her for seven weeks until she died in his arms on 25 July. 'It was the most touching thing,' he wrote in his diary that night, 'to see her trying with her poor emaciated hand to make the sign of the Cross.'

On the 27th, he 'put my dear mother in her coffin'. Two days later, Anaïs was buried in the cemetery at Montparnasse. Later that day, after seeing the notary about the sale of her house, Edward complained that the formalities would take several weeks and that 'every kind of annoyance is to be expected'.

Next morning, he received a letter of sympathy from Frederick Leveson-Gower, who had known Anaïs during his childhood in Paris: 'I know how much you will feel it, but your consolation must be that she is spared any more suffering and that you have always been to her the best of sons.' He also received a letter from General Henry Ponsonby, private secretary to Queen Victoria, whom he had first met in the Crimea:

I have to thank you for the excellent photograph for the Queen's book. Her Majesty is much pleased with it and it is placed in the album in the space which was waiting for your portrait ... I never understood your resignation. I knew Lord Lyons was strongly in favour of you, but all I could learn was that you had resigned ... and just at the moment when your intimate acquaintance with French military men would have proved most useful. Conolly no doubt is a worthy successor, but a new man always finds it difficult to take up a good predecessor's work.

On 28 July, Leveson-Gower had made 'an excellent speech' in the House of Commons during a second debate on the salaries and expenses of the Foreign Office:

I find myself called upon to defend the character, ability, prudence, and courage of General Claremont, a particular friend of mine, who has been most unjustly criticised and most unfairly represented. I am satisfied that public opinion will acquit him of the unjust censures which have been cast upon him – censures which he has not in any way deserved.

Above left: 1. Duvernay as Miranda in *La Tentation*, having just emerged from the cauldron. Mezzotint after painting by François-Gabriel Lépaulle, *c.* 1832.

Above right: 2. Yolande Duvernay, painted by Antonin Moine at the height of her celebrity, Paris, mid-1830s.

3. The cloister scene in Meyerbeer's opera *Robert le Diable*, Paris Opéra House (Salle le Peletier). Lithograph by J. Arnoult, 1840s. Yolande danced the role of the abbess in 1832.

Above left: 4. Dr Louis Véron. Engraving by Charles Carey, 1855.

Above right: 5. Contemporary caricature of Dr Louis Véron, showing the large cravats he wore to hide a skin infection, *c.* 1835.

Below: 6. A performance of *Giselle* in the Paris Opéra House (Salle le Peletier), 4 June 1867. Lithograph by Collen Imerton, *c.* 1870.

Above left: 7. Duvernay in *The Devil on Two Sticks*, painted 'from recollection' by Princess Victoria, 5 April 1837.

Above right: 8. Duvernay in *Cachucha* costume in Act 2 of *The Devil on Two Sticks*, painted by Princess Victoria, 26 December 1836.

Below left: 9. Duvernay as the Naiad in a scene from *La Belle au Bois Dormant* (*The Sleeping Beauty*). Lithograph after painting by John Rogers Herbert, London, February/March 1833.

Below right: 10. Duvernay wearing male costume in Act 3 of *The Devil on Two Sticks*, painted by Princess Victoria, January 1837. The costume was, wrote Victoria, 'very becoming … and she looks *so* handsome'.

11. *The Melton Breakfast*. Engraving after original painting by Sir Frances Grant, 1834. Stephens is sitting on the sofa behind the table, sixth from the left.

12. Chicksands Priory, painted by Thomas Fisher, *c.* 1815.

Above left: 13. Duvernay. Lithograph after painting by Alfred Edward Chalon, London, 1830s.

14–16. Duvernay in *Cachucha* costume. *Top right:* 14. Lithograph after painting by John Frederick Lewis, 1837. *Bottom left:* 15. Lithograph after painting by Alfred Edward Chalon, *c.* 1837. *Bottom right:* 16. Lithograph by Madeley, *c.* 1836.

17. Convent of the Sacred Heart, Roehampton, *c*. 1856. The chapel where Yolande attended Mass is on the left.

18. Grove House, Roehampton, photographed *c*. 1920. Front elevation.

19. Grove House, Roehampton, *c*. 1920. Rear elevation, showing the façade and terrace added by Stephens in 1851/52.

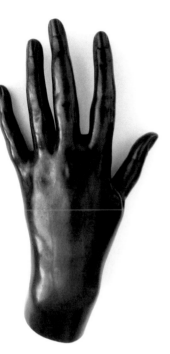

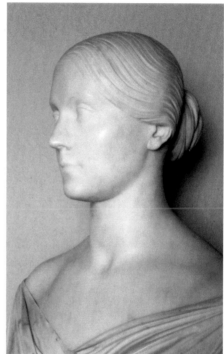

Above left: 20. Bronze cast of Yolande's left hand, 1845.

Above right: 21. White marble portrait bust of Yolande, sculpted in Florence by Lorenzo Bartolini, 1845.

22. Portman Square, north side, 1813.

Above left: 23. Stephens. Portrait by unknown painter, mid-1850s.

Above right: 24. Yolande, painted by Edouard Dubufe, 1853.

Below left: 25. Lyne Stephens coat of arms.

Below right: 26. Stephens. Watercolour sketch, late 1850s.

27. Hôtel Molé, Paris,
photographed *c.* 1920.
Courtyard view.

28. Hôtel Molé, Paris,
c. 1920. Garden view.

29. Hôtel Molé, Paris,
c. 1920. Grand salon.

Left: 30. Stephens. Portrait by unknown painter, *c.* 1859. He is holding a wad of banknotes in his hand to symbolise his status as the richest commoner in England.

Below left: 31. Yolande in mourning dress. Carte-de-visite by Bingham, Paris, 1861.

Below right: 32. Yolande. Carte-de-visite by Levitsky, Paris, *c.* 1862.

Above: 33. Lynford Hall, photographed in 1903. North front, showing the ornamental gates.

Below: 34. Lynford Hall, photographed in 1903. View from the south-west, showing part of the formal gardens.

Above left: 35. Yolande. Carte-de-visite by Le Jeune (Ancienne M. Levitsky), Paris, 1864.

Above right: 36. Colonel Edward Claremont, military attaché in Paris. Lithograph by C. W. Walton, c. 1868.

Below left: 37. Félix, Marquis de La Valette. Carte-de-visite by Levitsky, Paris, early 1860s.

Below right: 38. Frances Claremont with her youngest daughter Olivia. Carte-de-visite by Disdéri, Paris, 1859/60.

Above: 39. Yolande's barouche and coachman in the Bois de Boulogne. Carte-de-visite by Louis-Jean Dalton, summer 1867.

Right: 40. Yolande with Charlotte Claremont (aged thirteen). Carte-de-visite by Paul Coutem, Vichy, 1866.

Below left: 41. Harry Claremont. Hand-coloured photograph by Thomas Fall, London, early 1880s.

Below right: 42. General Edward Claremont in his uniform as military attaché in Paris. Hand-coloured cabinet print by John Edwards, London, 1887.

Above left: 43. Our Lady of Consolation and St Stephen, Yolande's chapel on the Lynford estate. (Bob Jones)

Above right: 44. Yolande Lyne Stephens, painted in Paris by Émile-Auguste Carolus-Duran, spring 1888. She is wearing the rope of pearls which she gave to the church in Cambridge six months later.

Below left: 45. Panel from a stained-glass window in the church of St Francis, Shefford, 1884. Yolande is depicted holding a replica of the church in her hands. (Photography by Davina)

Below right: 46. Interior of church of Our Lady and the English Martyrs, Cambridge, built entirely to Yolande's 'own taste and fancy'. (John Hagger)

Above left: 47. General Edward Claremont. Cabinet print by Étienne Giraud, Photographie Universelle, Paris, 1888/89.

Above right: 48. Harry Claremont, photographed *c.* 1892.

Below left: 49. Michael Dwane, Yolande's personal chaplain, photographed *c.* 1910.

Below right: 50. Stephen Lyne Stephens (*née* Claremont) in the uniform of the Army Service Corps. Photograph by J. Weston and Son, London, 1914.

Top left: 51. The Lyne Stephens mausoleum in winter, grounds of Grove House, Roehampton.

Left: 52. The sarcophagus inside the mausoleum. (Geoff Halsall)

Below: 53. The Claremont graves, photographed from the steps of the mausoleum. Left: Edward, Fanny, Teddy. Centre: Stephen. Right: Harry, Kitty.

In reply, Lord Enfield thanked him for his 'generous defence of that gallant officer' and said he was sure that Sir Robert Peel 'would never have made use of the expressions which he had used regarding General Claremont if he knew what pain they had occasioned one who had so gallantly defended his country'.[11]

'I think I made a good defence of you,' Leveson-Gower wrote to Edward on 1 August, 'and that it impressed the House favourably. Several Members complimented me upon it ... I am most anxious that you should return to England as soon as possible. I can hardly discuss the reasons, but you may rely on my advice being good.'

Edward was torn between returning to London to defend his conduct and staying in Paris to sort out his mother's affairs and manage the sale of her house in Louveciennes. During the next two weeks, as the correspondence about his resignation was printed as a Command Paper for presentation to the House of Commons, he disregarded his friend's advice and made the decision to stay in Paris.

The Command Paper was read in the House on 18 August. It was published in *The Times* the following day, together with a leader on the subject which filled an entire page. The leader explained that two questions arose from the publication of the correspondence, 'on the first of which we must speak with reserve ... the personal relations between General Claremont and the Foreign Office'.

The writer noted that Edward's reasons for leaving Paris had been corroborated by the foreign secretary when he spoke in the House of Lords. In Lord Granville's words: 'About the second week in December, Colonel Claremont, finding that the only other Military Attaché in Paris was about to leave, came away with that gentleman, in obedience to orders received.' As a result:

General Claremont's explanation is ... distinctly corroborated by his superiors at the Foreign Office; and if he thus acted in obedience to orders, it may seem somewhat strange that his resignation should have been so summarily accepted, especially when Lord Lyons's testimony to his previous services is accepted without qualification ... Whether he acted rightly is another question ... but he was not alone to blame, and it does not appear why he alone should be made the scapegoat for all the defaults of the Embassy.

There was a second question to be considered:

The fact cannot be explained away that none of the staff of the Embassy remained through the severest part of the siege, and that the member who was especially charged with military duties left his post at the crisis of a great military operation. We are totally at a loss to understand why General Claremont should ever have been instructed 'to follow the course adopted by other Military Attachés'. What had the course adopted by others to do with his own duty? ...

We do not doubt that he had, as Lord Lyons attests, done good service; but men are appointed to such posts not simply that they may do ordinary work in ordinary times, but that they may render special services in an emergency. That emergency had arisen, and General Claremont ought to be been at his post to the last moment. No excuse can be made for him, except that his superiors had expressly released him from this simple and strict view of his duty by telling him to follow the example of others ... His special duties required his presence at his post, and he was additionally bound to remain by the fact that his departure left the Embassy unrepresented ...

We have dwelt on General Claremont's defence, not because it exonerates him from blame, but because it shows that he was not alone in fault ... If the Diplomatic Service, with its various attachés, is to sustain the attacks to which it is now subject, it must show some better return of work than is afforded by the story of General Claremont and the British Embassy during the Siege of Paris.[12]

16

THE *MÉNAGE-À-TROIS*

General Claremont ... obtained the management of her property;
and with his wife and children became permanent members of her
family, and took up his abode wherever she was.

Constance Smith, *c.* 1912

Yolande had returned to Grove House in July 1870, a few days after
Louis-Napoleon declared war on Prussia. She missed Edward's
reassuring presence. She worried about his safety in a country at
war. When the Prussian army encircled Paris, she fretted about his
well-being in a city under siege. For three months she received no
news. His wife would not have passed on information from the
Foreign Office, nor would it have been wise for Edward to send
letters addressed to his mistress out of Paris by balloon post.

She moved to Lynford in October and Edward's arrival there in
January 1871 was an unexpected pleasure. When he returned to
Paris in February, she worried again about his safety, particularly
during the dangers of the Commune. She hoped he would return
to England in April after Colonel Conolly arrived in Versailles to
replace him. Instead, she had to wait another six months while he
tended his dying mother and dealt with her affairs.

This was the fourth pivotal moment of her life. The first was the July Revolution of 1830 which allowed Véron to lift her straight from ballet student to soloist. The second came seven years later when she accepted Stephens's offer against her inclinations. The third was in 1845 when the death of Lady Aldborough provided an opportunity to manipulate him into marriage. Now, eleven years after her husband's death, she wanted Edward Claremont, not just as a lover but as a constant companion, to share her life and take the weight of administration and management off her shoulders.

Edward was a highly effective officer in the field, as proved in the Crimea and during the Italian Campaign. He was valued by Queen Victoria and by ministers of state. He was popular in the army and in his diplomatic capacity at the embassy. He was respected by French army officers, as well as by Louis-Napoleon, and he was liked by British residents in Paris, at least until his departure during the siege. People had admired his *savoir-faire* since his early years in Canada.

His relationship with the Foreign Office, of which *The Times* had written 'with reserve', would appear to have been poisoned by the fifteen-day interval between the order to join Lord Lyons in Bordeaux 'without delay' and his reply written in Lynford Hall. His friend the Duke of Cambridge, commander-in-chief of the army, came to the same conclusion. 'I regret to hear of your having resigned,' he wrote from his office in Horse Guards Parade on 23 March, 'and of your resignation having been accepted, but your absence from Paris during the last part of the siege has been so much commented upon that I do not see how it was possible to escape from this unfortunate result. I have always regretted your not returning to Lord Lyons at Bordeaux when directed to. I thought it a mistake and I'm afraid that all this trouble may be regarded in this way.'

Edward's delay in replying to the order was crucial. An official of his standing, the military attaché to the British Embassy in Paris, should not have been out of communication for fifteen days during a critical period of the Franco-Prussian war as a result of – as he vaguely described it – 'a circumstance over which I had no control'. The Foreign Office may also have heard rumours about the nature of his relationship with Yolande, adding a whiff of scandal to his lapse of duty. What was considered normal in Second Empire Paris was a different matter in Victorian England.

If the despatch was sent to Edward at his London address, it is possible that his wife waited for several days before forwarding it to Norfolk. It is more likely that the delay was engineered by Yolande to keep him with her in Lynford Hall, to prevent him returning to the war in France where he would be placed in danger. It is not difficult to picture her, during those crucial few days, using her proven power of weeping to persuade him to stay a little longer in Lynford, to delay replying to the Foreign Office, to delay his departure for France. It seems to have been another occasion when he was detained in Norfolk 'very much against my will but I could not help it'.

With the active support of Lord Lyons, he had assumed that his resignation would not be accepted. He should have made more of an effort to defend himself, but he was angry at his treatment by the Foreign Office and grieving at the loss of his mother. He was also concerned about money. His salary as military attaché had come to an end and, even if he had been entitled to half-pay from the War Office, this would have been insufficient to support his family.

When he returned to London in September, he wrote to his old friend Lord Cowley, referring to a conversation he remembered about a pension from the diplomatic service. 'I must express the pleasure I had in seeing your handwriting again,' Cowley replied on 10 October:

I knew that you had been subjected to great distress but I did not know where you were. Now as to the matter on which you wrote to me. I cannot recall speaking to you about the subject ... I have no doubt that you report correctly what occurred but I could not positively speak as much. If you can give *about* the date when you spoke to me, I will look into my correspondence ...

I do not wonder at your being annoyed at some of the assertions which have been made upon you and which anybody with any knowledge of the subject must know to be unfounded, but I must own that I did not see the necessity for your resignation. Had I been near you, I should have done all in my power to dissuade you from taking the step. I fear that this may stand in the way of anything being done for you now.

Cowley wrote again five days later: 'I have looked through all my official correspondence both public and private ... and cannot find a trace of having brought your wishes before the government.'

Yolande was in Roehampton when Edward received these letters. He spoke to her of his disappointment about the pension, the loss of his salary, his financial concerns for the future. The appeal of her money had grown stronger during recent months when he had been faced with one disaster after another. With an excess of income over expenditure, she was building up a significant fortune of her own and had no close relatives to whom to bequeath it. She had often told him so, dangling the prospect of great wealth in front of him and his children.

The cards had fallen in her favour – and Cowley's letters about the pension provided her with another perfect opportunity. Edward was, as Cowley realised, 'in great distress'. It was easy for Yolande to persuade him that the simplest solution was for him to live with her on a permanent basis. He could take charge of her financial and business affairs, and he would never have to think about money again.

Stephens's will had not included the usual caveat about his widow's remarriage, so a second marriage would have made no difference to Yolande's financial position. Divorces had become easier since the Divorce and Matrimonial Causes Act was passed in 1857, but the cases were heard in public in the High Court in London and inevitably led to scandal. Edward, bruised by the recent publicity about his resignation, had no desire to have his private life raked over by the newspapers.

Yolande, already ostracised by society, might have preferred to have become the second Mrs Claremont; faced with Edward's refusal to have his adultery aired in public, she settled for his constant presence in her life. To formalise the arrangement, she gave him a plain gold ring which he wore every day. She also acquired a leasehold house in Gloucester Street, Portman Square, and transferred the property into Edward's name. It would be used as a London townhouse and also as a base for Edward's adult children.

Not only did Edward refuse to consider a divorce, he also insisted that his wife remain with him. Frances Claremont (Fanny) was a quiet, self-effacing woman who disliked large gatherings and had rarely accompanied her husband to the balls and functions of Second Empire Paris. She had been hurt and bewildered by the attentions he lavished on Yolande, as well as by his absences in winter when he spent several weeks in Lynford Hall. Now she had to move in with the woman who had effectively taken her husband from her. In late October 1871, she packed up her possessions and travelled to Lynford with her three unmarried daughters. It was the start of the *ménage-à-trois*.

Yolande was eager that Edward's friend Richard Wallace, who had moved to London after the Commune, should join them in Norfolk for a few days' shooting during their first winter together. Edward passed on her invitations and Wallace wrote several non-committal replies. In November, he had 'a great deal of business on hand which will require my presence in town [but] I shall certainly avail myself of her offer to run down some other time and spend a few days with her quietly'. In January 1872, referring to the dog which had accompanied him on the streets of Paris, he was still 'overwhelmed with business ... We always intend profiting from Mrs Lyne Stephens's kind invitation and when we do, Swipe shall accompany us and will, I hope, devour all the cats, rats and mice, but spare the poodles.'

In February, Yolande and the Claremonts moved to Roehampton, where the *ménage-à-trois* took the residents by surprise. Although most of them had never seen Yolande, they took a jaundiced view of Edward's motives. According to Constance Smith, who lived nearby:

General Claremont ... made himself so indispensable to her that he obtained the management of her property; and with his wife and children became permanent members of her family, and took up his abode wherever she was. He was not a man of good character, and his unhappy wife, who was an excellent person, disliked and resented the dependent position bitterly. She had, however, to submit, and we used to see her Sunday after Sunday in Roehampton church with her handsome daughters.[1]

In April, they moved to the Hôtel Molé in Paris, where Edward employed men to rebuild the fences and plant trees in the garden to replace those which had been cut down and burnt during the siege. He employed builders to restore the roof which had been damaged by shells during the battle to reclaim the city from the Commune.

Every year, the *ménage-à-trois* would follow the same routine: the shooting season in Lynford, the spring and early summer in Paris, the autumn and late winter in Roehampton. Edward made all the arrangements as Yolande's carriage horses and her household of servants – Italian butler, French under-butler, chef and lady's maid, English housekeeper, footmen, housemaids, coachman and grooms – moved from one house to another and crossed the Channel to and from Paris.

He took charge of her administrative and financial affairs, managed her properties, kept detailed accounts, and dealt with the household servants and ground staff. It was a very different life to the fifteen years he had spent as military attaché in Paris and involved the loss of many of his friends in the military with whom he could no longer converse on equal terms.

He had an opportunity to see his French friends again in January 1873 when the final act of the Second Empire was played out on English soil. After the war, Louis-Napoleon had joined his wife in England. A friend lent them a small stately home in Chislehurst and Edward visited them there in the spring of 1872. The emperor's health continued to decline and, when he died the following January, his funeral was an extraordinary event for a small town in Kent. 'It would be far easier,' wrote *The Times*:

> to give a list of the celebrated men of the Second Empire now living who were not to be found [at the funeral] than of those who were. The Imperial household, in all the magnificence of exalted rank ... was restored to the full strength at which it stood before the war, not one member, we were assured, being absent. Former ministers, ambassadors, councillors of state, and deputies might be counted by the dozens ... Meantime the crowds outside the gates had been growing until the half-mile of road between the lodge and the chapel was thickly lined on either side ... there were Frenchmen at every part of the road, and such a gathering of one foreign nation there has probably never been seen in England since William the Norman brought over his barons and their following.[1]

The funeral service was held in the Catholic chapel in Chislehurst, with an estimated 20,000 people lining the streets to watch the cortège pass by. A large number of French army officers were present, including Marshal Canrobert who had twice praised Edward's conduct during the Crimean War. 'Marshal Canrobert is ill and ought not to have travelled,' commented *The Times*, 'yet he is here.'

Edward also made the journey to Chislehurst to pay his last respects to Louis-Napoleon and renew his acquaintance with

Marshal Canrobert, General Trochu and other friends in the French military. He was not Yolande's only lover to attend the funeral. After the death of his American wife, Félix de La Valette had married a daughter of the Comte de Flahaut. They crossed the Channel for the occasion and the new Marquise de La Valette played her part at the funeral as 'a lady of the Empress's household'.

The Second Empire had fallen. There was no more royalty in France, no more glittering court balls at the Tuileries, but life had returned to the streets and rebuilding work was well underway. During their stays in Paris in the spring and summer, Yolande and Edward attended performances in the Salle le Peletier. As they watched the new generation of ballerinas, Yolande – now sixty years old – was overheard to murmur 'how shocking' at the amount of leg displayed on stage.

The wood-and-plaster building, the scene of so many of her triumphs as a dancer, burnt to the ground on the night of 28 October 1873. A new opera house was already under construction, ordered by Louis-Napoleon after a failed assassination attempt outside the Salle le Peletier in 1858. Realising that the narrow Rue le Peletier presented an opportunity to potential assassins, he instructed the architect Charles Garnier to design a more opulent theatre in a more open location.

The structure of the new building was complete by the time of the Franco-Prussian war, when it was used as a hospital and ammunition store. Work resumed a few months after the defeat of the Commune and the grandiose Palais Garnier opened its doors in January 1875, about the time Edward advised Yolande to give up the Hôtel Molé. It was too large a house to manage during the many months of the year that the *ménage-à-trois* was in England.

The Hôtel Molé was sold on 26 June 1875 to the politician Baron Gérard. In its place, Yolande rented a first-floor apartment at 122 Avenue des Champs-Élysées, an eighteenth-century mansion built around a central courtyard, which occupied a corner plot between the Champs-Élysées, the Rue Balzac and the Rue Lord

Byron. The rooms in the apartment led into one another around the courtyard and Yolande furnished them with the fine furniture and old master paintings from the Hôtel Molé.

The first eight years of the *ménage-à-trois* saw the marriages of four of Edward's children. The first was in June 1872 when his second son was married in St George's, Hanover Square. This was followed by his three daughters all marrying army captains: Charlotte to Cecil Thorold in September 1875; Emily to Fletcher Littledale in June 1878; and Olivia to the unfortunately named Algernon Bastard in September 1879. These marriages took place in St Mary's, Bryanston Square, the parish church for Gloucester Street.

Edward was now known as 'the General', even by his wife and children, and Yolande insisted on being called 'Madame'. Jealous of their youth, she showed little interest in the Claremont daughters. Of the three sons, George was a captain in the army, serving in the West Indies; Edward (Teddy) was in the navy, a lieutenant on HMS *Duke of Wellington*, the flagship of the Port Admiral in Portsmouth; and Henry (Harry) had left England in the summer of 1871 to join a cousin who owned a coffee plantation in Ceylon.

Only Teddy was in England during the early years of the *ménage-à-trois*. With an ability to charm, he became Yolande's favourite among the Claremont children; when he married in 1872, she gave him a settlement of £10,000 (£1 million).

Apart from Teddy and his sisters, no one visited Yolande in Roehampton. Life was more sociable in Lynford when Edward invited his friends to join him for shooting parties and Christmas was always celebrated in the hall. Edward's daughters brought their spouses and Yolande invited her neighbours and tenants to evenings of music and amateur theatricals.

Teddy retired from the navy in 1875. In the same year, Harry returned on leave from Ceylon and joined the family for Christmas. The two brothers performed in the amateur theatricals on 27 December in a farce titled *The Area Belle*. According to a local newspaper, 'Mr E. Claremont sustained with marked effect the character of Tosser, Mr H. Claremont appeared as Walker Chalks', and their future brother-in-law, Algernon Bastard, 'played the part of Pitcher with much ability and created frequent roars of laughter'.

The following year, Edward was appointed a trustee of the Lyne Stephens estate in place of Sir Richard Williams-Bulkeley who had died the previous summer. His fellow trustee was the younger Sir John Lubbock (whose father died in 1865), while the legal management was in the hands of Horace Pym, a young lawyer who had entered into partnership with the elderly Meaburn Tatham in 1870.

Horace Pym was a big man with 'an ebullient personality' and a gift 'for friendship and infectious sociability ... Invited to a party in the evening, he often appeared in the office next day, rubbing his hands, with a new job in his pocket.' He was always available to his wealthier clients and 'was once reputed to have sprung up from a dinner table and hurried away without hesitation when word came that a client required his help'. Aware of the opportunity offered by his legal management of the Lyne Stephens estate, he set out to flatter Yolande, making many visits to Grove House and Lynford Hall to discuss matters of detail.

The government had now repented of its treatment of Edward Claremont, of using him as a scapegoat for the failures of the British Embassy during the Siege of Paris. In March 1877, he was given an award for distinguished or meritorious service. Seven months later, he was promoted to the rank of lieutenant-general, an honorary rank because he was no longer serving in the army or the diplomatic service. This was, perhaps, some recompense for the ignominious end to his career.

After his service in the Crimea and as military attaché in Paris, he might have expected greater honours, probably a knighthood. He had, effectively, given up the prospect of such honours for Yolande, her money and her power of weeping. He was living in luxury, he was waited on by an army of servants, but he was also bound to a woman who was becoming more imperious and demanding as the years went by.

His failure to respond to the order from the Foreign Office in January 1871, his inability to stand up to Yolande when she begged him to stay in Lynford Hall, led inexorably to his decision to live with her in the *ménage-à-trois*, a decision made when he was in distress and not thinking clearly.

Nineteen years after making this decision, he wrote a letter to his sons, a letter which he attached to his will to be read after his death. It included these words: 'God knows I have plenty of faults and require mercy. I have often swerved from the path of duty – take my word for it, it does not answer even in this world. I have always suffered for it and always regretted it.'

17

MADAME AND THE GENERAL

*I know how ghastly it is when no one else is here and how very
uncertain the tempers are.*
Harry Claremont, Lynford Hall, 13 November 1881

Regret is not an emotion that Yolande would have recognised at
this stage of her life. She was just happy to have Edward with
her, looking after her affairs and constantly by her side. At the
same time, she was almost totally indifferent to his family. Fanny
she effectively ignored and, with the exception of Teddy, she was
ungenerous to his children. The daughters received no marriage
settlements; George, abroad with his regiment, formed no part of
her life; and she saw little of Harry before he returned from Ceylon
towards the end of 1880.

Harry had intended to run a coffee plantation but his arrival
in Ceylon in 1871 coincided with an outbreak of coffee-leaf
rust which devastated every plantation on the island. Several
planters converted their estates to tea production, which expanded
dramatically during the 1870s and became profitable at the end
of the decade, just as Harry decided to leave the colony. He

returned to London and, on 20 June 1881, he wrote to a Mr and Mrs Walker in Eastbourne:

> I write to tell you that I have asked your daughter to be my wife. I have known her only ten days it is true, but I love her dearly. I did not mean to let her know what my feelings were towards her just yet, but somehow I couldn't help myself ... I unfortunately have very little to offer her. What I have is all invested in Ceylon and I regret to say that investments there are not what they once were. I have enough however to make her comfortable and I think I can make her happy, at any rate I will do my best ... Please forgive me for trying to rush you. I can't help it.

Katherine Walker's parents were unenthusiastic about Harry's lack of prospects. 'I can quite understand your desire that we should wait for a time,' he wrote again on 23 June. 'I hope to get the promise of something to do shortly and then should ask you again to entrust your daughter to my care.'

In July, Yolande invited Katherine (Kitty) to stay in Grove House, where she could meet her future father-in-law. The visit was not a success. Edward's behaviour was, according to Harry:

> most disagreeable ... he did not see how we were to be married and thought that long engagements were such a mistake. He thought that I should never marry unless it was for money and that he did not wish me to have to go through all the bothers that he himself had ... He was so put out at the whole affair that he could not be at all himself.

Edward was feeling trapped. It was his financial 'bothers' which had led him to become dependent on Yolande and his irrational anger at Harry's proposed marriage is a clue to his state of mind. He took four months to calm down before he met Kitty again in Lynford Hall.

'I am glad to hear that you will be asked here,' Harry wrote from Lynford on 13 November. 'I hope you will enjoy your visit more than I am afraid you did the Roehampton one. I hope everything will come right, but you must have a little patience.' He would understand if Kitty chose not to come because the men would be out all day shooting and she would be left alone in the house with Yolande and Fanny Claremont: 'I know how ghastly it is when no one else is here and how very uncertain the tempers are.' He was, he wrote, 'very bored by it all'.

Harry may have been bored at Lynford, but he was learning to pay attention to Yolande, to flatter her as his father did. She had given Teddy a marriage settlement of £10,000 and he was hoping she might do the same for him. The offer was not forthcoming, although Yolande did offer an alternative. In February, a telegram addressed to Kitty arrived in Eastbourne: 'Mrs L.S. regular brick. Makes allowance four hundred a year. Just been told. Can't keep it in. Harry.'

This represents about £44,000 a year in today's money, enough for the Walkers to agree to their daughter's marriage. Edward, too, came round to the idea. He wrote to Kitty on 2 March:

I am credibly informed that you have made up your minds to disregard my advice and have determined to be very foolish and very imprudent! You know I must have my little joke, but seriously I hope to behave very well in future and do all I can to conduce to your happiness.

The marriage took place in St Peter's church, Eaton Square, on 1 June 1882. Fanny attended the ceremony, but Edward and Yolande were in Paris. The excuse for not returning to London was Edward's health. 'I am not at all the thing,' he explained to Kitty, 'and see no chance of being able to go over to England and being present at your marriage.' Yolande wrote too:

I am very sorry that circumstances have made it impossible for me to go back to England before the end of June. It will be a great privation but my sincere and affectionate wishes will accompany you at the foot of the altar … The General, I am happy to say, is getting alright. He is obliged to take much care of himself, the weather is so very treacherous just at present.

Harry and Kitty spent a few days in the West Cliff Hotel in Folkestone before crossing the Channel to spend their honeymoon in Yolande's apartment in the Champs-Élysées. 'We arrived in Paris yesterday,' Kitty wrote to her mother on 11 June:

Mrs Lyne Stephens and the General came to meet us in the carriage and were very cordial and nice. This apartment is too lovely. The rooms are all a dream, all opening out of each other, full of curios in the shape of china, pictures, tapestry, etc. My room is very pretty, the curtains of copper coloured brocade and pale blue walls … The General is going to take places for the opera and the theatres, and Mrs Lyne Stephens says she has a lot of jewels for me to choose from.

When Harry's first child was born in London eleven months later, Yolande wrote to Kitty in her spiky, forward-slanting handwriting:

I can understand your great happiness and joy at being a mother. I can well imagine what you feel. Many years of my life were passed in expectations and as much in regrets, till I became quite resigned to the will of God, thinking that whatever happens to me is done for my own good. Grandpapa seems very pleased with Miss Claremont and, as for myself, it will be so jolly to hug and kiss her. I hope she will let me do so without crying … Kiss baby for me and tell her that she must love me *a little*.

It is tempting to speculate about Yolande's feelings as she wrote this letter. No one in England ever knew that she had given birth to two children in Paris, that she may also have experienced the 'great happiness and joy at being a mother' – if only for a short time.

Meanwhile, events were unfolding which would soon bring her closer to Harry. In the summer of 1881, his brother Teddy, perhaps inspired by the amateur dramatics in Lynford Hall, had acquired the lease and management of the Royal Court Theatre in Sloane Square. Yolande lent him £2,500 towards the cost and the theatre reopened under the management of 'Mr Edward Clare' on 24 September.

Ten months after reopening, the theatre had to close again when the Metropolitan Board of Works insisted on 'extensive alterations ... for the prevention of the spread of fire'. Teddy employed an architect to design a new proscenium wall and an entrance porch, and the theatre reopened again, 'prettily redecorated', on 14 November 1882.

This three-and-a-half-month interruption was expensive, not only because of the cost of the work but also because of lost revenue. Teddy borrowed more money from Yolande and, without Edward's knowledge, also borrowed from several of his father's friends, including Richard Wallace and the Duke of Cambridge. In March 1883, he premiered a new play by Arthur Wing Pinero. This was followed by two further productions, but Teddy was now deeply in debt.

The last performance under his management took place on 30 June, after which he escaped his creditors by moving north to Settle in Yorkshire where, under the different pseudonym of Edward Clarke and with more borrowed money, he bought a printing and stationery business. This was not a success either and in June 1884, after incurring further debts, he fled again, this time back to London. He failed to attend meetings of his creditors in Yorkshire, using the excuse that he was too ill to travel, and when he was declared bankrupt in Bradford in August 1884, the official receiver suggested that a warrant be put out for his arrest.

Edward was appalled by his son's behaviour. His conduct, he wrote, 'has been so bad, the claims against him so numerous, that the only thing for me to do is to steadily refuse to have anything to do with him'. Teddy wrote humble and ingratiating letters to his father, ending one with a postscript which makes clear the order of priority in the family: 'Love to Madame and my mother.' He also wrote to Harry, complaining about being 'utterly broken in heart and spirit. Will nothing soften my father towards me ... I don't want money now, but I do want a little sympathy, a little encouragement.'

In September 1885, when the High Court of Justice confirmed Teddy's bankruptcy with liabilities amounting to almost £16,000 (£1.8 million), he wrote again to his father:

> The other person besides yourself whose forgiveness I crave is a person who has always been a true friend to me. I mean Mrs Lyne Stephens. I am writing to her now and it has cost me *many, many* a bitter pang to think of my base ingratitude. I was *mad*, I believe, and that is all I can say.

Edward's reply was curt: 'I hope sincerely that you are, as you say, an altered man and that you will prove it.'

Edward and Yolande were so disappointed in Teddy, 'so bitter and unforgiving', that they would not give him the £10 he needed to buy his dog back from the receivers. In their wills, drafted by Horace Pym and signed in early 1887, he was removed from any significant interest in their estates. He was named as a residuary beneficiary of Edward's will but he was not appointed a trustee, nor was he given an interest in the house in Gloucester Street. Yolande left legacies of £20,000 each to Edward's other five children, but Teddy was merely given an annuity of £200 a year, which would cease if 'he shall have done or suffered something whereby the whole or some part of the annuity ... would become payable to or vested in some other person'.

It was Harry, who had continued to flatter Yolande and spend time with her in Lynford and Paris, who gained the most from Teddy's bankruptcy. He now became her favourite among the

Claremont children. When his second daughter was born in Lynford Hall in January 1885, Yolande stood as godmother when the child was baptised in the Anglican church at West Tofts and given the name Marie Louise. In her will signed two years later, she left her personal fortune to Edward and, after his death, to his youngest son Harry – 'the precious boy who is heir to so much'.

In July 1885, the newspapers reported that 'a residence has been purchased in Norfolk for Prince Albert Victor. If the news be true, the Prince will have a charming sporting estate ... and Lynford Hall will lose a charitable lady in Mrs Lyne Stephens'. Albert Victor, eldest son of the Prince of Wales, was second in line to the throne and the news was reported in British colonies throughout the world. It reached the Chatham Islands, a remote archipelago in the Pacific Ocean several hundred miles from New Zealand, where a beneficiary of the Lyne Stephens estate, Edward Chudleigh, ran a sheep station. On 7 September, he made a note in his diary:

> Saw a paragraph in the Home News that Prince Albert Victor was going to purchase my good cousin's house and grounds of Lynford Hall Norfolk. She told me she would not sell it when I was at home. At that time the Prince of Wales and Lord Dudley had both offered for it. £800,000 I understood was refused.[1]

The prince did make an offer for Lynford but Yolande turned it down, mainly because of Edward's love of shooting. During the winter months, he managed the estate, supervised the ground staff, and dealt with disputes with neighbouring farmers who continued to complain about their land being overrun by hares bred for sport. Several of these disputes came before the magistrates at the Mundford Petty Sessions.

When the *ménage-à-trois* was in Roehampton, Edward attended court functions at Buckingham and St James's Palaces in his role as groom of the privy chamber to Queen Victoria. In June 1887, the queen celebrated her golden jubilee. It was fifty years since she succeeded her uncle William IV on 20 June 1837, seven weeks after writing in her diary that Yolande had danced the *Cachucha* during a performance of *Don Giovanni* looking 'wretchedly thin and pale'.

The jubilee celebrations lasted for thirteen days, from the 16th to the 29th, with Edward in attendance at several functions. At the service of thanksgiving in Westminster Abbey on the morning of 21 June, he was instructed 'to show Her Majesty's Guests and Suite to their places in the Choir'. The dress code was specific: 'Full Dress Coat and Trousers will be worn by the Gentlemen of Her Majesty's Household in Waiting. The Day will be observed as a Collar Day.'

Edward stayed in Gloucester Street during the two weeks of the jubilee. One day, he dressed himself in the uniform he had worn as military attaché in Paris and walked to a nearby photographic studio in Hyde Park Corner. He was portrayed leaning against a plinth, his plumed helmet by his side, his white gloves in his hands. He wore the Légion d'Honneur below the top button of his scarlet tunic. His other medals were displayed on his chest: Companion of the Order of the Bath, Crimean Medal with four clasps, Turkish Order of Medjidie, and the Italian Campaign medal awarded after the battles of Magenta and Solferino.

He had lost weight during the last sixteen years and the scarlet tunic hangs a little loosely about him. He also has a melancholy look, perhaps remembering past triumphs when he was friends with the emperor of France and with marshals and generals in the French army. His unique position as military attaché to a country where he was born and spoke the language and had served with its army in battle had given him a high reputation in both England and France. All this he had lost because he could not say 'no' to Yolande Lyne Stephens.

18

THE EYE-DOLL HOUSE

*What I have most at heart is Cambridge, and for this ... I must be
allowed to indulge my own taste and fancy.*

Yolande Lyne Stephens, 30 August 1884

By the time of the golden jubilee, Yolande had succeeded in putting
much of her scandalous reputation behind her. In its place, she had
acquired a reputation as a philanthropist.

The neighbours in Roehampton may have ignored her presence
among them, but she was popular with her tenants on the Lynford
estate who knew nothing about her early life. She would drive
around the villages to visit them in their homes and gave presents
at Christmas to every man, woman and child – inviting the children
into the hall to collect their presents from under a Christmas tree.
Older residents on the estate remembered her in the 1920s as 'a
real Lady Bountiful'.[1]

'Always be kind to your family', Stephens had told her – and
with no family of her own, she continued his generosity to
members of the extended Lyne family, not only in England but
also in the colonies. One example was Edward Chudleigh in the
Chatham Islands, to whom she gave £10,000 (£1 million) to

enable him to buy and stock 7,500 acres of land with sheep. On a visit to Auckland in 1877, he received two telegrams from his lawyer in Christchurch:

> 20 June: Have authority to inform you ten thousand Lyne Stephens absolutely yours. English mail just in.

> 21 June: Mrs Lyne Stephens gives you money outright. Instruct us to make gift complete.

'The great state of doubt and anxiety I have been in for the last two months,' Chudleigh wrote in his diary, 'makes this sudden success and good fortune a fact worth recording.'[2]

Yolande's first major gift to charity was in January 1866 when Sir John Lubbock handed £20,000 (£2 million) to the chairman of the Middlesex Hospital, ostensibly 'from an anonymous donor'. Five years later, on 2 February 1871, she gave the smaller – but still significant – sum of £500 (£54,000) to the Lord Mayor's Fund to provide food for the people of Paris. This 'munificent donation' was second in size only to that of the Bank of England, which contributed £1,000.

In 1882, she paid for an ornate fountain with drinking troughs to be installed in the village of Roehampton, using water supplied from a spring on Putney Heath. Her inspiration was Sir Richard Wallace, who was awarded a baronetcy for his efforts to help British residents during the Siege of Paris. Water supplies in the city had been damaged during the siege and the Commune, so Wallace paid for more than a hundred drinking fountains to be installed in the streets – fountains known today as *Les Wallaces*.

A single fountain was enough for Yolande and it cost her £3,000 (£322,000). She employed the Catholic architect J. C. Radford, and gave him precise instructions. According to Radford, the final design was 'the result of much enquiry and inspection throughout London and some of the big towns in the provinces and in France and Italy'.

The concept of the bronze sculpture, two cherubs riding a dolphin, came from a tomb in Italy; it was made in Paris by Henry Dasson and cast there under Radford's supervision. The grey and red granite was sourced from quarries near Aberdeen; 'the unusual size of the drinking troughs for horses made the granite work very expensive as a great many blocks had to be quarried before suitable ones could be obtained'.[3]

Water for the village had previously been pumped or drawn from wells, so the supply of fresh drinking water was welcomed by the people of Roehampton. An engraved address was prepared by the vicar and churchwardens offering Yolande 'our best thanks for the generous kindness ... of building in our village such a useful and ornamental structure. It is not the beautiful fountain alone which calls for the expression of our thanks but also the thoughtful consideration for the health and comfort of your neighbours.'

The fountain in Roehampton, the gifts to the Middlesex Hospital and the Lord Mayor's Fund, together with small contributions to charities such as the Fund for Ladies in Distress through Non-Payment of Rent in Ireland, were Yolande's only donations of a secular nature. The rest of her giving was to religious institutions, mainly in the Catholic diocese of Northampton which included the county of Norfolk. The woman who had faked a sudden desire to become a nun at the age of nineteen became increasingly devout as she grew older, a religiosity which had its roots in her friendship with an English nun.

During her early years in Roehampton, while Stephens attended Sunday service in the Anglican chapel near the gates of Grove House, Yolande had to travel further afield to attend Mass. In July 1850, nuns from the Sacred Heart, a French teaching order, acquired an adjoining estate with plans to use the house as a convent and boarding school for girls. Yolande made contact with the mother superior, Stephens gave £500 towards the construction of a chapel, and when the building was completed Yolande attended Mass at the convent, sitting in a side chapel for lay members of the congregation.

Twenty years later, Mabel Digby arrived in Roehampton to take over the duties of mother superior. The daughter of an heiress, she had converted to Catholicism at the age of eighteen, entered the order of the Sacred Heart four years later, and spent fourteen years in a teaching convent in France. As mother superior during the Franco-Prussian war, she had converted her school building into a hospital for wounded soldiers.

Yolande was in Grove House when Mother Digby arrived at the convent in August 1872. She called on the new mother superior and was delighted to learn that they could converse together in French. She was also struck by the nun's demeanour. 'When I first saw her calm sweet countenance,' wrote one of the novices, 'the impression lasted me for forty years.'[4]

Yolande made many visits to Mother Digby when she was staying in Roehampton, private visits of which the other nuns were unaware. At first the nuns lived in cramped accommodation in the old servants' quarters, so Yolande paid for a new building with greater space and comfort. She made many other gifts to the convent, money which was always handed over by Sir John Lubbock. As one of the nuns explained, 'a veil of mystery, almost of romance, hung over the benefactress when nobody ever saw her'.

She had a longer journey to make when she was staying in Lynford Hall: the nearest Catholic church was ten miles away in Thetford. 'The bustle and excitement of the arrival at the church door of the great lady and her attendants' was a regular Sunday event in the town. It was one of her guests, the Catholic Lord Lovat, who came up with the idea of a private chapel on the estate. 'Why don't you build a chapel here at Lynford,' he asked her in December 1875, 'and save yourself the trouble of taking your staff and guests to Thetford?'

Yolande selected a site close to the Home Farm and employed the Catholic architect Henry Clutton to design the chapel. She rehoused the farm tenants and converted the farmhouse for use as a presbytery. With permission from the Court of Chancery, she bought four acres of land from the Lyne Stephens estate.

As she had done with the mausoleum in Roehampton, she placed the land in trust and appointed Edward Claremont as a trustee. Building work began in the spring of 1877 and the chapel was completed eighteen months later at a cost of £10,000 (£1 million). Built of stone and local flint, it was given the grand name of Our Lady of Consolation and St Stephen.

The unorthodox ownership of the land led to legal difficulties with the diocese and, in 1882, Yolande agreed that the land, chapel and presbytery should be transferred into the hands of the diocesan trustees. At the same time, she endowed the chapel with £5,000 (£550,000) to enable it to remain in use for perpetuity. A resident priest had already been appointed: Father Michael Dwane had arrived in the presbytery in September 1881 to act as Yolande's personal chaplain.

It was a great occasion in Lynford when the chapel was consecrated on 7 October 1884 by Arthur Riddell, Bishop of Northampton, accompanied by six canons and eight priests, all of whom were entertained for three days in Lynford Hall. A crowd of local people came to watch the proceedings and one man was convinced that the service had been conducted by the pope. 'Nay, nay,' he said firmly when informed that the splendidly dressed prelate was only a bishop. 'It was the Pope of Rome. I saw him with my own eyes.'[5]

Arthur Riddell had been appointed Bishop of Northampton in April 1880. This was the largest Catholic diocese in the country (consisting of Bedfordshire, Buckinghamshire, Cambridgeshire, Huntingdon, Norfolk, Northampton, and Suffolk) but contained the fewest Catholics so it was always short of funds. 'Excelled by no one in the intensity of his religious beliefs', Riddell wasted no time in developing the diocese. He founded religious institutions and built churches 'in places where before the zealous Catholic had not easy means of joining in the elaborate ritual of his worship'.[6]

Yolande was already active in the diocese when Riddell was appointed to Northampton. She had built the chapel in Lynford and paid for a new building at the St Francis Home for Boys, a

Catholic orphanage in Shefford in Bedfordshire. The new bishop inspired her and, for almost a decade after his appointment, his zeal to build churches in a diocese starved of funds was matched by her zeal to pay for them.

Riddell visited Yolande in Lynford at least once during his first year of office. 'My dear Lord Bishop,' she wrote to him on 6 January 1881:

> I am soon leaving Lynford and it would have been very agreeable if you could have given me the pleasure to come again, but I am afraid your time is so ... taken up and my departure may be before the end of the month, so that in mentioning this wish of mine, I am not at all hopeful you could grant it. In that case, I would, when I come back to these parts, beg you to appoint your own time.[7]

The bishop's next visit was on 24 August, when Yolande made a special journey to Lynford Hall to meet him. '*Monseigneur*,' she said to him in French as they sat in one of the grand reception rooms, '*je voudrais vous bâtir une petite maison*' – 'I should like to build you a little house'. Fifteen months later, in early December 1882, Riddell wrote a letter about his ideas for the location and size of the property. Yolande replied from Lynford Hall on the 20th:

> I have been so extremely busy of late, with a house full of people and with my usual Christmas gifts and the tree to a great number of children, that it has been quite impossible for me to answer your letter ... You know so much better than I can myself the requirements for a Bishop's House, that I should hardly like to interfere with any plan which may meet with your approval, nor certainly to constrain it, as I think it would be a pity building the house and not doing it well.[8]

In May 1883, the bishop wrote to her in Paris explaining that the diocese had borrowed money to buy four plots of land bordering Marriott Street in Northampton and that the architect 'is now engaged on the working drawings'. After their return to England, she and Edward visited Riddell on 18 July to see the site of the new house. 'As I am very awkward travelling by myself,' she had written a few days earlier, 'I hope you will not mind General Claremont accompanying me.' On 21 July, she wrote again:

> I have been thinking a great deal about our conversation ... and I cannot bear the idea of your having incurred a debt for the purchase of the ground on which your house is to be built. Therefore I feel that I *must* enclose a cheque which I think will make you free on that score, leaving still £5000 for the building. This will, I suppose, enable you to sign the contract and to begin the work as soon as possible. Before I close this note, I wish to tell you how much I enjoyed my visit to you, and also how much more interested I am now that I have seen everything.[9]

The Bishop's House – Yolande's *petite maison* – was completed in 1884, a large, imposing residence set in four acres of grounds. She paid for the land, the building costs, and the furniture and furnishings, including the oriental carpets. She also presented the house with a religious painting by the seventeenth-century artist Pierre Mignard, the frame inscribed with the words 'Presented by Mrs Lyne Stephens, October 7th 1884' – the date of the consecration of her chapel in Lynford.

She and Edward visited Northampton again on 12 March 1885, this time to inspect the finished building. 'We talked about your house all the way back,' Edward wrote to Riddell from Gloucester Street two days later, 'and we both agreed that it is perfect inside and out. The appearance is dignified and original, and the internal arrangements so well planned.'[10]

At the same time as paying for the Bishop's House, Yolande had funded further buildings at the orphanage in Shefford, including the new church of St Francis which was also completed in 1884. A panel in one of the stained-glass windows portrays her on her knees, wearing a black dress with a white shawl over her head and shoulders, holding a replica of the church in her hands.

Edward accompanied her to the opening service during the first week of July, followed by a luncheon in the town. 'It was a very great pleasure to be in Shefford last week,' she wrote to Riddell on the 14th. 'I only wish I should live long enough to assist at many such ceremonies. The General was much alarmed when you mentioned his name and relieved when he found he had not to make a speech!'[11]

She made many other gifts to the diocese. In 1882, she gave £2,500 to the Episcopal Income Fund; three years later, she contributed £4,000 (£500,000) towards the cost of building the church of Our Lady of the Sacred Heart in Wellingborough; but her crowning gift was the church of Our Lady and the English Martyrs in Cambridge, one of the largest Catholic churches in the country.

In the past, the hierarchy had dissuaded Catholics from studying at university. Before 1856, those Catholics who did attend were prevented from taking their degrees because of the religious test required. Numbers had increased only slightly since then because students still had to obtain their bishop's approval, and most bishops – stressing 'the dangers to the faith of an atmosphere of liberalism and scepticism' – continued to oppose the entry of Catholics to university except with special permission.

By the time Arthur Riddell was appointed to the diocese, several bishops had begun to change their minds and it became clear that the small church of St Andrew, which had served Catholics in the town for forty years, was too small for the expected increase in Catholic students. The clergy decided to build 'a new and imposing church ... more worthy of the old faith of Cambridge'. With a donation from the Duke of Norfolk, a plot of land was purchased on a corner of the major crossroads in the city, the intersection of Lensfield Road and Hills Road known as Hyde Park Corner.

In 1883, Canon Christopher Scott was appointed to St Andrew's with instructions to raise money for the new church. Having worked as vicar-general of the diocese, he already knew Yolande. He had blessed the chapel in Lynford in November 1879 and had visited her several times since then. He was a man of great charm and, when he visited Lynford during the winter of 1883/84, Yolande listened intently as he told her of the land at Hyde Park Corner and the church he hoped to build there.

Cardinal John Henry Newman also visited Lynford that winter and lent his support to the cause. He wrote to Scott on Yolande's headed notepaper, a letter marked 'for publication':

Cambridge, as being the seat of a great university, has a hold on the hearts and minds of Catholics in all parts of England. This is why I feel a special satisfaction in learning from you that … you are receiving subscriptions with a view of building there a new Church on a new site, an undertaking which, though local in its purpose, is not local in the interest which attaches to it, nor in the call which it makes on our co-operation. I pray God to bless so important a work.[12]

Scott and Newman sowed the seed in Yolande's mind. She nurtured the idea for several months and by 14 July, as she wrote to Arthur Riddell after attending the opening service in Shefford, 'I am rather under a promise to Dr Scott about helping him at Cambridge'.

A month later, on 15 August 1884, she and Edward made the journey from Roehampton. It was the Feast of the Assumption and she had brought a bouquet of flowers from the gardens at Grove House. She asked Scott to lay the bouquet on the altar of St Andrew's, then asked him – with no trace of irony – 'Will you allow poor me to build your church?' As he would write ten years later:

What hopes should we have had of utilising the site unless we had looked to her who had already done so much, but who crowned her many deeds of munificence by erecting the church? … There had been no need of repeated requests, of urgent appeals to persuade to it; the work was as spontaneous as it was lavish in its generosity.[13]

Yolande intended this to be her church, funded entirely by her own money and built and furnished entirely to her own taste. As she wrote to Riddell on 30 August: 'What I have most at heart is Cambridge, and for this ... I must be allowed to indulge my own taste and fancy, for I think it would not do building a church there which could not be worthy of the surroundings.'[14]

She would pay for the entire cost of the church and the rectory. She would pay for the furnishings and furniture in both buildings, as well as ceremonial accoutrements in the church and vestments for the clergy. She agreed to just one exception: she would allow Baron von Hügel, a prominent Catholic in the town, to donate a medieval processional cross, although it was she who would pay to have it restored and studded with precious stones.

Yolande and Scott agreed that the church should be dedicated to Our Lady of the Assumption, in honour of the Feast Day when she made her offer. Scott also wished to commemorate the English Catholic martyrs who died for their faith between the Reformation of 1535 and the reign of Charles II, many of whom had been educated at Cambridge.

He employed the Catholic architects Dunn and Hansom of Newcastle to design the church in Gothic Revival style. Builders were appointed, and ecclesiastical artists and craftsmen selected to produce the carvings, sculptures, and stained-glass windows. The land at Hyde Park Corner was cleared and, in the summer of 1885, foundations were laid for the church.

At the same time, work began on the rectory which was completed two years later, a large red-brick building with an open quadrangle, reminiscent of a university college. Work now began on the church and, on the afternoon of 30 June 1887, Yolande was guest of honour when Arthur Riddell laid the foundation stone. She and Edward had taken the train from London that morning after he performed his last duty at Queen Victoria's jubilee. The town was decorated in celebration of the jubilee and 'at no spot in the borough were the decorations more chaste and artistic than on the gateway to the new Roman Catholic church ... where a bust of

Her Majesty crowned the edifice of flags, evergreens and Chinese lanterns'.

The bishop entered the site of the church in a long procession, 'preceded by candle-bearers and followed by the greater part of the chapter and clergy' of the diocese. A platform with a large wooden cross had been erected where the altar would stand, 'the foot of which was adorned with choice roses and behind which were plants'. He blessed the stone and sprinkled it with holy water before giving a brief address from the platform. He concluded with a tribute to Yolande: 'Almighty God moved the heart of a lady who came forward to bear the whole of the expenses of this beautiful church, which will vie with many of the churches of the good olden days.'[15]

While Catholics in Cambridge delighted in their new church, Protestants in the town were enraged by the size of the building. The interior measured 156 feet long by 71 feet wide. The nave would be 50 feet high and the spire – at over 213 feet – would be the highest landmark in the whole of Cambridgeshire, visible for miles in all directions. As one of Scott's friends, Edward Conybeare, later recalled:

> Though a generation or more had passed since Catholic Emancipation, the penal laws ... were still remembered and some non-Catholics considered that a religion so recently ... outlawed ought to avoid making itself conspicuous. Yet the new church was the most outstanding landmark in the whole town. Hostility was thus aroused; shoals of letters, of bigotry now almost unthinkable, were sent to the local Press, and the great poplar tree which then stood at Hyde Park Corner was white with ultra-Protestant posters and leaflets.[16]

Low-church evangelicals were particularly incensed. 'Dolls' eyes for idols,' they chanted, aware that this 'eyedollatrous' building was funded from a fortune made in a glass factory. The church became known as the 'eye-doll house', giving rise to rumours – still prevalent today – that Stephens had made his money by the invention of moveable eyes for dolls. E. M. Forster included the legend in his novel *The Longest Journey*, published in 1907:

> They waited for the other tram by the Roman Catholic Church, whose florid bulk was already receding into twilight. It is the first big building that the incoming visitor sees. 'Oh, here come the colleges!' cries the Protestant parent, and then learns that it was built by a Papist who made a fortune out of moveable eyes for dolls. 'Built out of dolls' eyes to contain idols' – that at all events, is the legend and the joke. It watches over the apostate city, taller by many a yard than anything within, and asserting, however wildly, that here is eternity, stability, and bubbles unbreakable upon a windless sea.[17]

During the winter of 1887/88, Yolande and Edward made the occasional journey by train from Brandon to Cambridge to see the walls of the church rise from the ground. In November, Arthur Riddell travelled to Rome where he took the opportunity of having a word with Pope Leo XIII about Yolande's activities in the diocese. He wrote to her from Rome on 30 December, a letter to which Yolande replied on 19 February: 'Thank you for ... the gratifying intelligence that the Holy Father granted a special blessing to the Lady *qui vous bâtit une grande église*. It is very good of you to have thought of me.'[18]

Three months later, she received a letter from the Vatican, dated 30 April and signed by Cardinal Giovanni Simeoni, Prefect of the Sacred Congregation for Propagation of the Faith. The pope had asked Simeoni to congratulate her on 'the zeal with which she has promoted the advancement of the Holy Faith, as well as her generous donations towards the building of churches'. He was sending her a rosary of agate beads mounted in silver, together with the 'Apostolic Blessing'.

In July, Christopher Scott found himself in a quandary. He was ready to sign a contract for further work to the church when news arrived that 'Mrs Lyne Stephens was lying seriously ill at

Paris, and it was believed in danger of death'. Had Yolande made arrangements for completion of the church in her will? Scott thought not. The solicitor for the diocese offered to travel to Paris but was informed that Yolande 'was not permitted to see anybody'. As a result, Scott had 'several sleepless weeks in which he was haunted by visions of an uncompleted church which would be known for all time as Scott's Folly and which it would be almost impossible to get anyone to finish because of its great cost.'[19]

According to Scott, Yolande recovered from her illness and, after returning to England, 'one of the first acts of her convalescence was to come to Cambridge'. At their first meeting in the autumn of 1888, she unclasped 'a magnificent pearl necklace worth many thousands of pounds' from around her neck and placed it in his hands. As he wrote a few years later:

> Her great gift to Cambridge was not merely an easy one out of superfluous wealth, but it involved some personal sacrifice. Friends of late had missed the sight of costly jewels, which for years had formed a part of her personal adornment. What had become of a necklace of rarest pearls now no longer worn? They had been sacrificed for the erection of this very church.[20]

Work on the exterior was complete by the spring of 1889 and, on 6 May, Scott climbed the scaffolding to lay the capstone on the spire. The weathervane was fixed the following day. On the 8th, 'the tower was illuminated by coloured lights and a display of fireworks took place from the top of the scaffolding. This produced a very beautiful effect and was seen for miles.'

Although the interior of the church remained 'quite devoid of ornament', the stonework was finished. Above the rose window of the north transept were inscribed these words: 'Pray for the good estate of Yolande Marie Louise Lyne Stephens, Foundress of this church.'

19

PENAL SERVITUDE

*Madame never varies. She turns everything round and makes
a row out of nothing.*

Harry Claremont, 24 April 1889

Yolande was seventy-five years old. The generosity she bestowed
on the diocese of Northampton, the charm she displayed to Arthur
Riddell and Christopher Scott, were rarely reflected in her private
behaviour. Over the years, she had become spoilt, imperious and
irritable. She insisted that Edward be with her at all times and
the unfortunate Fanny sometimes took refuge in the house in
Gloucester Street, particularly when Yolande and her husband
were in France. As Harry wrote to his mother-in-law after the birth
of his third child, a boy, on 3 April 1888: 'The Heir is fit and *round*
with a lot of dark hair like his father ... Madame and the General
went off yesterday to Paris.'

A few weeks after their arrival in the Champs-Élysées, Yolande sat
for the eminent society portraitist Émile-Auguste Carolus-Duran.
Sitting with her head slightly tilted to the left, she watched the
flamboyantly dressed painter at work on the canvas, his dark

curls streaked with grey, his wrists festooned with gold chains and bracelets. She wore a black silk dress, a black velvet head-dress, and the string of pearls that she would donate to the church in Cambridge a few months later. Her iron-grey hair is combed forward into a fringe; her large, wide-apart eyes gaze directly into the eyes of the viewer.

A demanding woman, accustomed to having her own way, she was no doubt a difficult sitter but Carolus-Duran was expert at gazing into the soul of his subjects. Seating her against a deep red background, he captured the contrasts in her personality and the portrait has an almost hypnotic power. The art dealer who restored the painting a few years ago described its impact:

> I was struck by ... the subject's face, particularly her expression. At a glance, one might think she is gently smiling, but a longer look reveals something else – and it is hard to be quite sure what. Her expression seems to segue between gentle warmth, near contempt and tragic regret. Which of these very different takes is most persistent is perhaps dependant on my own mood, but that it is capable of this transition gives the painting enormous, almost haunting vitality – as though there is something of her still here.[1]

At the same time as sitting for Carolus-Duran, Yolande wrote a will disposing of her assets in France. She left legacies to five people in Paris, including 'my friend Madame Frédéric Reiset' and Josephine Trochoux, her housekeeper in Paris. She left 20,000 francs to the priest of her parish, Saint Philippe du Roule, 'to make distributions among the poor of his parish as he shall think fit', and 20,000 francs to the Home for Incurable Children in the Hospital of Saint Jean de Dieu in Vaugirard. Finally, she bequeathed her residuary estate in France – her financial assets and the contents of her apartment in the Champs-Élysées – to Harry Claremont.

A few weeks later, according to Christopher Scott, she was close to death and not permitted to see anyone from Cambridge. There is no evidence for this illness, and perhaps it was not Yolande who was in poor health. Edward had been unwell in Lynford during the previous winter and this had delayed their return to Roehampton, as well as their onward journey to Paris. As Yolande explained to Arthur Riddell on 19 February:

> I have had this winter a great deal of sickness in the house and now I am stopped by the state of the weather. It would be so bad travelling in these snow storms and it would hardly be safe for General Claremont who ... has not been at all well the whole winter. When I do start, I hope you will not mind my taking *mon petit chaplain* as he is really in want of some rest and a little change.[2]

By March, Edward was 'improving by slow degrees' and he was well enough to leave for Paris on 3 April. If he did fall ill again in July, Yolande would have been too distraught to deal with anything, even matters concerned with the church in Cambridge.

Back in Lynford in September, she and Edward spent a second winter making the occasional visit to Cambridge to see the church under construction. Still encased in scaffolding, the exterior was now almost complete and builders were at work on the roof and the spire. 'Altogether,' wrote the *Cambridge Chronicle*, 'the building is one possessed of considerable beauty. The interior being lofty and the character of the stone-groined roof exceptional, the view from the west end is very striking.'[3]

In the spring of 1889, while Fanny Claremont moved into the house in Gloucester Street, Yolande and Edward crossed the Channel, *en route* for the Hôtel de Paris in Monte Carlo. Three of the Claremont children joined them there: Harry, who had left his wife and children in London; Teddy, partially reconciled with his father now he was gainfully employed as a manager with the Edison and Swan Electric Light Company;

and Emily Littledale and her husband. The party was completed by Yolande's chaplain, Michael Dwane, who had received permission to make a second visit to France for 'some rest and a little change'.

On 24 April, while Fletcher Littledale stayed in the hotel, Harry and Emily accompanied Yolande and Edward to Nice. 'Madame was despicable,' Harry wrote to his wife that evening. 'Emily and I came back from Nice alone. We thought Madame was better left with the General. She cannot bear anyone else being with him.'

He wrote again the next day, complaining that the weather was 'filthy' with a strong mistral blowing:

Madame never varies. She turns everything round and makes a row out of nothing. That arch humbug the Padre was here yesterday. He sat holding her hand and stroking it, saying she was without fault! Dwane told me this. If I had heard it myself, I should have said something. As soon as the Padre had gone, she went for Dwane and ranted at him like a lunatic. Emily had some roses on her dress, so she told her that only *cocottes* wore flowers. It is all very well for you seven hundred miles off saying 'bear with her' ... I am dispirited and hate everything at present. However, the term of penal servitude will soon be over.

By the 26th, Harry and Emily had decided to return to England:

Madame has been more amiable since I announced my departure. I think she is pleased for several reasons. First, the expenses will be less. Second, she is jealous of any of us, especially the girls. Third, she can say 'Your children leave you and I remain to take care of you'. The General is dead against our leaving but I have been 'firm' or, as he says, 'obstinate'. I told him straight that Madame is jealous of everyone, even Dwane, and that if he wanted peace for the remainder of the trip, he had better absent the Padre.

Madame is angry about my reasons for going and talks of the precious boy who is heir to so much. So far I have just laughed at her, but I think I shall give her one before leaving, just to show that my spirit is not quite broken! I never see her hardly except at meals. I find that is quite sufficient and as much as one can put up with. I have been here exactly a month and it seems like a year. It is such a relief to know that there are only two more days to put up with. It has been too beastly for words.

Yolande was still in Monte Carlo when Scott laid the capstone on the spire of her church in Cambridge. By late June, she and Edward had returned to Paris, by which time another Exposition Universelle was underway in the city. Built to celebrate modern technology and industrial production, the newly completed Eiffel Tower formed part of the exhibition and served as the main entrance. 'I do not hurry the General to go back to England,' Yolande wrote on 10 July, 'as he is so much better that it would be a pity to leave without the agreement of his doctor.' Edward had already visited the exhibition, 'so I do not like his going a second time for taking care of me'.

They returned to Roehampton at the end of the month and moved to Lynford a few weeks later. During the winter, they made several visits to the church in Cambridge where work was proceeding on the immensely rich interior. Yolande took an interest in every detail. She sometimes met the architect to order alterations: the carving on the organ case; the design of the altar rails. 'She knew what she liked and what she disliked,' wrote a parishioner who was present at one of these meetings, 'and this time it was the carving of the organ case that displeased her.' Scott asked the architect how much the alteration would cost. 'About £1,000,' he replied. Yolande 'handed him a cheque for that amount before she left'.[4]

In March 1890, she and Edward returned to Paris, leaving Fanny alone in Gloucester Street. Edward had been unwell again during the winter, probably with stomach cancer, and the French physician treated him with several unsuitable remedies. 'I had my doctor yesterday,' he wrote to Kitty on 18 April:

> who is giving me what, if I were a horse, I should call correction powders. I have to take them at the beginning of each meal. Then I take homeopathic medicine five times a day, a liniment for my legs, another for my chest, coffee before I get up, mulled wine when I go to bed. It requires a good memory to keep up with it all. The last engraving of Madame's portrait is a great success.

'I have somewhat better news to give you of the General,' Yolande wrote on 13 May. 'The doctor finds him better and, if his appetite would increase, I think he would get stronger. I am under the doctor for the painful ailment of eczema and I hope I may get rid of it.' This prompted a letter from Fanny, written from 4 Gloucester Street on 27 May:

> Harry's account of the General is not very satisfactory and I am much worried about him ... I am glad Mrs Lyne Stephens is so much better. I am afraid she thinks more of her own health and not enough of other people's, but as we cannot change how we must be, the best one can do is to try and bear things patiently, and if she would not worry the General, one would manage to get on. I feel very angry with her sometimes, for she must see how weak and ill he is, and how unable to put up with it.

She wrote again three days later:

> I would rather know the worst than be kept in the dark ... It is so hard to be away so far, but the General does not seem to wish me

to go to Paris. Harry says it would only worry and alarm him if anyone went, so I can only try to be patient and hope for the best. Do let me know the truth.

At the end of the month, the doctor advised Edward that sea air and rest might do him good, so Harry accompanied his father to the Grand Hotel in Arcachon, south-west of Bordeaux. The journey by carriage was tiring, 'the dust fearful', and Edward was looking weak and tired when they arrived. He improved after a few days of peace and quiet. 'He ate a capital dinner last night,' Harry wrote on 6 June:

> The weather is heavenly, bright sun and a nice breeze so it is not too hot. We sat for a long time by the seaside *en plein soleil* this morning. The hotel is right on the beach and at high tide the sea washes up against the foundations. There is not a soul here, five people beside ourselves and some of them go today ... Yesterday afternoon we drove through the pine forest for two and a half hours and he was not a bit tired ... We dine by the open window and are in the air day and night ... I can't tell you how glad I am we came. It is marvellous what the change has done.

Aware that the improvement was only temporary, Harry wrote to Yolande to prepare her. 'She takes such a time to gather anything,' he explained to Kitty, 'that it is as well to begin to try and impress upon her the inevitable.' He also wrote to his mother in Gloucester Street, suggesting that she should now come to Paris. Fanny set out immediately and arrived in the Champs-Élysées a few days before Harry and Edward returned from Arcachon at the end of June. Michael Dwane also arrived in Paris, to attend to Yolande's spiritual needs.

'The General is much weaker and has fallen away about the face and neck terribly,' Harry wrote from the Champs-Élysées on 3 July:

It is too sad to see him in such a reduced state. He seems to take very little interest in anything and doesn't seem able to keep his mind on anything for long. Mother was very much shocked at his appearance. Madame I think knows how bad he is and so has been very nice to Mother. I hope it will last.

Harry now wrote to Kitty every day, describing Edward's condition and complaining about Yolande's behaviour. 'Madame is very nice to everyone except Dwane,' he wrote on the 4th:

She goes at him rather, poor old thing. She is very nearly broken already. I had a drink with her yesterday and she broke down completely. She was very nice and very kind and said she had me only to look to and she knew I would take care of her as the General had told her, so of course I said that, though I never would be what he had been, I would do my best. She spoke quite sensibly but was fearfully upset and I am afraid she will collapse utterly. Mother is very funny – she said she felt for Madame more than she did for herself!

The loss of Stephens in 1860 had been painful for Yolande, but the imminent loss of Edward Claremont felt like a far greater tragedy. Her power of weeping was of little use to her now. As Harry wrote on the 6th:

Madame hangs on to me and turns to me in everything. It will be an awful blow to her after thirty years, as she said last night, of having every wish and whim fulfilled, and every trouble and anxiety taken off her shoulders. She was quite dazed. I found her standing against the wall in her dressing room almost in a faint. She said she can't cry. She said she would give anything to be able to.

The following day, Yolande pulled herself together to write a coherent letter to Arthur Riddell in Northampton about vestments and altar furniture for the church in Cambridge. She seems to have had hopes of a deathbed conversion:

> The dear General is more unwell than when you saw him last. His illness is excessive and the doctor does not give any encouragement. He has now for the last two days taken to his bed. When I showed him your letter, he said 'how very nice and kind of the Bishop, thank him very much for me'. His wife is here and she has already sent for a clergyman who came this morning and gave him the sacrament. You see that any attempt the *right way* would be impossible. The opposition would be great and I fear nothing would result of it. I feel quite distressed.[5]

The five other Claremont children arrived in the Champs-Élysées on the 7th and Harry made a visit to Sir Richard Wallace, who had returned to live in Paris: 'I saw poor Wallace today. He sent for me. Poor fellow, he is very ill and suffers agonies. He looks dreadful but is full of anxieties about the General. Madame has been most trying. She is nearly off her head, poor old thing.'

On the 8th, Edward told Yolande that 'yesterday he had hope, today not. The poor woman is in a dreadful state in consequence and wanders about aimlessly. Mother does nothing but look terribly anxious and worn.'

On the 10th: 'Madame has been quite detestable to everyone today. Dwane left the house on being called a liar and swears he will return to England tomorrow. This happened after she had been to church and offered two candles to Notre Dame des Victoires. She seems better now. I suppose she has worked it off.'

On the 11th: 'Madame has calmed down a bit, but every now and then she works herself up and fires off. No one pays any attention to her rantings, so she is forced to shut up.'

On the 13th: 'Madame is very nice to me but resents any suggestions of any sort. Sometimes she is in the depths of despair; at other times she is generally despicable. We all feel for her, but her grief is purely selfish, her one refrain being what will become of *me* and *my* affairs.'

Next day, Edward became delirious, his voice so weak that no one could hear what he was saying. For two days, he passed in and out of consciousness until, on 16 July:

> He passed quietly and peacefully away before us all. He looks so beautiful, so handsome and restful ... Madame goes to Méry for which I am thankful, though I shall have to return here to settle up and fetch her. She is calmer than I expected and trusts to me implicitly.

The Château de Méry-sur-Oise, twenty miles north of Paris, was the family home of Edgar, Comte de Ségur-Lamoignon. He was a diplomat and politician of great religious zeal; his wife Marie was the daughter of Yolande's friend Madame Reiset. Yolande visited Méry every year when she was in Paris, leaving the Claremonts in her apartment in the Champs-Élysées. Now, after Edward's death, she would go to Méry for comfort.

'Our first great grief', Harry wrote to Kitty on the 18th. 'We leave Paris tomorrow morning and arrive at Victoria at seven o'clock in the evening.' Two days later, Yolande wrote from Méry:

> Yesterday I tried to follow you all day during that dreary and most miserable journey. Your telegram only came this morning and has relieved my mind. It is over, God be praised ... Consolation is impossible. I like to be alone more than with other people and, still, returning to my house will be a terrible trial, in fact my place is awful to me. But no remedy! *Je me sens bien malheureuse.*

On 21 July, Horace Pym read the will in Edward's house in Gloucester Street which Fanny now made her permanent home. There was a letter attached to the will, written in Lynford Hall in January 1890 and sealed in a black-edged envelope. It was addressed to two of his sons, George and Harry, 'to be given to one or to the other of them when I am dead':

> When you read this I shall be no more ... It would be very nice of you, when you go to Paris, to see that my mother's grave is kept in order. I am a trustee for the mausoleum at Roehampton and you must both look after it. You all may sometimes have thought me harsh, but believe me when I say that I have been actuated solely by my desire that you should be honest men and women ... I only trust that you will cherish my memory and think kindly of me, as I always have done of my own father and mother.

Yolande was still in Méry when the funeral service was held in the Anglican church in Roehampton on 23 July. Edward had requested a simple service, with no flowers, and had also asked to be buried 'in the most unostentatious manner and in the ground in front of the mausoleum at Roehampton if possible'.

Although his wife would surely have preferred a different place of interment, he was buried according to his wishes. After the service, his coffin was carried into the grounds of Grove House and lowered into a grave dug in the consecrated ground below the steps to the mausoleum.

20

FIRST GREAT GRIEF

I cry and sob enough to break my heart. The trial is too great, too awful for anyone to bear.

Yolande Lyne Stephens, 27 December 1890

Most newspapers reported Edward's death with a brief paragraph. The longest obituary was written by the Paris correspondent of the *London Evening Standard*:

> Many friends in England and France will feel sincere regret at the death of General Claremont, which took place in Paris ... after a protracted illness. The late gallant officer was better known here as Colonel Claremont, when ... he occupied the position of Military Attaché to the British Embassy, and became deservedly popular, not only with the Commanders of the French Army, but also in social circles ... He had reached his seventy-first year.

A few days later, there was a further announcement: 'The death of General Claremont makes a vacancy in the Royal Household for a Groom of the Privy Chamber. The salary is £120 a year, with some allowances, and there are no duties whatsoever.'

On 29 July, Harry returned to Paris to bring Yolande home to Roehampton, the 'terrible trial' which she had been dreading so much. She was inconsolable when the carriage turned into the drive and she saw her servants, dressed in mourning, lined up outside the front door to greet her. Letters of condolence were waiting for her, including letters from Lady Wallace, widowed four days after Edward's death, and General Trochu, who wrote that 'we have lost the best, the most sure of our friends'.

During the next few weeks, Horace Pym often came to see her with legal matters to discuss. On 9 September, she signed a codicil to her will replacing Edward as the residuary beneficiary of her English estate with Harry Claremont. Two days later, Pym accompanied George and Harry when they proved their father's will in London. He had discovered that Edward held securities in Turkey with a value of £7,000 and the will was proved in the sum of £21,290, sufficient to give Fanny an allowance of £1,000 a year.

On 15 September, Yolande wrote to Arthur Riddell who had asked about accessories and accounts for the church in Cambridge, which was now complete and ready for consecration:

> Dr Scott has assured me that there is nothing owing which could delay in any way the consecration of the church … I am not well and I find that, in my present state, all the work I see before me is a great deal too much. I hope and trust that Dr Scott will be able to supply the altar linen and altar cloth. As for the summary of account, I never had anything to do with it, and cannot possibly understand the least thing about it. I am afraid that if I am trusted with this great business, I shall fail *quite* to be of any use.[1]

Yolande had lost interest in the church which, for six years, had absorbed so much of her enthusiasm, her energy and her money. During the next three weeks, Christopher Scott sourced the outstanding items ready for the consecration on 9 October. At the same time, arrangements were made for the opening service six days later. 'Dr Scott asked me to join Baron von Hügel on the secretarial work entailed,' wrote Maurice Croucher, one of Scott's helpers:

> There was a lot to do and arrangements had to be made to find accommodation for all the Bishops and Abbots and others who were to be invited to the opening ...What struck me was that the Bishops seemed totally unable to look up their local train service themselves; by the time we got them finally fixed up, Baron von Hügel and I could have passed an exam in Bradshaw.

Yolande forced herself to make the journey to Cambridge on 15 October, accompanied by members of the Claremont family and by Horace Pym and his wife. She had been looking forward to this occasion for more than six years; but now Edward Claremont was gone, the pontifical High Mass in the church she had built to 'indulge my own taste and fancy' would give her no pleasure.

'The doors were opened,' wrote Maurice Croucher, 'and the huge congregation began to flock in. Admission was by ticket only, but we soon discovered that people who had tickets for the aisles were passing into the seats reserved in the nave. I got into a hansom and tore down to Sayles, where I obtained a lot of rope twist which we tied round the ends of the benches.'

The choir of the Brompton Oratory had travelled from London for the occasion and the entire Catholic hierarchy attended the service, except for the Archbishop of Westminster, 'who was too old and feeble', and the Bishop of Salford, who was unwell. Large numbers of clergy and members of the monastic orders were also present, together with several leading Catholics, including the Duke of Norfolk.

Yolande sat in one of the front pews, 'a frail little figure in black', accompanied only by her lady's maid. At the end of the service, Croucher took the collection in the nave:

> I started, with an empty plate, to where Mrs Lyne Stephens was sitting. She seemed lost in contemplation, with bowed head, and

the impertinent thought, 'You have done so much and I won't disturb you', crossed my mind. I was passing on when a small hand waved and I came back. She picked up her reticule, found a little purse and after much peering therein, placed a coin on the plate. It was a shilling.[2]

After the service, a luncheon was held in the Devonshire Assembly Rooms, which Yolande had neither the strength nor the inclination to attend. The Duke of Norfolk took the chair, with Arthur Riddell on his right and Christopher Scott on his left. There were toasts to 'The Pope' and 'The Queen', after which Scott 'proposed the health of Mrs Lyne Stephens, who is absent on account of her recent bereavement'.

During the speeches, Scott 'condoled with Mrs Lyne Stephens upon her loss by the death of General Claremont, who had taken such a great interest in the building of the church, although himself a Protestant'. He referred to 'the interest taken … by poor people', including 'a poor woman who died in great distress but, forgetting her own misery, asked God with her last words to bless this church'. He told the story of a 'hearty workman who came all the way to Cambridge on purpose to see the church and who asked God's blessing on Mrs Lyne Stephens'.[3]

By the time Scott made this speech, Yolande was already in Lynford Hall, having taken the train to Brandon immediately after the service. She remained in Norfolk for five weeks before summoning up the energy to return to Roehampton on 22 November. 'I need not tell you how I felt in entering this place,' she wrote to Harry on the 27th. 'It was more dreadful than ever.'

This was the fifth turning point in her life. Now there was only Harry to take charge of her affairs but he had recently been diagnosed with tuberculosis. Shortly after the opening service in Cambridge, he was 'laid up with congestion of the lungs'. Ordered by his doctor to spend the winter months in Switzerland, he and his family left for Davos in November and would remain there until the spring. As Yolande wrote to Arthur Riddell at the end of the month:

> I wish I could write to you in my own language ... I cannot say much yet about myself. My health could help me a little in what I wish to do, but the state of my spirit is still unequal to the requirement of my work. The illness of Mr H. Claremont, which has obliged him to leave England at once for some months, has added a new misfortune to the existing one ... I need not say that this will cause me much discomfort, being now quite alone to manage everything.[4]

She had only her servants for company. 'I cry and sob enough to break my heart,' she wrote to Harry on 27 December. 'The trial is too great, too awful for anyone to bear ... a very cruel time, so much sorrowful recollections. All is gone, never to come back.' Two days later, she wrote again to Arthur Riddell:

> Many thanks for your most kind letter. It has done me great good in my extreme solitude. May I say in return that my heart is full of gratitude and I should like to express to you all that I feel ... You are very right, my affliction is great. I have lost a friend so devoted and unselfish that no one could ever replace him. Every day I feel it more and more. I try to think, as you tell me, that all happens for the best, but I do not yet see it and my misery speaks louder than the voice of resignation. I am living quite alone ... Mrs Claremont is not with me, nor anyone else. She found it too great a trial being here.[5]

'I find Mrs Lyne Stephens in health but fretting dreadfully for the dear General,' Horace Pym wrote to Harry after a visit to Grove House in January. 'There is no doubt in my mind that it is exceedingly bad for her being alone at Roehampton and I shall be very glad when the weather permits her to get to Paris, and still more so when you are well enough to return to her assistance.'

One morning in mid-January, when thick layers of snow lay on the terrace outside the drawing room windows and the lake was covered in ice, Yolande wrote to Kitty who was with her husband in Davos:

> I have no news to give you. What I could tell you of my wretched life would make you very melancholy. To talk of what one feels constantly would be misery. Solitude is not a word to express what I endure. Picture to yourself a poor woman whose mind and body is lost in this house much too big for a party of six, having to sit to every meal without a soul. I had no idea I could bear so much. I am so enervated, so terribly low that I hardly know what I can do to allow me to end this letter without saying a word more.

It was during this cold spell that Yolande's neighbour, Constance Smith, was surprised to find her in residence:

> Romance and mystery hung around Grove House for, though Mrs Lyne Stephens had lived there for many years, no one visited her ... and hardly anyone had even seen her ... She allowed us to skate on her lake in her habitual absence in winter but, that year, I found she was living in the house and I called to apologise for unintentional trespassing ...
>
> I was received by a very tiny, very slight little old lady, with large eyes and the saddest face I ever saw. She was very amiable and very friendly, but received my apologies with tears – as the fact of her spending the winter at Roehampton was owing to General Claremont's death. He liked the shooting at Lynford, but now that he was gone there was no one to enjoy it.
>
> Her broken English and her French were hard to understand, but we got on well together, and parted affectionately. I saw her several times more, and on the cold winter days when I went to see the children skate, her sad little form in deep black was constantly to be seen, taking slow solitary walks in the garden.[6]

Harry was still in Davos when the 1891 census was taken during the evening of 5 April. In the entry for Grove House, Yolande is listed as head of a household of fourteen servants: a butler, housekeeper, cook, French lady's maid, three laundry maids, three housemaids, a still-room maid, a dairymaid, and two footmen. Living in cottages on the estate were a coachman, two grooms, four gardeners, and a lodge-keeper/carpenter.

That same evening, in Gloucester Street, Fanny Claremont listed the names of the people who would be sleeping under her roof that night. In addition to the servants, she included her eldest son, George, who was staying for a few days in London.

A lieutenant-colonel in the Worcestershire regiment based in Malvern, George had married Marianne (Daisy) Hamilton, the widow of one of his fellow officers, in 1887. Having begun to suffer from epileptic fits, he retired from the army two years later and moved to Daisy's home town of Larkhall near Glasgow. Unknown to George, Daisy had incurred debts in Larkhall which she now asked him to repay.

Yolande had refused to give George a marriage settlement, or any other financial help, so he mortgaged his house and furniture in Malvern. On 18 May 1890, when there was no money left, he wrote to his father in Paris asking Yolande to lend him £450:

Daisy has been in bad health all the winter. She has been quite prostrate. She has hardly eaten a thing or slept a wink for a week. I feel all this very much as I am so utterly helpless in the matter. I have neither securities nor capital to offer, so please ask Mrs Lyne Stephens to advance the money. She shall be paid back and I will put by a portion of my retired pay to pay the interest on the loan. Remind her with my love of her kindness to me when we spoke of my marriage in the morning room at Lynford and she said that, though she could not make a settlement on me then, I should never be any the worse of it hereafter.

Edward had less than two months to live when he received this letter. He decided not to show it to Yolande; instead he wrote his own cheque for £450 (£53,000). Despite this generosity, George's marriage became increasingly unhappy and, when he was staying with his mother in April 1891, he told her 'what a comfort four days of peace in London had been to him and how he disliked having to go back to Larkhall on the Monday'.

Fanny was worried when she answered the enumerator's questions during the early evening of 5 April. George had been restless during the morning; he told her that he was going out for a walk but had never returned. He was found later that night in his London club, slumped in one of the lavatories. He had suffered an epileptic fit, fallen forwards and hit his head on the floor. The duty attendant was taken ill that day and had not been replaced, so George remained in the closet, his head on the floor, for five hours.

Next day, Yolande took the news 'most complacently'. When the family suggested that George should be buried close to his father in the consecrated ground outside the mausoleum, she refused to allow it. To one member of the family, she explained that she would not like Daisy to have access to the mausoleum; to another, she said firmly that 'no one is to be there except the General and his wife'.

George's body was taken to Malvern where he had lived before his retirement. He was buried there on 11 April, with Daisy, Teddy and his three sisters as mourners. Fanny stayed in London and suffered a visit from Yolande. 'Mother keeps well,' Teddy wrote to Harry on the 12th. 'Mrs Lyne Stephens went to see her yesterday and rather upset her.'

The arrival of warmer weather in May did little to lift Yolande's spirits. Five weeks after George's death, she wrote another letter to Arthur Riddell:

I am still here and in the same state of mind. I have been all the time not wishing to do anything or go anywhere. The weather was for many months the principal cause of it, then so much business to attend to and so little knowledge and energy to do it all. It is not easy for one who had never done any serious work of that sort to take to it or understand it at once ... However, the spring cheering me a little, I hope some day I may get more what I was before all my troubles which have been all along very great.[7]

THAT TEARLESS CRY

I come in for a lot of ill-humour. Nothing gives
pleasure or satisfaction.

Canon Michael Dwane, 16 February 1892

Harry's eldest daughter, Sybil, would remember Yolande as a '*très grande dame*', a small, dainty old lady with a strong French accent. Her grey hair was parted in the middle and she was always dressed in black. When the children stayed with her in Grove House, she would give them a wrapped sweet before they went to bed and insisted that they curtsey to her before leaving the room. Sybil also remembered 'a wonderful French chef who was very good with rabbit'.

Yolande tried to hide her grief when Harry and his family were visiting. In private, she was hysterical, howling in anguish in what Michael Dwane referred to as 'that tearless cry which is so painful to witness'. She was unable to cope without Edward's emotional and administrative support. Harry did his best to take over his father's duties, but he was away in Switzerland during the winter months and was becoming increasingly unwell. '*Très cher ami*,' she wrote in an undated letter when she had not heard from him for several weeks:

All the days I have passed for ten days now have been most anxious ones. I have been wishing to have a few words from you, but nothing has come. How is it, if you could not come, a line would have calmed my anxiety. I have counted the hours but all is a blank. What shall I do, waiting, waiting all the time is cruel! I cannot give you an idea of my wish to know something about you. I am most anxious.

In July, she returned to Paris, arriving shortly after the first anniversary of Edward's death. Harry joined her there in August. With the agreement of Sir John Lubbock, he had succeeded his father as trustee of the Lyne Stephens fortune and, after a few weeks in Paris, he travelled to Norfolk to learn about the administration of the Lynford estate. Yolande wrote to him from Paris on 28 September:

Your letter from Lynford has made me nearly happy, though I would be more completely so if you had said you were stronger. Only I am dreadfully afraid all that knowledge of every department could not be acquired without much fatigue. Do take care, do not be anxious. It would have been better for you to rest after the Lynford work, but one cannot do anything without exertion.

Now for what you ask about me. I got better of the attack of diarrhoea and I thought it would be soon alright, but the exertion made me very unwell. They were obliged to give me pills which yesterday morning had too strong an effect and made me feel very seedy. Pills are terrible and what is to be done. I cannot remain as I am. If I could get things as it ought to be, I could at once begin putting all my things in the packing boxes and try to find my way to Roehampton ... All in this life is disappointment.

She returned to Grove House in early October. Shortly after her return, Harry left again for Switzerland and, on 29 October,

Yolande signed a codicil to her will which raised the possibility that he might die before her. On 8 November, she wrote him a rather garbled letter:

> I am pretty ashamed of myself to be still in your debt of letters to such an extent. I can hardly tell you how it has happen, but this is a plain fact and nothing of what I can say will make it less bad. I am in great fault. However, you know all my faults and you know that I could do my best to avoiding displeasing you if I could help it.
>
> You are quite right saying that a few lines would be sufficient occasionally. That is true but when I begin I try to make up for the loss of time, but I plunge in more and more in difficulty and I cannot get out after. Since I am here I have taken again to the way I left this last year, though I made a promise to avoid it. It is not so easy to give up bad habits. I ought to exert myself in getting as I should like myself to be, but I cannot do it …
>
> People who have not seen me for some time say I look well. I think it may be to please me a bit but why would they say that if it was out of humbug only? Of course I am happy to hear it … *À vous, toutes les forces de mon coeur.*

She wrote again on the 27th, having encountered a problem with gifts of game, an annual ritual which Edward had handled in the past:

> I find myself in an awful difficulty. I have to send, as in preceding years, game to people, schools, etc., and I have not the book we used to refer to, to whom and to know also the quantity. If you have seen anything referring to what was done, tell me, as they ask and I have not the least idea of what was done, and if you have seen, in books, anything of the sort, answer me at once as I cannot get on.

Yolande stayed in Roehampton for a second winter, a decision attributed by Michael Dwane to 'the proximity of her solicitor'.

Pym came regularly to see her and Dwane also kept her company, returning by train to Norfolk at weekends to say Mass in the chapel at Lynford.

In November, Christopher Scott came from Cambridge to spend a week in Grove House. His visit calmed her. 'For some time before Christmas,' Dwane wrote to Harry on 18 January 1892, 'our times have been more peaceable. Of course you will understand that spasmodic outbursts have taken place.' Yolande wrote ten days later:

> It is very true that I should write oftener and little at a time to you, so that you should know what I am about. My saying that I have no time to write much is perfectly true but if it is merely to let you hear what, besides business, I am able to do, well and good. I can do so to a certain extent. My mornings generally are spent in a little letter writing, mixed with doing little jobs about my rooms. The short days in winter make the day work very indifferent for utility. Still, one can always have plenty of little talks and the time passes ... *Je vous embrasse tendrement.*

According to Constance Smith, Yolande complained of being 'very much neglected by her servants, so neglected that her doctor threatened to expose their conduct if they did not behave better to her'. If this was true, the servants had cause for their behaviour for Yolande was now a bitter, self-absorbed and bad-tempered old woman who had become miserly with small amounts of money.

Her butler resigned in the summer of 1891, after which her main victims were Michael Dwane and her lady's maid, Marie Marque. She treated Dwane as a servant, rather than a man of the church. 'How kind you were to have dear Dwane with you,' she wrote to Harry when he was in Lynford in September 1891, 'and to give him a meal of potatoes and bread and butter.'

Dwane expressed his anger in long letters to Harry. 'I might make many a letter out of my own too-wounded feelings,' he wrote on 6 February 1892:

> but this would not be *news* to you. Perhaps the hardest thing to bear is the oft-levelled charge that I am useless, wasting my time, unable to do anything, while all the time I am not allowed to do the least thing. I'm told I'm no good, I do nothing for her, etc. When this is said with feeling, as you know it can be, it is hard to bear in the face of a fixed determination that I shall not be trusted to do anything. I exercise a great deal of self-control. I am often astonished at my self-restraint. It is best to treat what is said in anger and violence as if it had been said in coolness and deliberation. That style on my part leads to coldness on her part, and I have a most trying time of it.

Two days later, he wrote again:

> I come in for a lot of ill-humour. Nothing gives pleasure or satisfaction. I have been called useless, that I do no good, that my time is spent without an object, etc. Though I was boiling over, I took a seat, looked into the lady's face, and in the mildest of tones, asked if she really wished me to be near her or not, that I was there as her companion, and as she well knew, had nothing else to do (she takes care of that), but if she was unhappy on that account and would prefer me to be in Lynford, she had but to say the word ... Dr Marshall comes once a day and Marie says he will be favourite until he has to send in his account.

Yolande queried Dwane's expenses on his third-class railway journeys to Norfolk at weekends, 'which she said were cooked – she vowed that the third-class fare was nothing near so much as I had charged, 7/3'. The station in Brandon was five miles from

Lynford and the early months of 1892 were particularly cold. 'On Monday,' he wrote on 2 March:

> I was taunted with the expense I am causing by having the old grey horse from the farm take me from Brandon to Lynford. And frost! Nothing is said about the expenses of Pym and his clerk coming here three times a week, for very little, and they would not like to go third class. ... Last week, I was told I was no good. There was no use in my being here. I might just as well be at Lynford and she would have to tell me to stay there. Very well, I replied, you have only to say so once. Ah, she said, you threaten me.

The following afternoon, Yolande discovered Edward's jewel and watch cases hidden away at the back of a drawer. In his will, he had left her 'all the jewels and trinkets she has given me and which she is to point out and select also the plain gold ring which I always wear'. The cases had been brought to Grove House for her to make the selection, but she was so overwrought that they were wrapped in paper and put away for another time. On the evening of 3 March, Dwane wrote a long letter to Harry:

> I have had such a trying afternoon. Madame was routing in the drawer of her table in which the cellar book is kept, and she complained that there was a packet at the back which was in the way. She took it out and impatiently asked me to open it, saying it was doubtless papers. There were two cases and I divined at once what they were from knowledge derived from your mother. One was your father's jewel case; in the other were his various watches.
>
> Such a scene I hope never to witness again. Madame was completely unnerved. She collapsed and began that tearless cry which is so painful to witness. Her reading of the situation is that your father himself put them there, in a place to which he knew no one had access but herself, so she would be sure to find them. 'It was so like him, so like his thoughtfulness for her in everything', etc. 'Now she was alone, desolate and dreary,' etc., etc.

There was no use arguing but I did my best to calm her. Later on, I tried to make her recall whether or not she had put them there herself, but in vain. 'He had put them there, with his own hands.' I tried as delicately as I could to show that that was unlikely, that your father had taken his watches and jewellery to Paris with him, and that in conformity with the terms of his will (this is what I understood from your mother), the jewels were sent to her that she might select what she liked from them. 'No, no, that could not be,' etc. The shock was terrible in its effects, construed as it was by her as a proof of your father's kind thoughtfulness.

Yolande assumed that all the jewels were hers, without a thought for Edward's wife and children. 'I have suggested to Madame,' Dwane continued:

that she should get you all together and either let you choose or make a distribution, but I do not think I am likely to prevail. No doubt Madame will tell Pym, who could disillusion her and have the will carried out by restoration of jewels. Your mother told me that he had declined to suggest such a thing to Madame last year when asked to do so but, if the way was opened for him, he surely would not shrink from reminding her of the terms and conditions of the will. Or am I to mind my own business?

Yolande wrote to Harry five days later – making no mention of the jewels:

I know well that I do not deserve praises for my *épistolaire* work. I am always backward for answering letters, not that I absolutely wish to be lazy and doing nothing. Oh no, I am sometimes very angry with me but I have not in me the energy to live as I used to do not so very long ago, and what is the point is that I have so little to say. If you can fancy how my days are passing, it would not surprise you, living almost quite by myself. I do not find the least thing that could have an interest for any of you.

Ten days earlier, Christopher Scott had arrived in Roehampton to discuss the final fittings for the church in Cambridge. Sitting in the drawing room in Grove House, he talked about the work that remained unfinished, but according to Michael Dwane, 'he simply ceased to go on when he was treated in a way to which we are accustomed but he is not. People know little of Madame if they think they can *force* money out of her.'

Apart from Michael Dwane, Yolande had never shown this side of her personality to any member of the clergy. A few days later, she received a letter from Arthur Riddell conveying the pope's blessing for her work in Cambridge. She replied on 4 March, the day after the scene about Edward's jewel and watch cases, confirming that she was about to send Scott a cheque for £4,000 (£450,000):

> I cannot thank you enough for your extremely kind letter which, besides being full of kindness to me, conveyed also the invaluable approval on the part of the Holy Father of the work it has been my privilege to carry out in Cambridge. The blessing which his Holiness has graciously conferred on me has filled me with happiness and gratitude ... It will, I think, interest your Lordship to know that Dr Scott was staying with me last week and we then decided to complete at once what remains to be done for the Church. Accordingly it is my intention to forward to him the sum ... which is needed to finish everything.[1]

The cold winter had affected Yolande's feet and ankles which were crippled with arthritis, one reason perhaps for her bad temper. They had been damaged by her years as a dancer and the arduous training she underwent as a child. Ballerinas in the 1830s danced *en pointe* with no blocks in their shoes, just a mass of darning at the points, so they had to work hard to strengthen the muscles in their toes, feet and ankles. One of Edward's daughters visited her in Roehampton on 19 March and, according to Fanny, found her 'looking ill, complaining of sciatica, and was hardly able to crawl along'.

Yolande visited Fanny in Gloucester Street at least twice a week, driving in an open carriage from Roehampton even in the coldest weather. Fanny found her 'very cross and tiresome' and wished she would not come so often. 'I pity poor Dwane,' she wrote to Harry. 'He says from the time he comes down in the morning until ten at night when she goes to bed, she hardly lets him out of her sight and finding fault with him all the time. He even seems afraid to go into the garden without permission.'

In April 1892, Yolande plucked up courage to return to Lynford Hall. Harry had arrived in England a few weeks earlier, but his lungs had deteriorated and he was ordered back to Switzerland, this time to Montreux. Michael Dwane wrote to him there on 1 May:

On her arrival and for some days afterwards, she was very sorrowful and broke down on first speaking to a person. Now, for more than a week, she has been much better. She suffers martyrdom from her feet and can walk but little, but otherwise I would pronounce her very well indeed. I need not say that she will not admit that she is any better, or ever will be, but that is because we say so and, of course, what we say is wrong. I dare not ask questions and conversation is hard if not impossible. I wish somebody else was staying here.

Yolande wrote five days later, thanking Harry for his attention during his brief stay in England:

You are so kind and tried to do everything to show me your utmost interest that if you did not say even so much, my heart would be full of gratitude. You must guess what I feel and I can only thank you heartily for all. I feel dull to think that you are gone away. I wish I was gone with you, or you with me, but this cannot be. I do not know what my short evening will do for me, but time may do still a little, very little comfort for me. Perhaps you may some day help me in that. *Je vous embrasse.*

On the 16th, Dwane wrote a rather indiscreet report on her health:

> The doctor says that she is as clear in memory and as keen in intellect as ever. But in body? Well, I hardly know what to say. She has had attacks of what the doctor calls bile or 'intestinal indigestion', commonly called diarrhoea, and all last week she has been ill at ease. The worst of it is that it is accompanied by want of power of retention. Now this is simply *entre nous* ...
>
> And temper? Ah, only this afternoon there was an unusual amount of perversity about my going out in the carriage. I offered several times to go with her but 'No' she said. 'Had I nothing better to do?' At last she said that Marie was going with her, so I thought I was not wanted. I was leaving when I was asked 'Was I not going in the carriage?' I said 'No'. 'But you *shall* go,' was shrieked in all violence and vehemence, and repeated several times.

Fanny Claremont was relieved that she had moved to Norfolk; she had been exhausted by the constant visits from Roehampton. Yolande wrote to tell her that she was 'very miserable' in Lynford and, when Fanny heard rumours that she was thinking of returning to Grove House at the end of May, she expressed the hope that she would stay in Norfolk. She was seventy-eight years old and suffering from liver failure. She did not feel well enough to cope with any more visits from Yolande.

When Harry returned to London in early June, he wrote to Lynford about his mother's health. 'I was happy to get your letter,' Yolande replied on the 6th, 'but I feel much upset that you had to give me a very poor account of the state you found the dear mother, with a little attack of bile. She is not subject to that generally and I hope it will soon get right.'

Harry made a brief visit to Lynford before returning to London and taking his mother to the Granby Hotel in Harrogate, a spa hotel where he hoped she might feel more comfortable. He suggested to Yolande that it would be a kindness to write to Fanny at this late stage in her life. 'I could not write to her,' Yolande replied on the 20th. 'What could I say? I pray for her. It is all I can do. I want to be at Roehampton but cannot take any decision about going. I am miserable and want to see you all. Can I do anything useful?'

Next day, she received more news from Harrogate. 'I am most unhappy that the news is no better,' she replied:

> I had a slight hope that the shade of a little comfort should have continued but your letter this morning takes away my hope. Do you like the consulting doctor and does it give a hope for us to feel less anxious? I wish I could be with you all, but I am always very fidgety when there is a question of moving.

Fanny may have been an unwelcome member of the *ménage-à-trois*, but she had lived with Yolande for twenty years – and while she lay dying in Harrogate, Yolande fretted about the journey to Roehampton. 'She wants to go and I feel sure she will go,' wrote Michael Dwane on 22 June, 'only she will not fix a day. She is upsetting herself – and others – very much owing to her nervousness about the details (and *expense*) of the move.'

Yolande finally made the journey on 30 June. Four weeks later, Fanny Claremont died in the Granby Hotel in Harrogate. 'It was so merciful,' Harry wrote to his wife that evening. 'She had no suffering and simply seemed to sleep out, just like the General did.'

He brought his mother home to London. After a funeral service in the Anglican church in Roehampton, the coffin was taken into the grounds of Grove House and buried in Edward's grave outside the mausoleum. Yolande showed no grief as the Claremont family gathered in Grove House. She was happy to spend time with Harry and his children. 'I wish I could have the dear children in my pocket,' she had written during the winter, 'to take them out for recreation and play with them till I am tired to have been pulled about.'

22

A SOLITARY DOVE

I do not know what my short evening will do for me, but time may
do still a little, very little comfort for me.

Yolande Lyne Stephens, 6 May 1892

There are two – very different – accounts of Yolande's personality
towards the end of her life. The first is from the letters of Harry
Claremont and Michael Dwane. The second is from the memoirs
of Horace Pym. Yolande perceived Pym to be a friend as well as a
lawyer. In his presence, she displayed the wit and charm that had
captivated the men of society so many years before, just as she had
done with Arthur Riddell and Christopher Scott.

After several visits to Lynford in the spring of 1892, Pym
wrote that he had found her 'excessively bright and quite equal
to the labour of all her business affairs'. He would remember her
in old age as 'full of physical vigour and intellectual brightness,
and still remarkable for her personal beauty, finding life to
the last full of many interests, but impressed by the sadness of
having outlived nearly all her friends and contemporaries'. In
his opinion, she was:

A simple-lived, brave, warm-hearted, generous woman ... Her conversation and power of repartee was extremely clever and brilliant. A shrewd observer of character, she rarely made a mistake in her first estimate of people, and her sometimes adverse judgements, which at first sight appeared harsh, were invariably justified by the history of after-events. Her charity was illimitable, and was always, as far as possible, concealed.

His memoirs continue with an interesting account of Yolande's background and her whereabouts during the Siege of Paris and the Commune:

The history of this admirable woman is deeply interesting in every way. She was the daughter of Colonel Duvernay, a member of a good old French family, who was ruined by the French Revolution ... She was educated at the Conservatoire in Paris, where they soon discovered her wonderful talent for dancing ... For thirty-four years, as a widow, she administered, with the utmost wisdom and the broadest generosity, the large trust placed in her most capable hands ...

During the Franco-German war of 1870, she remained in her beautiful home in the Rue du Faubourg Saint-Honoré and would daily sally forth to help the sufferings which the people in Paris were undergoing. No one will ever know the vast extent of the sacrifice she then made. Her men-servants had all left to fight for their country, and she was alone in the big house, with only two or three maids to accompany her.

During the Commune she continued her daily walks abroad, and was always recognised by the mob as a good Frenchwoman, doing her utmost for the needs of the very poor. Her friend, Sir Richard Wallace, who was also in Paris during these troubles, well earned his baronetcy by his care of the poor English shut up in the city during the siege; but although Mrs Lyne Stephens's charity was quite as wide and generous as his, she never received, nor did she expect or desire it, one word of acknowledgement from any of the powers that were.[1]

Pym had known Yolande since he took over the legal management of her husband's estate in 1870. It is difficult to understand how he could have believed these stories. Perhaps he included them in his memoirs to put a better light on the large sums of money he received under her will.

For ten years, Pym and his family had lived in Foxwold, a large house near Sevenoaks in Kent which he had built to his own designs. He had borrowed heavily to fund the building and, in a codicil dated 6 October 1892, Yolande left him a legacy of £10,000 'as a mark of my affectionate regard and gratitude for all he has done for me during many past years of friendship, with the desire (but not as a condition) that he will use the legacy in reducing any encumbrances existing at the time of my decease upon his Foxwold estate'.

In an earlier codicil dated 12 December 1891, she left £10,000 to Pym's wife and £5,000 to each of his four children. These two codicils gave Pym and his family a total of £40,000 (£5 million). In addition to this, in a codicil to her French will dated 22 July 1893, she appointed Pym as her residuary beneficiary in France in place of Harry Claremont. Altogether, Pym and his family would receive £92,000 (£11 million) from Yolande's will, in addition to his legal fees for administering the estate.

This was not all. Over the years, she had given him several old master paintings, including a Watteau, and many pieces of valuable porcelain and *objets d'art*. He would also inherit the contents of her apartment in the Champs-Élysées. As the fortunate lawyer wrote in his memoirs:

To the inmates of Foxwold, she was …. a true and loving friend, paying them frequent little visits, and entering with the deepest sympathy into the lives of those who also loved her very dearly. The house bears, through her generosity, many marks of her exquisite taste and broad bounty, and her memory will always be fragrant and beautiful to those who knew her.

While Harry was forced to spend increasing periods of time in the mountains of Switzerland, Pym visited Yolande frequently in her old age, taking care to avoid matters which might cause friction, such as the restitution of Edward's watches and jewels to his family. In September 1893, when Yolande moved to Lynford after spending fourteen months in Grove House, he came to see her as soon as she had settled in. 'I came here by very fast train,' he wrote to his daughter on the 23rd, 'and as I drove through the park, there were hundreds of pheasants running about and their kind old nurses, the hens under whose wings they had been hatched, were looking at them with surprise at their bright colours and flighty ways'.

He made many visits to Lynford during the next twelve months, staying overnight and providing her with the pleasures of his company. There were also legal matters to discuss, not least the matter of her executors. In her will of 1887, she had appointed Harry Claremont, Sir John Lubbock and Horace Pym. By early 1894, it was clear that Harry Claremont did not have long to live, while Sir John Lubbock – a remarkably busy man – was unlikely to take much interest in the administration. Pym told Yolande that she should appoint another executor.

George Claremont was dead, his brother Teddy was unsuitable, and apart from Horace Pym she had no male friends. Pym's solution was to nominate his brother-in-law, Joseph Gurney Fox. She agreed to this and, in a codicil signed in Lynford Hall on 15 February 1894, she appointed Fox as the fourth executor and trustee of her will.

Yolande was transformed in Pym's company; she missed him when he was gone. It is easy to conjure up an image of a little old woman dressed in black hobbling around the enormous rooms of

Lynford Hall, dwarfed by the high ceilings and ornate furnishings, alone among her many servants, reliant for company on her chaplain and her lady's maid. Spoilt by more than thirty years of more wealth than she knew what to do with, by Edward Claremont looking after all her affairs, there was nothing left to give her pleasure, just the constant pain in her feet and an aching loneliness.

On 5 July, she put pen to paper for the last time, writing to Harry in weak handwriting and in French:

> I am surprised to start this letter as I have not written any letters since I have been here. It is such a long time since I picked up my pen that I am almost incapable of writing. I know you are easy to please and you will be happy that the first letter I have written for an infinite time is for you. In the past, I used to write without difficulty. Now slowness makes it hard for me and yet it feels as if I am speaking to you. This gives me pleasure. I wish to tell you that I have become so immobile that I prefer not to go out. I am happy to embrace you because I love you. My hand wants to repeat this – I embrace you because I love you. When are you coming to see me?

A few days later, Christopher Scott came to Lynford to tell Yolande that prayers would be read for her soul on 15 August, the Feast of the Assumption, the tenth anniversary of her offer to pay for the church of Our Lady and the English Martyrs. That morning, while the promised prayers were intoned in Cambridge, Yolande tripped and fell in her bedroom, hitting her head on the parquet floor. Her lady's maid heard her cry out. She rushed in and lifted her on to a sofa. Then, 'all of a sudden', Yolande fainted and remained unconscious for several hours.

An urgent message was sent to Harry who had returned to London a few weeks earlier. When he arrived in Lynford the following day, Michael Dwane was shocked by the change in his appearance. Gaunt and skeletally thin, Harry was weak, tired and fatigued, and frequently overcome by spasms of coughing. 'I got here all safe,' he wrote to Kitty that evening, 'not too tired and did not cough at all really ... Madame is better, not all there but she knew me and is most affectionate. Kissed me over and over again and wouldn't release my hand. I stayed till she dozed off.'

The doctor talked of 'suffusion of blood on the brain', probably a stroke or a haemorrhage. 'Marie never leaves her,' Harry continued, 'and is very devoted, in fact too much so.' The distraught lady's maid was waking Yolande up every few minutes to thrust a crucifix in her face, 'giving her no peace and not letting her sleep. Madame has received the last sacraments and seems to know she is dying and is quiet and resigned and grateful for the attention.'

The last rites had been performed by Christopher Scott who was summoned from Cambridge on the morning of the 16th. When the ritual was over, he rose from his knees and stood at the bedroom window:

From her room, I looked abroad upon the view without, the spacious gardens on the terrace, with their winding well-kept walks, flowers of every hue, the marble statues, the flowing waters beyond, the long stretches of stately trees shutting in the princely mansion from the world outside; the summer sun ... shining upon the whole in all its glory, the soothing notes of a solitary dove the only sound which broke the stillness ... a scene of peace and entrancing beauty ... I have said the only sound was the song of a solitary bird, but there was another, the laboured breathing of her to whom all that fair scene belonged, now lonely indeed, separated from friends, now to complete the sacrifice, and herself to quit all.[2]

Yolande rallied during the night of the 18th. 'Madame is decidedly better,' Harry wrote the following day:

Her pulse is stronger and she is taking nourishment, chicken broth, calf's foot jelly with brandy in it, and champagne. All this *naturally*, besides two injections of six ounces of beef tea. It is really marvellous how she has rallied. She kicked up a row last night at being changed – quite like old times – and astonished the nurses by her strength. She talked to me for some time.

Horace Pym came twice to Lynford as Yolande lay dying: on 17 August and again on the 21st. In his memoirs, he would recall 'her affectionate gratitude to all who watched and tended her, her bright recognition when faces she loved came near, her quick response to all that was said and done … beautiful and touching to see, and very sweet to remember'. A few hours after Pym left on the morning of the 22nd, Harry wrote a more brutal description of the deathbed scene:

> She lies all day in a sort of stupor you can't call sleep. She is never dry and the sheets are changed every hour. Last night the smell was so awful that both the nurse and Marie were nearly sick. The doctor said this was decay of the internal organs and he recognised the smell … Madame told me I was not to leave her and made me stay with her a long time till I said that the doctor would pitch into me for staying too long. I told her I couldn't keep you away any longer and that you would be here on Saturday. She smiled and said 'I am very glad. You are all very good to me.'

Kitty joined her husband on 23 August, so there are no more letters. Harry kept his promise and remained with Yolande until she died on 2 September 1894. For the next three days, her body lay in state in the chapel in Lynford. On the 6th, she was taken to Brandon station and then by train to Cambridge, where she was received by Christopher Scott at the main door of the church of Our Lady and the English Martyrs.

The coffin of 'handsome polished oak' was carried into the church and laid before the altar. The church was arrayed in mourning, the altar steps covered in purple cloth, the pulpit and communion rails draped in black. In the evening, Scott conducted a short service and the choir of the Brompton Oratory, who had travelled from London for the occasion as they had done for the opening service four years earlier, sang a funeral dirge. Four nuns of the Poor Sisters of Nazareth kept watch during the night.

The following morning, a Requiem Mass was conducted by Christopher Scott and Arthur Riddell in the presence of a large congregation. Scott preached the eulogy, taking his text from Hebrews 6: 'God is not unjust that He should forget your work, and the love that you have shown in His name':

The departed benefactress, whose remains now lie before the altar, has claims upon us why she should be remembered. We have towards her a debt of gratitude for deeds, on account of which she will not, we trust, be forgotten by God into whose presence she has been called ... Greatly indeed was she indebted to God; richly had she been endowed with gifts of every kind; of natural character, of special intelligence, of winning attractiveness, which compelled homage from all who came under the charm of her influence; with the result of widespread renown and unbounded wealth – the possession of which, blessings as they might be, only too easily obtain from us an idolatrous devotion which excludes God from our hearts ...

Therefore it was that the blessing of God came in another form – by the discipline of suffering and trial. There was the trial of loneliness. Soon bereft, as she was, of the husband, of whose affection we may judge by the way in which he laid all he possessed at her feet; French and Catholic, living amongst those who were not of her faith or nation, though enjoying their devoted friendship; deprived of the surroundings of Catholic sympathy, she was thrown entirely upon herself in all that which is of the deepest concern. With advancing years, deprived by death even of intimate friends, she was lonely in a sense throughout her life.

These were her crosses, destined doubtless as a corrective to the fascination of wealth, and which led her to become, in addition to her contributions to general charities, the great benefactress of our large and poverty-stricken diocese.[3]

After the service, the coffin was taken to Grove House in Roehampton where Yolande lay in state for the rest of the day and night. The coffin was surrounded by floral tributes, from members of the Claremont and Pym families, the clergy of churches she had funded, and Lady Wallace, the French *parfumerie* assistant who had married Richard Wallace, a wreath from one Frenchwoman to another, both of them risen from poor backgrounds to marry Englishmen of great wealth.

Nuns knelt in prayer by the coffin and continued their vigil through the night. At noon on 8 September, a small number of people gathered in the house to attend the interment in the mausoleum. The mourners included the Claremont children and their spouses; Horace Pym and his wife; Arthur Riddell and Christopher Scott; the Catholic Bishop of Southwark; the chaplain of the Convent of the Sacred Heart; Michael Dwane and Marie Marque; and Yolande's friend from Méry, Edgar de Ségur-Lamoignon.

Constance Smith came to watch the proceedings and was invited into the house by the lady's maid:

> The drawing room was filled with flowers and there were nuns kneeling by the little coffin – such a very little coffin – which lay in front of the temporary altar where two Bishops were presiding. Then the procession formed and headed by the Bishops the tiny coffin was carried across the garden to the mausoleum she had built for her husband's body.
>
> The chief mourner was General Claremont's youngest son, but he seemed too feeble to be able to follow the funeral, and sank into a chair as it left the house. There were the Claremont daughters as mourners, but I saw no sign of grief, nor any tears except in the eyes of the little French lady's maid who had invited us into the house, recognising us as neighbours.[4]

The procession crossed the terrace and passed through the rose garden to the mausoleum. Yolande might have preferred to have joined Edward in his grave outside the building, continuing the *ménage-à-trois* for all time, but the bearers continued up the steps and into the gloom of the interior. The sarcophagus had been opened and, as the clergy spoke the words of committal, Yolande's small coffin was lowered into the tomb alongside the large one which held the remains of her husband.

Two days later, Harry received a letter, in almost indecipherable handwriting, from his father's friend General Trochu. Calling himself 'an octogenarian relic and an invalid', Trochu explained that he had sent a letter to Yolande every year on the anniversary of Edward's death, to commemorate the passing of a man 'who held so great a place in my life'. This was the first year that she had not replied. He sent his condolences to Harry and also to Michael Dwane, 'who showed such extraordinary devotion to her soul'.

In his advent address on 28 November, Arthur Riddell paid tribute to the woman who had given so much to his diocese:

> We commend to your prayers the soul of one who has recently passed away … Her innumerable works of religion and charity during her life, and especially in recent years, force us to acknowledge our indebtedness to her … Gratefully remembering these gifts we ask our beloved clergy to remember her at Holy Mass and we ask them and you all often to pray for her soul. Her name has been inscribed in our Liber Vitae among the great benefactors whether living or dead, and for these we constantly offer up Mass and prayers that God may bless their good estate in life and after death receive them to their reward.[5]

Obituaries in the newspapers also referred to Yolande's charitable works and her building of churches. Only a very few mentioned her years on the stage. 'To 99 per cent of the present generation,' explained the *Pall Mall Gazette*:

the names of Duvernay and Lyne Stephens convey nothing whatsoever; yet the lady who bore these successively and who passed away last week at a very ripe old age was, more than sixty years ago, the subject of much comment and the object of much admiration with our grandfathers, who crowded old Drury Lane to see her.[6]

An elderly journalist in Cambridge recalled her *Cachucha*:

I wonder if there are many people who know that this venerable and untiringly charitable lady was, prior to her marriage to Mr Stephens Lyne Stephens, famous throughout the civilised world as the enchanting operatic dancer, Yolande Marie Louise Duvernay. This wondrous ballerina made her first appearance in Drury Lane in 1833, but it was in a *pas seul* – the Spanish dance of the *Cachucha* – that I especially remember her. I can see her now, in my mind's eye, in her modest pink skirt with black lace flounces ... and hear the merry clatter of her castanets.[7]

23

THE PRECIOUS BOY

He spends money at such a rate that I wonder how he will manage to live … He seems to have no idea what he spends. His extravagance makes me uneasy on his account.

Kitty Bedingfeld, *c.* 1922

Two weeks later, a Catholic newspaper published a mean-spirited tribute to the woman who had given so much to the Church: 'The operatic boards are not the exact spot to spend an apprenticeship to the great aims of existence, but when one is naturally good and desirous of obeying the commands of the Church, one can work out salvation anyway.'[1]

The *Pall Mall Gazette* was more prosaic, referring to Yolande as 'the wealthiest lady in England'. On 3 January 1895, 12,000 miles away in the remote Chatham Islands, Edward Chudleigh made a note in his diary: 'Mail arrived with account of Mrs Lyne Stephens's death leaving nearly two millions of money.'

Her financial assets were valued at £647,759, her Roehampton estate at £57,210, and her assets in France at £49,274, giving her a personal fortune of £754,243 (£89.5 million). She had also had sole use of her husband's estate which was valued at an additional

£1,057,430 (£125 million), providing a total of £1.8 million (£214.5 million).

There was a rumour that Yolande was even richer than Queen Victoria. This was probably untrue – but it may have been close. Wills of British monarchs are not in the public domain, but some estimates put Victoria's wealth at about £2 million when she died in 1901. This compares with Yolande's £1.8 million, a difference of just 10 per cent.

In her English will written in March 1887 and ten codicils signed between September 1890 and June 1894, Yolande disposed of her assets in England. She left an immediate legacy of £30,000 to Harry Claremont; £20,000 each to his three sisters; and (in a codicil in 1893) £5,000 to Teddy in addition to his annuity of £200 a year. She bequeathed £1,000 to the long-suffering Michael Dwane; £500 to William Marshall, her doctor in Roehampton who made several professional visits to Lynford; £500 each to her housekeeper and coachman; and a year's wages to all her servants: twenty-two indoor servants and 129 outdoor servants, most of whom worked on the Lynford estate.

Her bequests to charity totalled £29,000, including £5,000 each to the Bishops of Northampton and Southwark, to be used for charitable purposes, and £2,000 to the orphanage in Shefford. In a codicil signed in May 1892, she left £5,000 to Christopher Scott and Arthur Riddell to invest on behalf of the church in Cambridge, 'for upholding and keeping in repair the fabric'.

She gave a legacy of £2,500 to each of her three executors, Sir John Lubbock, Horace Pym and Joseph Gurney Fox. Pym also received her financial assets in France, the contents of her apartment in the Champs-Élysées, and the legacies of £40,000 for himself and his family. The wording of the will confirmed that 'Horace Pym shall by himself or his firm act as Solicitor in the trusts and execution of this my will'.

Yolande's relationship with Sir John Lubbock, who had been a trustee of Stephens's estate for thirty-four years, had not been a happy one, so she was flattered when he brought his five-year-old son Harold to see her in the spring of 1893. When Pym next came to Roehampton, she dictated a codicil: 'To Harold Lubbock, son of Sir John Lubbock, as a mark of gratitude for all his father and grandfather have done for me, the sum of £5,000.'

Finally, she left her property in Roehampton and her entire residuary estate in England to Harry Claremont, a fortune worth £452,000 (£54 million) after payment of legacies and death duties. He inherited this in trust, to be passed on 'in male tail' down the generations. Her 'household effects', including most of her celebrated art collection, were included in the trust, to be 'held and enjoyed by the person entitled to the Roehampton estate'. She made this request:

> I direct that my Roehampton estate is not to be sold or disposed of by my trustees for any purpose whatever, and I declare that [this] limitation ... is made with the earnest hope and strong desire that the estate will not be sold by any tenant for life thereof or any person becoming entitled thereto ... and I desire that any person who shall become entitled to the Roehampton estate ... shall take and use the surname and arms of Lyne Stephens ... in lieu of his or her own surname.

Yolande's will was proved by Harry and Horace Pym on 5 October. Four days later, Harry signed a new will which appointed Kitty and Pym as his executors and divided his personal assets between his three daughters. In mid-October, after signing the papers to change his name by deed poll to Lyne Stephens, he and his family travelled to the Royal Hotel in Monte Carlo where it was hoped that the warmer sea air might benefit his lungs. He died there on 30 December 1894, having outlived Yolande by less than four months.

Kitty brought his body home to England, crossing the Channel four and a half years after Edward's body had made the same journey. After a funeral service in Roehampton, Harry was buried on 10 January in a second grave outside the mausoleum, a few yards from the grave of his parents. Constance Smith watched the cortège as it made its way from the church:

> I was walking in Roehampton Lane when I saw a funeral procession moving along the lane towards the entrance lodge of Grove House. I enquired whose funeral it was, and was told that it was the funeral of Mrs Lyne Stephens's heir, Mr Claremont, and I remembered how feeble and ill he looked when chief mourner at the ceremony in September.[2]

Harry's will, signed only four months earlier, was proved in the sum of £44,000 (£5 million). His inheritance from Yolande was in trust and not included in his estate, although the probate value did include her immediate legacy of £30,000.

Thirty years of looking after Yolande's affairs had availed Edward Claremont very little, apart from a luxurious lifestyle and the shooting he enjoyed so much on the Lynford estate. Harry, too, gained little from his years of attendance, his 'penal servitude' as 'the precious boy who is heir to so much'. He had neglected his wife and children to be with her in Lynford, Paris and Monte Carlo. He knew that he was dying, that his six-year-old son Stephen would inherit her fortune, although he would not have use of it until he reached the age of twenty-one. In the meantime, the boy was made a ward of the Court of Chancery, his fortune administered by Yolande's trustees.

In her English and French wills, Yolande had bequeathed forty-eight of her most valuable paintings to the National Gallery and her best pieces of china, furniture and *objets d'art* to the South Kensington Museum (now the Victoria and Albert Museum). Most of these items were in Lynford Hall and Grove House, and the bequests were made on condition that they 'shall be known, described and marked as the Lyne Stephens Collection and deposited ... in some suitable position for their proper exhibition to the public'.

Six weeks before her death, outraged by the introduction of the Finance Bill (1894) which introduced estate duty on the full value of all property, both real and personal, she signed a codicil to her English will revoking these bequests. Instead, the items would:

> fall into and form part of my residuary personal estate and shall not form part of the bequest of household effects, provided always that it shall be lawful for the trustees to postpone ... the sale of the pictures, ornamental china and objects d'art ... and to permit the same to be enjoyed and remain in the possession of the person entitled to the income of my residuary personal estate.

The bequests to the gallery and museum included two paintings and a few items of furniture from her apartment in the Champs-Élysées. Although she failed to write a similar codicil to her French will, Horace Pym (her residuary beneficiary in France) chose to honour her original intention.

This involved some bureaucratic difficulty. Yolande's French executors required proof from the National Gallery and the South Kensington Museum that, 'according to English law, they are entitled to receive the legacies'. The proof required was two powers of attorney, prepared by the consul at the French Embassy, which had to be signed by all the trustees of the gallery and museum before they could be passed on to an attorney in Paris. It took time for the National Gallery to obtain the necessary signatures, giving rise to a letter of complaint from Horace Pym dated 9 January 1895:

> Owing to the delay in obtaining the authority of the trustees of the National Gallery to hand over the pictures left to them by the deceased lady, I have had to pay a French tax for 1895, amounting to 2,000 francs (£80) because these goods were remaining in the

apartment in Paris on 1 January. I am also unable to accept a
tenant for the apartment for the same cause, and am paying a rent
of £800 per annum for the rooms. I think it well that you should
know these facts, and also that I claim from the National Gallery
the sum of £80 tax paid, as above stated. Pray accelerate the
completion of the French authority with all despatch.[3]

The gallery replied on 7 February, pointing out that it knew nothing
about the tax and had no intention of reimbursing the £80. Pym
left it to one of his clerks to write again the following day:

This payment has been personally made by our Mr Pym and
cannot be made a charge against the late Mrs Lyne Stephens's
estate. Looking to the great value of the gift you have received,
we feel that it is very ungracious on your part to decline to recoup
Mr Pym a payment he has made under such circumstances ... Had
you offered to meet Mr Pym by paying even half the sum he has
disbursed, he would not have felt, as he now has reason to do, that
he has been treated ungenerously.[4]

At the same time as feeling annoyed at the delay in Paris, Pym was
making arrangements to sell most of the Lyne Stephens Collection
at auction in London. Yolande's will included this clause:

It shall be lawful for my trustees ... at their discretion if the said
tenant for life is an infant, to sell the said household effects ... and
in such case, the monies to arise from such sale shall ... form part
of my residuary personal estate.

The tenant for life was six years old. Of the three trustees, Sir John
Lubbock showed little interest in the administration, so it was
Horace Pym and his brother-in-law Joseph Gurney Fox who used
their discretion. Instead of restricting the sale to the most valuable
items which had reverted to the estate by codicil, they decided to

sell the 'household effects' as well: the entire contents of Lynford Hall and most of the furniture and paintings in Grove House. Inevitably, this would raise more for money for the trust which Pym was paid to administer.

The auction took place at Christie's in May 1895 and lasted for nine days. A whole day was devoted to pictures, including seventy old master paintings, five paintings of horses in Melton Mowbray, and one of a royal shooting party at Compiègne. Another day was allocated to the sale of silver items and jewellery. 'Messrs Christie's rooms,' explained *The Times* on 8 May:

> are now filled with the old pictures, fine French furniture, and Sèvres and other porcelain, for the possession of which the late Mrs Lyne Stephens was celebrated in London and Paris for some forty years or more. She was Mademoiselle Duvernay, the famous dancer ... the adoration of our fathers and grandfathers ... She married Mr Lyne Stephens ... both had excellent taste, were well advised, and were large buyers of fine things, so the announcement that the whole collection would be sold was received with unusual interest by amateurs all over the world.

The sale included three Velasquez portraits: Philip IV of Spain, the Infanta Maria Teresa, and an unnamed infanta. There were paintings by Bellini, Boucher, Greuze, and Veronese; a Rubens-Brueghel collaboration; an Elisabeth Vigée Le Brun; two paintings by Watteau; three by Murillo; a painting by Albert Cuyp of the Prince of Orange on horseback; a Claude Lorrain; a portrait of Louis XIV by Hyacinthe Rigaud; and the full-length portrait of Cardinal Richelieu by Philippe de Champaigne.

The furniture was French, mostly Louis XIV and Louis XVI. Lots included a gilded sixteenth-century Italian sedan chair; marquetry tables; secretaires and chests of drawers; sofas and chairs; tapestries; carpets; and an armchair 'reputed to have been the property of Cardinal Wolsey'.

There was a large quantity of porcelain, including three Sèvres dinner services of eighty, forty-eight and fifty-three pieces, and the Montcalm Vase, 'one of a pair presented to the Marquis of Montcalm, the defender of Quebec, by Louis XV'. There were clocks and barometers, and two 'large chimerical dragons inlaid with enamel' from the Summer Palace in Peking.

Jewellery included several gifts from men of society during Yolande's years on the stage: 'a pair of long brilliant earrings ... formerly the property of Marie Antoinette'; 'a necklace formed from forty-one large graduated pearls' which sold for £4,200. Among the objects of vertu was 'an old French fan of ivory, finely pierced and inlaid ... with a white silk mount painted with garden scenes ... presented to Mademoiselle Pauline Duvernay by Count d'Orsay'.

According to Horace Pym, the sale was 'the great attraction of the season', with 'buyers from Paris, New York, Vienna, and Berlin eagerly competing with London for the best things'. Prices obtained were 'very far in excess of those paid for the various objects, in many cases reaching four and five times their original cost'.[5]

The proceeds of the sale, £141,000 (£17 million), were added to Yolande's estate in trust for the now seven-year-old Stephen, increasing his total trust fund to £593,000 (£70 million). Kitty was angry that Pym had sold so much of the collection, stripping Grove House of many of its contents. 'I am thinking,' she wrote, 'of what my kind and generous friend Mrs Lyne Stephens would have wished if she had not been tricked by a rascally lawyer.'

Pym had written regularly to Harry about legal and financial matters, and was solicitous to Kitty, writing several times to enquire about her husband's health. Kitty was unimpressed. 'Mr Horace Pym benefited largely under Mrs Lyne Stephens's will,' she wrote in the notebook she used to record matters of business:

Towards the end of her life, she added one codicil after another, leaving large sums to members of Mr Pym's family, as well as the contents of her apartment in the Champs-Élysées which consisted of the choicest art treasures in pictures, china, furniture, etc., together with a sum of money invested in France. All of this French property had originally been left to my husband, but the legacy was revoked in a codicil ... and left absolutely to Mr Horace Pym.

In addition to this, the firm of Tathams and Pym, of which Mr Pym was then the sole representative, was appointed sole solicitors to the Trust. Under these circumstances, I was advised to appoint a lawyer to act for me ... The result was that I obtained from the Court of Chancery a provisional allowance of £3000 a year for maintenance during Stephen's minority. My actions in taking my affairs out of Mr Pym's hands angered him considerably. His object appeared to be to persuade me that I was entirely in his power in everything.

Kitty had given birth to a third daughter, Winefride, on 7 March 1894, less than ten weeks after her husband's death. A few months later, she left Harry's house in Chelsea and moved into Grove House with her children. Under Yolande's influence, she had converted to Catholicism and, in April 1897, she married Raoul Bedingfeld, a Catholic from Norfolk whom she first met at the opening service of the church in Cambridge. Constance Smith dined with them in Grove House towards the end of the year:

The house was much emptied of its beautiful contents ... but some very fine tapestry still remained, and in the billiard room hung two portraits of Mrs Lyne Stephens. One was of her in her early bright days; very handsome, with curling hair, and gay hopeful expression. The other was by Carolus-Duran, painted of her in her old age, a very melancholy picture. Not a smile left on her face and with most pathetic large dark eyes.[6]

Stephen reached his majority on 3 April 1909. He had already instructed a lawyer to draw up a disentailing deed, breaking the entail on the Grove House estate and 'vesting the same in himself in fee simple'. The deed, which was signed on his twenty-first birthday, also broke the entailed trust on Yolande's residuary estate.

Kitty's second husband died in 1910, after which she left Roehampton and returned to the house in Chelsea. The following year, Stephen let Grove House and thirty-three acres of land to Charles Fischer, an American merchant, with an option to purchase the freehold. The remaining acreage was let to the Roehampton Polo Club, with a similar option to purchase.

As Grove House was emptied for letting, more items from the Lyne Stephens Collection were sold at auction. Among the old master paintings sold at Christie's in June 1911 were two by Greuze, three by Guardi, and a view of Venice by Canaletto. The furniture and furnishings included several Gobelins tapestries, 'a set of six Louis XIII walnut-wood chairs', and several items of Sèvres porcelain and *objets d'art*. Stephen and Kitty retained six paintings to hang in the house in Chelsea: a Veronese; a Murillo; portraits of Louis XIV, Marie Antoinette and Madame de Pompadour; and a double portrait of Charles I and Henrietta Maria.

Stephen volunteered for military service at the outbreak of the First World War, but was rejected because of poor eyesight. Instead, he joined the Army Service Corps and drove ambulances at the front. In January 1917, despite his need to wear glasses, he was transferred to the West Yorkshire regiment. He was, wrote the colonel of the eleventh battalion, 'capable of carrying out the duties of a subaltern in the infantry without further training ... he has constantly been under fire and has a considerable knowledge of general conditions and requirements of the infantry in the present campaign'.[7]

Wounded during the third battle of Ypres in October 1917, he was repatriated to a hospital in England. 'He was injured on right cheek by fragment of shell which was extracted and the wound drained,' reported the medical board on 31 December. 'It healed in November but there is still inability to open mouth properly on account of scar tissue ... He can separate his teeth half an inch.'[8]

In February 1918, while convalescing in England, Stephen married his cousin, Joan Northey. Two months later, he wrote to the War Office to request a 'wound gratuity', pointing out that the fragment of shell had caused 'considerable and permanent facial disfigurement, in addition to which the shock has greatly affected my general health'. He re-joined his battalion in September, three months before the armistice, and was demobilised in March 1919.

He took to alcohol after the war, perhaps to mask the chronic pain in his face. He set out on a world tour after demobilisation and was away for several months, sending postcards to his mother from Hawaii, Tunis, Java and New York. Joan divorced him in 1921, after which he became a playboy; he raced motor cars, gambled in casinos, had affairs with actresses, and mixed with what Kitty called 'a racy crowd'. In 1922, he spent several months in Rhodesia.

Kitty confided in her notebook that, although his income was £13,000 a year (£700,000), she was concerned about his extravagance: 'He spends money at such a rate that I wonder how he will manage to live within this income! Not at the rate he is going! He seems to have no idea what he spends. His extravagance makes me uneasy on his account.'

She had left London after the war and moved to the Villa Borghese in Torquay. Stephen rarely came to see her. He made a brief visit in October 1920, to inform her that he intended to reduce her allowance. He visited again in July 1922 before he sailed for Rhodesia. A few weeks later, she wrote a letter which she attached to her will for him to read after her death:

> I trust that your religion and the faithful practice of it will be your abiding consolation until the end of your life. May the remembrance of your early years, and Catholic surroundings, bring you back entirely to God. May he in his mercy grant my prayers. Perhaps even in this world, I shall have this supreme consolation.

On 9 September 1823, a telegram was sent from Swanage in Dorset to the priest-in-charge of the Roman Catholic presbytery in Torquay: 'Will you please bring news to Mrs Bedingfeld at Villa Borghese that her son was killed in a motor accident Saturday evening.' The story was told in a local newspaper:

> A shocking motor fatality occurred on the Kingston to Swanage road on Saturday evening. A private car driven by Captain Lyne Stephens ... after passing a char-a-banc about a mile from Langton Matravers, swerved across the road and crashed into a telegraph pole. Captain Lyne Stephens was killed instantly ... He apparently applied the brakes suddenly to the motor, which was a powerful car of Spanish make, and was pitched through the windscreen, his head striking one of the lamps. Another car containing friends was following close behind, but suffered no damage.

At the inquest, the coroner gave a verdict of 'accidental death caused by negligent driving on part of deceased'. It was concluded that the two cars were racing.

Kitty arranged for her son's body to be brought to Roehampton and buried in a third grave outside the mausoleum, between the graves of his father and grandparents. There were no children from his brief marriage and only one beneficiary of his will: his sister Winefride who lived with him in Chelsea.

His estate was valued at £205,000 (£11 million), a third of the amount he had received from Yolande at the age of six. Her fortune would soon be reduced even further: according to family tradition, Winefride lost her inheritance from her brother, partly because of the Wall Street crash of 1929 and partly because of a fraudulent lawyer.

It was not just Yolande's fortune that vanished. Her name disappeared too. Created in 1826 when Charles Lyne inherited the Stephens fortune from Portugal, the name of Lyne Stephens came to an end in 1923 as two cars raced each other down the country lanes of Dorset.

24

THE LONG WAIT ENDS

This great outspread of benevolence, giving a joyous
independence which may extend downwards
through generations.

Mary Chudleigh, 13 April 1860

At the time of Yolande's death in 1894, the Lyne Stephens estate was valued at £1,057,430, so each ninety-third share was worth £11,370 (£1.3 million). Forty-eight of the original beneficiaries were still alive – and they had grown tired of waiting. When the drama critic Lewis Clifton Lyne died in December 1889, the *Western Mail* published an obituary:

One who knew Mr Lyne well tells me that he was a co-heir to about a million of money left years ago by a wealthy old lawyer named Lyne Stephens. Unfortunately for him, a life interest in this vast fortune was bequeathed to a French ballet dancer who, by prolonging her life to over ninety, has managed effectively to keep him out of his share.

Two weeks after Yolande's death, the *Cornish Times* announced that the Lyne Stephens fortune would now be distributed according to the will:

> To those whose memories carry them back some thirty or forty years, the announcement that the great fortune belonging to the late Mr Stephens Lyne Stephens is now to be dispersed among his heirs must revive many interesting recollections ... How the colossal fortune was accumulated by Mr Lyne Stephens's father when a merchant at Lisbon is an interesting story. Suffice it to say here that a number of representatives of the Lyne family of Cornwall will now benefit under the will.

At last the Court of Chancery could begin the slow process of winding up the Lyne Stephens estate. The first action taken by the court was to authorise the sale of Lynford Hall. It was advertised in May 1895:

> A princely freehold domain of about 7720 acres, well known as one of the finest sporting estates in England ... a noble mansion erected in the most substantial and costly manner, lavishly fitted and decorated in fine order throughout, suitable in every way for the accommodation of the family and guests of a wealthy owner.
>
> The mansion comprises some fifty bed and dressing rooms, lady's boudoir, spacious saloon opening from the grand entrance hall, a fine oak staircase, a palatial suite of grand reception rooms, the most complete domestic offices, and very fine cellarage ... surrounded by lovely pleasure grounds and a beautiful richly-timbered park intersected by a branch of the River Wissey, which flows through the estate, and includes a series of ornamental lakes, the resort of wild fowl in great numbers.[1]

The property was marketed by Horace Pym's legal firm, Tathams and Pym, and the auction was held on 23 July at the Mart, near the Bank of England.

Meanwhile, a dispute had arisen over the garden ornaments. Did they belong to Stephens's ninety-three beneficiaries or to Harry Claremont's infant son? The matter was referred to the Court of Chancery which, over thirty years earlier, had sanctioned the use of money in the Lyne Stephens estate to fund the completion of the mansion, although Yolande herself had bought 'a large number of marble and bronze statues and vases' for the formal gardens. In late July, Mr Justice Stirling ruled that the ornaments belonged to Stephens's estate, on the questionable grounds that Yolande had bought them to complete the gardens as designed by her husband.

The court began to divide the financial assets in the estate into ninety-three parts, although the wheels of Chancery still turned exceedingly slowly and the beneficiaries would have to wait another fourteen years before they received their full entitlement. The shares of those who had died while retaining their interest in the estate had to be distributed according to the wording of their wills – and sometimes according to the wills of those to whom their interests had been bequeathed.

Meanwhile, the poor families in Cornwall who believed they had a claim to the fortune were stirred into action. Attics and cellars were scoured for papers and, for more than a decade, they employed people to inspect parish registers and feed their hopes. In October 1905, a Thomas Varcoe wrote to his brother and sister:

> I refer to the case of between two and three millions of money in Chancery left by a Mr Stephens who amassed it at Lisbon. Perhaps you remember the stir that has been made many times in the case? Well, I received a note from a gentleman a short time since, requesting me to call upon him. I did so, and he informed me that they have made great discoveries and there is to be a meeting of all

the kindred on Wednesday next. I know you have father's certificates from registers proving our identity and relationship and if you will let me have copies of them I shall be glad, or any information you can supply me which will throw light on the mystery. They all seem confident they can prove themselves of the stock. So must we.

At the meeting, the families were told they had a valid claim to the money if they could prove direct descent from Lewis Stephens, the grandfather of the Stephens brothers of Portugal. 'They seemed confident that all will be right in the course of time,' explained Varcoe. 'John James Stephens's will is proved to be a forgery. He died without making one.'

William Philp of Liskeard was still on the case. 'As regards your being descended from the Lisbon Stephenses, doubtless is true,' he wrote to the family in September 1906. 'In my mind, there is not the shadow of doubt, and all the registers and certificates that have been found make you the right and lawful claimants to the paternal grandfather of John James Stephens that died in Lisbon.' All they needed to do was to find one marriage certificate: 'If you can find that one, your claim is at once lawful.'

In living memory, an old man called John Stephens told his daughters about the fortune: 'We should all be millionaires, you know, but we've been basely defrauded.' He told an interesting version of the facts:

A Stephens ancestor had estates in Lisbon. When this Stephens died, the foreman, Mr Lyne, forged the will, pinched the money and changed his name to Lyne Stephens. The will was disputed by another member of the family, but failed. The solicitor tried to persuade great-grandfather to try again. 'You'll be riding in your carriage in a month,' he said.

It was not only honest families who were trying to claim the money. In 1890, a young man called Frank Thompson was convicted of fraud at the Old Bailey. He had taken a loan in the name of one of the beneficiaries, Frederick Manley Glubb, who was living in Hong Kong at the time. Evidence was given by a moneylender in Great Russell Street:

> The prisoner called and gave the name of Frederick Manley Glubb. He asked me to lend him £100 and said that he was entitled to £10,000 under the will of Mr Lyne Stephens, at the death of Mrs Lyne Stephens, the widow. I asked him for references and he gave me the solicitors, Messrs Tathams and Pym, and his mother's name as Mrs Fanny Glubb … He said he was a gentleman and, believing his representations, I gave him a cheque for £70 … He gave me a charge on the reversion as security.

In December 1894, three months after Yolande's death, Tathams and Pym wrote to one of the beneficiaries, an elderly man with one brother and two unmarried sisters:

> A Mrs Beuce claims to be a sister of Charles Lyne of Bournemouth and therefore she would be a sister of your own. She also claims, as such sister, to be entitled to a share of the Lyne Stephens estate. Will you kindly tell us if you have ever heard of Mrs Beuce? We are having an enormous amount of trouble with persons presuming they are claimants to this estate, and whose claims we must at once put an end to in order to prevent those who really are entitled being put to trouble and expense.

Another possible beneficiary – and this time a genuine one – was the illegitimate daughter of Richard Benjamin Lyne, conceived in 1836 when he was working as a merchant in Argentina. He moved to Brazil less than two years after his daughter was born but he corresponded with her throughout his life and often sent her money. His family first learnt of her existence when the unmarried Richard Benjamin died in June 1899, aged ninety-six. In his will, he left an annuity of £4,000 to his 'daughter, Carolina Lyne, born in January 1837 and now residing with her half-brother, Dr Carlos Durand, in Buenos Aires'.

It came as a shock to Richard Benjamin's executors, both of whom were husbands of beneficiaries, when the will was read by Tathams and Pym, together with a letter confirming that Carolina was his natural daughter. Now there might be ninety-four beneficiaries instead of ninety-three. One of the executors, Paul Ewens, wrote to a friend in Argentina asking for further information. 'I have the pleasure of informing you,' the friend replied from Buenos Aires:

> that through the *Oficina de Investigacíon* (Secret Police), I discovered that Carolina Lyne is still alive. One of the employees saw Dr Carlos Durand and inquired about the lady. The doctor told him that she was enjoying good health and lived near his house, but refused to give her address and said that, if anyone wanted to know about her, he should communicate directly with him. The doctor was not aware that he was speaking with a member of the Secret Police as he was disguised as a porter.

The executors hoped that Carolina was an imposter, conspiring with Carlos Durand to claim the annuity. Ignoring the difficulties faced by children born out of wedlock (she had been passing herself as Durand's full-sister), they demanded that she prove her identity. When she failed to provide evidence of her baptism, Ewens sent her a strongly worded letter:

> You seem to be either unable or unwilling to produce one witness, in addition to your brother, to sign the necessary documents to prove your identity. On the face of it, and till I am further advised, there would seem to be some mystery connected with the matter which I am unable to fathom. I shall await a proper interval after this letter but, in the event of not receiving a satisfactory reply, we shall take such steps as our solicitor shall advise.

At this point, the assurance company arranging the annuity took up the matter, employing a private investigator in Buenos Aires. 'Mr Carlos Durand, retired medical doctor, lives retired from all society and is little known,' reported the investigator. 'As to his character, he seems strange, rough and not very scrupulous. Ever since their childhood, he and his sister have lived together and she is known as Carolina Durand.'

In a second meeting, the doctor him told a different story: 'Although, in our previous conversation, he had spoken of Miss Carolina Lyne as his sister, he now declared that the Miss Carolina who lived in his house was his sister, while Miss Carolina Lyne was a different person altogether.'

This was enough for the assurance company to turn down the annuity, so Ewens asked another acquaintance in Buenos Aires, George Watts, to carry out further enquiries. Watts visited Durand in his house in January 1903. His initial impression was favourable:

> I had half an hour with Dr Durand and my conversation with the old gentleman was entirely on plants. He only speaks Spanish but I got on well with him. If you are prepared to go to some expense, I have little doubt that something can be ferreted out through undertakers, banks, municipal registers, etc.

Five months later, he had changed his mind:

> From all I can gather, Dr Durand is a deeply-dyed blackguard. If the woman living with him is Carolina Lyne, she is quite under his thumb. A good deal of patience is required, as no doubt Durand is on the alert. I have thought of seeing the Chief of Police on the subject, but great caution is necessary.

Watts enclosed some notes written in Spanish, which explained that Durand had been separated from his wife for several months and inferred that he was 'having marital relations with a woman whom he formerly passed as his sister'. This shocked the executors, both upright members of Edwardian society. 'It is likely,' wrote Ewens, 'that one of the reasons for Durand's separation from his wife was his relationship with the woman now living with him called Carolina. It is hardly conceivable that she can be his half-sister.'

During the next three years, letters were sent to and from Buenos Aires; investigators were employed to peruse legal documents, parish records and Durand's divorce papers; and the executors offered to pay the chief of police for proof of Carolina's identity. By 1905, Durand had died and Ewens was trying to obtain a copy of his will. 'The consul is obtaining a copy bit by bit,' wrote George Watts, 'as the will is guarded and can only be got at surreptitiously. An illegitimate son has now cropped up. The case is interesting but for the time it occupies.'

In October 1906, when the executors learnt that Carolina had died, they prepared a deed stating that capital for the annuity would be retained in London and, if no claim was received from Argentina within the next seven years, the funds would revert to Richard Benjamin's estate. The deed referred only to the annuity, but the executors were more concerned about her status as a beneficiary of the Lyne Stephens fortune. Her heirs were three adopted daughters who would, if her identity was proved, be eligible to receive a one ninety-fourth share of Stephens's residuary estate.

At no time during their correspondence had Ewens informed Carolina of her interest in the Lyne Stephens fortune – but even if her adopted daughters had been aware of the situation, they would have had little time to make a claim. On 21 May 1906, a summons was issued by the legal firm of Robbins, Billing and Company. This requested the surviving trustee of Stephens's estate, Sir John Lubbock (now Lord Avebury), to produce a full set of accounts so that taxes and legal costs could be deducted from the funds in Chancery, after which the fortune would be divided into ninety-three parts and distributed to the beneficiaries, their heirs, or the assurance companies which had bought the reversions.

The final distribution was made two years later. 'On enquiry at the Pay Office,' explained another legal firm on 7 April 1908, 'I am informed that the cheques have not yet been prepared as they are waiting for a statement from Messrs Robbins, Billing and Company, who have the carriage of the order. I have seen Messrs Robbins who promised to lodge the statement without delay.'

Eight weeks later, the matter was finalised. As Tathams and Pym wrote to Paul Ewens on 25 May: 'We have received out of Court a further part of the one ninety-third share of Lewis Jedediah Lyne, deceased, being a final division of Stephens Lyne Stephens's estate.' One lucky man received, in addition to his own share, the shares of five of his deceased siblings.

At last Lord Avebury could file away his papers. He was a young man of twenty-five when Stephens died in 1860. By May 1908, he had spent forty-eight years involved in an administration in which he had no personal interest. It was not quite over yet for he remained a trustee of Yolande's estate until Stephen broke the entailed trust in April 1909. Lord Avebury died four years later, aged seventy-nine, having had been involved with Yolande's financial affairs for two-thirds of his life.

25

THE LEGACY

*French and Catholic, living amongst those who were not of her faith
or nation ... she was thrown entirely upon herself in all that is of the
deepest concern ... she was lonely in a sense throughout her life.*

Canon Christopher Scott, 7 September 1894

The story of Yolande Lyne Stephens can be divided into four incarnations: the sexy, witty young girl who entranced the men of society in the 1830s; the well-padded matron who became one of the *grandes dames* of Second Empire Paris; the devout Catholic with a zeal for building churches; and the bad-tempered old lady who persecuted her chaplain and lady's maid.

There is little left of the first Yolande. The Salle le Peletier in Paris is long gone, but the Passage Saulnier (now the Rue Saulnier) still exists; the stage door of the Folies Bergère faces the spot where the Duvernay lodgings once stood. The Theatre Royal in Drury Lane is a landmark of London; you can walk in Yolande's footsteps through subterranean passages which lead from the dressing rooms to the stage. Her Majesty's Theatre in the Haymarket (the King's Theatre in Yolande's time) still stands too, the scene of her meeting with Félix de La Valette while Stephens waited with pistols outside the door.

The second Yolande can be found in grand houses in England and Paris. The Hôtel Molé in the Rue du Faubourg Saint-Honoré and her apartment in the Avenue des Champs-Élysées are still standing, although it is difficult to see them because of more recent buildings which line the streets. The garden façade of the Hôtel Molé can be seen from a vantage point on the Avenue Matignon; a few windows of her apartment at 122 Avenue des Champs-Élysées can be glimpsed from another vantage point between two houses in the Rue Lord Byron.

The Hôtel Molé remained in the family of Baron Gérard for more than seventy years. It was sold in 1947 to an assurance company which, after several incarnations, is now known as the AXA Group. For twenty years, between the late 1970s and the late 1990s, it was leased to *Le Figaro*, the oldest newspaper in France. In 1998, AXA took over the property as its headquarters, using the original name of the Hôtel de La Vaupalière. It restored the building to its original magnificence and built a new glass-and-steel frontage on the Avenue Matignon.

In London, the Portman Square house was demolished many years ago, but its spirit lives on in Home House which occupies three buildings (numbers 19, 20 and 21) and is a private members' club. Like number 32, these houses were designed in the 1770s by James Wyatt and completed by Robert Adam, and Yolande would feel at home here, having lived with Stephens in Portman Square for four years.

Grove House in Roehampton remains much as it was in Yolande's time. Despite her 'earnest hope and strong desire' that the house should never be sold, Charles Fischer exercised his option and bought the freehold in 1912. When he disappeared during the First World War, having failed to pay the full purchase price, ownership reverted to Stephen who sold it again in 1921 to Dr Claude Montefiori on behalf of the Froebel Educational Institute. Grove House now forms part of the University of Roehampton which, by happy coincidence, boasts the foremost dance department in Britain.

The third Yolande can be found in ecclesiastic architecture in the old Catholic diocese of Northampton. Regular services are held in the church of St Francis in Shefford, the bishop still lives in the house she built for Arthur Riddell in Northampton, and the church of Our Lady and the English Martyrs is one of the great buildings of Cambridge. Christopher Scott's hopes that it would soon be filled with Catholic students were dashed in 1895 when the hierarchy decreed that a separate chaplaincy should be established for Catholics at the university. For a while, this left the church with a capacity exceeding the needs of its congregation; today it is a parish church with a wide reputation.

Hanging in the dining room of the rectory is a copy of Yolande's portrait by Carolus-Duran, which the artist (or his studio) completed in the summer of 1890. Her head is carved in stone near the ringer's doorway in the church porch. The dripstone terminations on the windows of the south aisle include the heads of Cardinal Newman; Christopher Scott; the Duke of Norfolk; the two architects, Dunn and Hansom; and General Edward Claremont, referred to in the guidebook as 'the foundress's agent'.

There are rumours that Yolande built the church in honour of the children she failed to conceive with her husband. If she had a motive other than religious zeal, and if this motive was connected with children, it is more likely to have been the memory of the two babies she had to give away during her youth in Paris. Perhaps the legacy she bequeathed to the Home for Incurable Children in Vaugirard is a clue to the fate of at least one of these children.

The fourth Yolande can be found in Lynford Hall where she spent the last year of her life. The Jacobean-style mansion still stands in the Breckland of Norfolk and is now a hotel specialising in weddings. Not a single bidder came forward when the property was put up for auction in July 1895; it was finally sold to Henry Alexander Campbell three years later. As a staunch Protestant, Campbell was offended by the presence of a Catholic chapel on the estate. He planted trees to hide what he called 'the terrible eyesore' from view.

Michael Dwane continued to live in the presbytery, holding services in the chapel and saying Masses for Yolande's soul every Sunday until he died in February 1913. He was remembered in Lynford with great affection: 'His kindliness and tact, his sincerity and amiability, made him a universal favourite. He was well-known for miles around and was looked upon as a friend of all, poor and rich.'[1]

Lynford changed hands several times during the early twentieth century. By the 1920s, it was in the possession of Frederick Montagu, who sold more than 6,000 acres to the Forestry Commission for the creation of Thetford Forest Park. In 1928, the hall was gutted by fire which destroyed the entire east wing. Two years later, it was bought by the Forestry Commission which offered a lease to the Scottish distiller, Sir James Calder, a man with glamorous friends. Ernest Hemingway is reputed to have propped up the bar and Joseph Kennedy, US ambassador to London between 1938 and 1940, came to stay for shooting parties, sometimes accompanied by his son John F. Kennedy, future President of the United States. As Catholics, they attended Mass in Yolande's chapel.

After the Second World War, the hall was used as a Forestry Commission training school. From the late 1960s to the early 1990s, episodes of television series were filmed here: *Dad's Army*, *The Professionals* and *You Rang, M'Lord*. A corner of the stable block was used for the exterior of René's café in *'Allo 'Allo!* – a series with a surreal echo of Yolande's strong French accent.

Foxwold, Horace Pym's house in Kent, featured in the 1985 Merchant Ivory film *A Room with a View*, as the home of the Honeychurch family. Several of Yolande's paintings were in the house during filming, as well as many pieces of *objets d'art* which she had given him over the years. When Pym died suddenly in May 1896, at the age of fifty-one, he was worth £12.5 million in today's money.

Another building connected with the Lyne Stephens name, a little before Yolande's time, is Chicksands Priory in Bedfordshire. Yolande was still in ballet school when Charles Lyne Stephens rented the priory. By the time he gave up the house, she was at the height of her celebrity in Paris and would soon captivate London for a third time.

During the Second World War, Chicksands was used as a listening post for the team at Bletchley Park working on decoding the German Enigma code. After the war, it was used as a US Air Force base and is now the Officers' Mess of the Defence Intelligence and Security Centre. Among the pictures displayed on its walls is a coloured lithograph of *The Melton Breakfast*, in which a youthful Stephens sits unobtrusively on a sofa while several men of title lounge about in the foreground.

Five of Yolande's paintings hang today in the National Gallery in London. Two were handed over by Horace Pym from her apartment in Paris: *Portrait of a Lady* by the workshop of Rogier van der Weyden, and *Virgin and Child with Saints and a Donor* by Gerard David. Two more were acquired at the sale of her collection in 1895: *Cardinal de Richelieu* by Philippe de Champaigne, and *Philippe-François d'Arenberg meeting Troops* by François van der Meulen. The fifth painting, *La Gamme d'Amour* by Watteau, was bequeathed to the gallery in 1912.

Several items of furniture in the Victoria and Albert Museum were also handed over by Horace Pym. These were described on Yolande's inventory as: 'a sofa and four easy chairs of carved and gilded wood covered in old Gobelins tapestry of the time of Louis XIV or Louis XVI; an old Louis XV chest of drawers of rosewood ornamented with gilded bronze objects, the upper portion being of red Italian marble; and two triangular lamps with three lights of old Sèvres china.'

These nationally owned works of art with a Lyne Stephens provenance are dwarfed by the size of the Wallace Collection on display in Hertford House in London. Sir Richard Wallace brought his art collection to Hertford House in 1872; twenty-two years later, his widow left the house and the collection to the British nation. When Lady Wallace died in February 1897, she was worth a little less than the value of Yolande's assets in her own name. These two Frenchwomen, born in poor circumstances in Paris, both married Englishmen of fortune, became custodians of art collections of immense value, and died in their old age less than three years apart.

Harry Claremont's eldest daughter Sybil married Sir Henry Bedingfeld of Oxburgh Hall, a fifteenth-century moated manor house in Norfolk, one of the most romantic houses in England. Brought up in the Catholic faith because of Yolande's influence on her mother, Sybil was a suitable bride for this long-established Catholic family. In 1950, she was instrumental in saving Oxburgh Hall from demolition and giving the property to the National Trust. It seems appropriate that the white-marble portrait bust of Yolande, sculpted in Florence by Lorenzo Bartolini, stands in the entrance hall, the first work of art that visitors see as they walk through the door.

The bones of Yolande and Stephens lie side by side in the white stone sarcophagus in the mausoleum at Roehampton. Three gravestones stand on the consecrated ground outside the building. Under the first are Edward and Fanny Claremont, joined in 1935 by their second son Teddy. Under the second are Harry and his wife Kitty, who was interred beside him in 1939. In the centre, between the other two, is the grave of Stephen, his body brought here from Dorset in September 1923.

In this Romanesque Revival building, and under this small plot of land, lie the remains of five major players in the life of a celebrated French ballerina. It is a truism that money does not buy happiness – but a truism writ large in the story of Yolande Lyne Stephens, the richest woman in Victorian England.

NOTES

Quotations from letters and papers in the Bedingfeld MSS and other private collections are not referenced.

AN   Archives Nationales, Paris
DN   Diocese of Northampton
GL   Guildhall Library, London
NA   National Archives, Kew
NGA   National Gallery Archive
NDRA   North Devon Record Office
OLEM   Church of Our Lady and the English Martyrs, Cambridge
RA   Royal Archives
UR   University of Roehampton
WSA   Wiltshire and Swindon Archives
WSRO   West Sussex Record Office

1 *The* Petit Rat

1. Quoted in Second, pp. 149–151.
2. Roqueplan, pp. 44–46.
3. Chambre, Major Alan, *Recollections of West-End Life* (London, Hurst and Blackett, 1858), I, p. 57.

4. AN, AJ/13/126, dossier 3.
5. Véron, III, p. 227.
6. Chasles, Philarète, *Mémoires* (Geneva, Slatkine Reprints, 1973), I, p. 275; Drysdale, John D., *Louis Véron and the Finances of the Académie Royale de Musique* (Frankfurt am Main, Peter Lang, 2003), p. 63.
7. Second, p. 217.
8. Véron, III, pp. 205, 225.

2 *The Fair* Danseuse

1. Quoted in Chazin-Bennahum, Judith, *The Lure of Perfection: Fashion and Ballet 1780–1830* (New York, Routledge, 2005), pp. 210–211.
2. Séchan, p. 210; Mahalin, pp. 112, 114.
3. Tamvaco, I, pp. 198–199, 220; De Boigne, pp. 27–29.
4. Quoted in Peacock, p. 82.
5. RA, VIC/MAIN/QVJ (W) Lord Esher's typescript, 21 February, 5 March 1833.
6. *Theatrical Observer*, 15 March 1833.
7. Ibid., 20 March 1833.
8. RA, VIC/MAIN/QVJ (W), Lord Esher's typescript, 19 March 1833.
9. Thackeray, William Makepiece, *Roundabout Papers* (London, Smith, Elder and Co., 1863), p. 117.
10. *The Satirist*, 9 June 1833.
11. Véron, III, pp. 211–212.
12. *Bell's Life in London*, 9 March 1834.
13. Quoted in Beaumont, p. 16.
14. Creevey, II, p. 273.

3 *The Idol of All the Dandies*

1. Tamvaco, I, p. 291.
2. Véron, III, pp. 189–190.
3. De Boigne, p. 29; Mahalin, p. 117.
4. *The New Satirist*, 21 November 1841.
5. Tamvaco, I, p.111.
6. Brontë, Charlotte, *Jane Eyre* (London, Penguin edition, 1953), pp. 142–146.
7. Bunn, II, pp. 91–92, 212–214.
8. Tamvaco, I, pp. 221–223.
9. *Town Magazine*, 25 November 1837.
10. Théophile Gautier, describing a performance by Elssler. Quoted in Guest, *The Romantic Ballet in Paris*, p. 152.

11. Quoted in Guest, *The Romantic Ballet in Paris*, p. 153, also describing a performance by Elssler.

12. YouTube clips danced by Margaret Barbieri of the Sadler's Wells Royal Ballet, and Gabriela Komleva of the Mariinsky Ballet. Choreography from Labanotation score, transcribed from Zorn notation by Ann Hutchinson Guest. See Guest, Ann Hutchinson, *Fanny Elssler's Cachucha: Labanotation Score* (London, Dance Books, 1981).

13. RA, VIC/MAIN/QVJ (W), Lord Esher's typescript, 21 December 1836.

14. *Bell's New Weekly Messenger*, 1 January 1837.

15. *The Theatrical Observer*, 30 January 1837.

16. RA, VIC/MAIN/QVJ (W), Lord Esher's typescript, 1 April 1837.

4 *A Princely Fortune*

1. WSRA, Add MS 8123.

2. GL, 11021/5, ff. 241–243.

3. *Report from the Select Committee Appointed to Inquire into the Cause of the High Price of Bullion* (London, 1810).

4. Lyne, Charles, *A Letter to the Rt. Hon. George Rose M.P., Vice-President of the Board of Trade, in which the real causes of the scarcity and consequent high price of gold and silver are stated and exemplified* (London, 22 November 1810), ii, 8, pp. 46–47. See also: Huskisson, William, *The Question concerning the Depreciation of our Currency Stated and Examined* (London, 1810).

5. Koster, John Theodore, *A Short Statement of the Trade in Gold Bullion* (Liverpool, 1811), pp. 71–72.

6. Lyne, Francis, pp. 215–242.

7. GL, 11021/11, ff. 322–327.

8. Bulwer-Lytton, Edward Robert, *The Life, Letters and Literary remains of Edward Bulmer, Lord Lytton* (London, Kegan Paul & Co, 1833), I, pp. 12–13.

9. Anon., *Real Life in London* (London, Jones and Co., 1822), II, pp. 519–521.

5 *The* Parvenu

1. Lyne, Francis, p. 174. Lord Eldon served as Lord Chancellor 1807–1827.

2. Gronow, *Anecdotes of Celebrities*, p. 83.

3. Ibid., p. 85.

4. Quoted in Bovill, E. W., *The England of Nimrod and Surtees 1815–1854* (Oxford University Press, 1959), pp. 106, 89.

5. *Morning Post*, 26 July 1830.

6. Martineau, Harriet, *History of the Peace: Pictorial History of England during the Thirty Years' Peace, 1816–1846*, revised edition (London, W. & R. Chambers, 1858), VII, pp. 347–348.
7. NDRA, flyer, 2 July 1832.
8. *Leicestershire Mercury*, 28 January 1854.
9. *Morning Post*, 17 October 1839.
10. *Essex Standard*, 26 December 1834.
11. Lyne, Francis, pp. 176–177.

6 *The Last Adventure*

1. Duncombe, T. H., *The Life and Correspondence of Thomas Slingsby Duncombe* (London, Hurst and Blackett, 1868), I, pp. 174–175.
2. RA, VIC/MAIN/QVJ (W), Lord Esher's typescript, 29 April, 30 April, 6 May 1837.
3. RA, VIC/MAIN/QVJ (W), Lord Esher's typescript, 26 June 1838.
4. Tamvaco, I, pp. 264–267.
5. R. H. Barham (under the pseudonym Thomas Ingoldsby), 'The Execution – A Sporting Anecdote', first published in *Bentley's Miscellany*, VI, June 1837. Later published in *The Ingoldsby Legends*. Maria Malibran was an opera singer who died in September 1836.

7 Mistress *Lyne Stephens*

1. De Boigne, pp. 29–30.
2. *L'Entr'acte*, 15 March 1857.
3. Cardigan and Lancastre, Countess of, *My Recollections* (London, Everleigh Nash, 1909), p. 4.
4. Cecil (Cornelius Tongue), *Records of the Chase and Memoirs of Celebrated Sportsmen* (London, Longman, Brown, Green and Co., 1854), pp. 429–431.
5. Véron, III, p. 204; Mahalin, pp. 117–118.

8 *The Richest Commoner*

1. UR, Autobiography of Mrs Smith.
2. Lyne, Francis, p. 182.
3. *Royal Cornwall Gazette*, 13 April 1860.
4. Letter to *Leeds Times*, 27 October 1894.
5. Buckle, G. E., and Moneypenny, W. F., *Life of Disraeli*, (London, John Murray, 1910–1920), II, p. 157.
6. Anon. (Diprose), p. 18.

7. Sale particulars, Lynford Hall, May 1856.
8. Lyne, Francis, p. 197.

9 *The Bill of Complaint*

1. Dickens, Charles, *Bleak House* (London, Penguin edition, 1996), preface, pp. 5–6.
2. *Bulkeley* v. *Stephens*, Bill of Complaint, July 1860, paras. 9, 11.
3. *Country Life*, 28 November 1903, pp. 758–768.

10 *A Lawyer's Will*

1. *Royal Cornwall Gazette*, 13 April 1860.
2. Lyne, Francis, pp. 189–192.
3. Bertouch, Baroness Beatrice de, *The Life of Father Ignatius, the Monk of Llantony* (London, Metheun, 1904), pp. 231–232.
4. Hare, Augustus, *The Years with Mother* (London, Century Publishing, 1984), pp. 237–238.
5. Lyne, Francis, pp. 190–191.
6. Extracts of Statements, pp. 1396–1398 (22 August 1887).

11 *The Still Sumptuous Duvernay*

1. NA, PRO 30/22/54.
2. NA, PRO/30/22/14C.
3. NA, FO 519/168.
4. Ibid.
5. Ibid.

12 *The First Military Attaché*

1. Leveson-Gower, pp. 6–7.
2. *The Times*, 7, 17 February 1855.
3. Quoted in Douglas, I, pp. 376–377.
4. NA, FO 519/168.
5. Ibid.
6. *Glasgow Herald*, 14 July 1858.
7. NA, FO 519/168.
8. Ibid.
9. Ibid.
10. Malmesbury, Earl of, *Memoirs of an Ex-Minister: an Autobiography of the Right Hon. The Earl of Malmesbury* (London, Longmans Green and Company, 1884), I, p. 496.
11. NA, FO 519/168.

12. WSA, 2057/F8/V/B/1390.
13. Quoted in Douglas, I, p. 334.

13 *The* Grande Dame

1. Blount, pp. 265–266.
2. Graves, Gertrude Montague, *Reminiscences of the Family of Captain John Fowle of Watertown, Massachusetts* (Boston, Press of David Clapp & Son, 1891), p. 27.
3. NA, FO 519/168.
4. Quoted in Vandam, Albert D., *Undercurrents of the Second Empire: Notes and Recollections* (London, William Heinemann, 1897), p. 364.
5. *Norfolk Chronicle*, 6 January 1866.
6. NA, FO 519/168.
7. *Bury and Norwich Post*, 23 April 1867.

14 *A Mere Point of Etiquette*

1. Quoted in Séguin, Philippe, *Louis-Napoléon le Grand* (Paris, Bernard Grasset, 1990), p. 394.
2. Gordon, p. 233.
3. Ibid., pp. 233–234.
4. NA, FO 146/1531.
5. NA, FO 146/1484.
6. Labouchere, pp. 89, 183–184.
7. NA, FO 146/1483.
8. Labouchere, p. 199.
9. *Daily News*, 23 December 1870; *The Times*, 20 December 1870.
10. NA, FO 146/1514.
11. NA, FO 146/1530.
12. NA, FO 146/1510.
13. Blount, pp. 192–212.

15 La Semaine Sanglante

1. NA, FO 146/1515.
2. Blount, pp. 227–228.
3. NA, FO 146/1871; FO 146/1532.
4. Command Paper 427, 18 August 1871.
5. NA, FO 146/1534.
6. Ibid.
7. NA, FO 146/1535.
8. Ibid.
9. Quoted in Legh, I, p. 386.

10. Edwin Child. Quoted in Horne, p. 478.
11. *Morning Advertiser*, 29 July 1871.
12. *The Times*, 19 August 1871.

16 *The* Ménage-à-Trois

1. UR, Autobiography of Mrs Smith.
2. *The Times*, 16 January 1873.

17 *Madame and the General*

1. Chudleigh, p. 336.

18 *The Eye-Doll House*

1. Flint, p. 138.
2. Chudleigh, p. 257.
3. UR, quoted in 'Notes on the Lyne Stephenses of Grove House'.
4. Quoted in Pollen, Anne, *Mother Mabel Digby: A Biography of the Superior General of the Sacred Heart, 1835–1911* (London, John Murray, 1914), p. 117.
5. Flint, p. 140.
6. *The Tablet*, 15 July 1905.
7. DN, original letter used by permission.
8. Ibid.
9. Ibid.
10. Ibid.
11. Ibid.
12. OLEM, undated MS letter.
13. Scott, *A Sermon*, pp. 16–18.
14. DN, original letter used by permission.
15. *Cambridge Chronicle*, 1 July 1887.
16. Quoted in Rogers, pp. 110–111.
17. Forster, E. M. *The Longest Journey* (London, Penguin edition,1960), pp. 63–64.
18. DN, original letter used by permission.
19. Scott, *The Story of the Building of the Church*.
20. Scott, *A Sermon*, p. 16.

19 *Penal Servitude*

1. Simon Little, Lefays Fine Arts, 2013.
2. DN, original letter used by permission.
3. *Cambridge Chronicle*, 10 May 1889.

4. Croucher, p. 59.
5. DN, original letter used by permission.

20 *First Great Grief*

1. DN, original letter used by permission.
2. Croucher, pp. 58–61.
3. *Cambridge Chronicle*, 17 October 1890.
4. DN, original letter used by permission.
5. Ibid.
6. UR, Autobiography of Mrs Smith.
7. DN, original letter used by permission.

21 *That Tearless Cry*

1. DN, original letter used by permission.

22 *A Solitary Dove*

1. Pym, Horace, pp. 143–145, 151–160.
2. Scott, *A Sermon*, pp. 19–20.
3. Ibid., pp. 11–13.
4. UR, Autobiography of Mrs Smith.
5. Riddell, pp. 475–476.
6. *Pall Mall Gazette*, 11 September 1894.
7. *Cambridge Independent Press*, 11 October 1890.

23 *The Precious Boy*

1. *The Universe*, quoted in Rayner, p. 196.
2. UR, Memoirs of Mrs Smith.
3. NGA, NG7/181/20.
4. NGA, NG7/182/1.
5. Pym, Horace, pp. 143–160.
6. UR, Memoirs of Mrs Smith.
7. NA, WO 339/92736.
8. Ibid.

24 *The Long Wait Ends*

1. Sale particulars, Lynford Hall, May 1895.

25 *The Legacy*

1. Flint, pp. 140–141.

BIBLIOGRAPHY

Manuscript Sources

Archives Nationales, Archives of the Paris Opéra, Paris
   Duvernay dossier (AJ/13/126, dossier 3)
Bank of England
   Court book, 1811
   Drawing account ledgers: Lyne, Hathorn and Roberts, 1804–1819
Bedingfeld MSS, Oxburgh Hall, Norfolk
   Claremont papers
   Lyne Stephens papers
Church of Our Lady and the English Martyrs, Cambridge
   Church archives
Diocese of Northampton
   Diocesan archives
Greater London Archives
   Lyne Stephens deeds and papers
Guildhall Library, Corporation of London
   Archives of Antony Gibbs and Sons
National Archives, Kew
   Foreign Office papers (FO)
   Lord John Russell papers (PRO)
   Tenth Royal Hussars: muster books and pay lists (WO)
   War Office papers: officers' services, First World War (WO)
National Gallery Archive, London
   Lyne Stephens bequest

North Devon Record Office
  General election papers, Barnstaple, 1830
Royal Archives, Windsor
  Queen Victoria's Journals
University of Roehampton Archives and Special Collections
  Extract from autobiography of Mrs Smith of Mount Clare, c.1912
  Notes on the Lyne Stephenses of Grove House (prepared by English Heritage)
Victoria and Albert Museum
  Duvernay dossier (playbills and press cuttings)
West Sussex Record Office
  Stephens, Philadelphia, account of the royal visit to Marinha Grande, 25 July 1788
Wiltshire and Swindon Archives
  Herbert papers
Private collections
  Charles Lyne Stephens account book, 1827–1847
  Lyne family papers

Published Sources

Anon. (Diprose, John), *Life in Paris before the war and during the siege …* (London, Diprose and Bateman, 1871)

AXA Group, *Hôtel de La Vaupalière* (Paris, Société Française de Promotion Artistique, 2008)

Beaumont, Cyril W., *Three French Dancers of the Nineteenth Century: Duvernay, Livry, Beaugrand* (London, C. W. Beaumont, 1935)

Blount, Edward, *Memoirs of Sir Edward Blount*, ed. Stuart J. Reid (London, Longmans, Green and Co., 1902)

Boigne, Charles de, *Petits Mémoires de l'Opéra* (Paris, Delcambre, 1857)

Brownlow, Jack, *Melton Mowbray, Queen of the Shires* (Wymondham, Sycamore Press, 1980)

Bunn, Alfred, *The Stage: Both Before and Behind the Curtain,* 3 vols (London, Richard Bentley, 1840)

Butler, J. R. M., *The Passing of the Great Reform Bill* (London, Longmans, Green and Co., 1914)

Calder-Marshall, Arthur, *The Enthusiast: an Enquiry into the Life Beliefs and Character of the Rev. Joseph Leycester Lyne alias Fr. Ignatius O.S.B. Abbot of Elm Hill, Norwich & Llanthony Wales* (London, Faber and Faber, 1962)

Cannon, Richard, *Historical Record of the Tenth, the Prince of Wales Own Royal Regiment of Hussars* (London, Parker, Furnival and Parker, 1843)

Christie, Manson & Woods, *Catalogue of the Celebrated Collection of Pictures, Porcelain, Objects of Art, and Decorative Furniture of Mrs Lyne Stephens, deceased* (London, May 1895).

Christie, Manson & Woods, *Catalogue of the Collection of Fine Old English and Foreign Silver Plate and Casket of Beautiful Jewels of Mrs Lyne Stephens* (London, May 1895)

Chudleigh, E. R., *Diary of E. R. Chudleigh, 1862–1921,* ed. E. C. Richards (Christchurch, Simpson and Williams, 1950)

A Collection of Addresses, Squibs etc. which were circulated in reference to the Election of Members to serve in Parliament for the Borough of Barnstaple in the year 1832 (Barnstaple, 1833)

Country Life, 'Lynford Hall, Norfolk, the seat of Mr H. A. Campbell' (28 November 1903)

Creevey, Thomas, *The Creevey Papers, a Selection from the Correspondence and Diaries of the Late Thomas Creevey M.P.,* ed. Sir Herbert Maxwell, 2 vols (London, John Murray, 1903)

Croucher, Maurice, 'The Opening of the New Catholic Church in Cambridge', *Cambridge Catholic Magazine* (Cambridge, August 1933)

Davidson, Hilary, 'The History of Elm Grove', *The Chronicle* (Roehampton, Digby Stuart College, 1958–1961)

Douglas, Sir George (ed.), *The Panmure Papers ... a selection from the correspondence of Fox Maule, second Baron Panmure, afterwards Eleventh Earl of Dalhousie,* 2 vols (London, Hodder and Stoughton, 1908)

Flint, James Canon, 'Lynford', *St Francis' Magazine* (Northampton, April 1925)

Foulkes, Nick, *Last of the Dandies: the scandalous life and escapades of Count d'Orsay* (London, Little Brown, 2003)

Gerhold, Dorian, *Villas and Mansions of Roehampton and Putney Heath* (Wandsworth Historical Society, 1997)

Gordon, Sir Charles Alexander, *Recollections of Thirty-nine Years in the Army* (London, Swan Sonnenchein and Co., 1898)

Gronow, R. H., *Anecdotes of Celebrities of London and Paris* (London, Smith, Elder and Co., 1873)

Gronow, R. H., *Reminiscences and Recollections,* 2 vols (London, Nimmo, 1889)

Guest, Ivor, *The Romantic Ballet in England* (London, Phoenix House, 1954)

Guest, Ivor, *The Romantic Ballet in Paris* (London, Dance Books, second edition, 1980)

Guest, Ivor, *Fanny Elssler: The pagan ballerina* (London, A. & C. Black, 1970)

Bibliography

Horne, Alistair, *The Fall of Paris: The Siege and the Commune 1870–1871* (London, Penguin edition, 1981)

Howarth, T. E. B., *Citizen-King, The Life of Louis-Philippe King of the French* (London, Eyre & Spottiswoode, 1961)

Labouchere, Henry du Pré, *Diary of the Besieged Resident in Paris* (London, Macmillan and Co, third edition, 1872)

Legh, T. W. (Lord Newton), *Lord Lyons: A Record of British Diplomacy*, 2 vols (London, Longmans, Green and Co., 1913)

Leveson-Gower, Frederick, *Bygone Years: Recollections by the Hon. F. Leveson-Gower* (London, John Murray, 1905)

Liddell, R. S., *The Memoirs of the Tenth Royal Hussars* (London, Longmans, Green and Co., 1891)

Lyne, Francis, *A Letter to Father Ignatius on the Death of his Mother* (privately printed, 1878)

Mahalin, Paul (un vieil abonné), *Ces Demoiselles de l'Opéra* (Paris, Tresse et Stock, 1887)

Mansel, Philip, *Paris between Empires* (New York, St. Martin Press, 2001)

McCrea, Frederick Bradford, *Tree and Services of the Wetherall Family* (privately printed, 1912)

Olivier, Juste, *Paris en 1830* (Paris, Mercure de France, 1951)

Peacock, Bernard, 'Paris, London, Lynford,' *East Anglian Magazine* (Ipswich, December 1958)

Pym, Francis, *Sentimental Journey* (privately printed, 1998)

Pym, Horace, *Chats in the Book Room* (privately printed, 1896)

Rayner, Eric, 'The Lovely Lady Bountiful,' *Catholic Fireside*, CLXXI, no. 4151 (19 September 1969)

Riddell, Arthur, *A Pastoral Letter by Arthur, Bishop of Northampton, Advent, 1894* (Northampton, 28 November 1894)

Roberts, Jenifer, *Glass: The Strange History of the Lyne Stephens Fortune* (Chippenham, Templeton Press, 2003)

Rogers, Nicholas (ed.), *Catholics in Cambridge* (Leominster, Gracewing, 2003)

Roqueplan, Nestor, *Les Coulisses de l'Opéra* (Paris, Librarie Nouvelle, 1855)

Saunders, Edith, *The Age of Worth* (London, Longman, Green and Co., 1954)

Scott, Christopher, *A Sermon preached in the Church of Our Lady and the English Martyrs* (Cambridge, September 1894)

Scott, Christopher, 'The Story of the Building of the Church of Our Lady and the English Martyrs', *Cambridge Chronicle* (27 October, 3 November 1915)

Séchan, Charles (ed. Badin, Adolphe), *Souvenirs d'un Homme de Théâtre* (Paris, Calman Lévy, 1883)

Second, Albéric, *Les Petits Mystères de l'Opéra* (Brussels, Société Belge de Librarie, 1844)

Tamvaco, Jean-Louis, *Les Cancans de l'Opéra: Chroniques de l'Académie Royale de Musique et du théâtre, à Paris sous les deux Restaurations*, 2 vols (Paris, CNRS Editions, 2000)

Vaillat, Léandre, *La Taglioni ou la Vie d'une Danseuse* (Paris, Albin Michel, 1942)

Véron, Louis, *Mémoires d'un Bourgeois de Paris*, 5 vols (Paris, Librarie Nouvelle, 1857)

Weston, Peter, *From Roehampton Great House to Grove House* (Roehampton Institute, 1998)

Wilkins, Philip, *Our Lady and the English Martyrs, Cambridge*, 4th edition (Cambridge, 1995)

ACKNOWLEDGEMENTS

I should like to thank Sir Henry and Lady Mary Bedingfeld, who gave me access to the Lyne Stephens and Claremont papers, as well as providing generous hospitality at Oxburgh Hall; Ivor Guest, who shared his research into the dancing years of Pauline Duvernay; Gilly King, History and Heritage Adviser at the University of Roehampton; Philip Wilkins, who introduced me to the church of Our Lady and the English Martyrs in Cambridge; Christophe Rizoud, Caroline Pacheco and Johanna Zhang of AXA who showed me around the Hôtel de La Vaupalière (Hôtel Molé) in Paris; Lady Sarah Backhouse, for providing a great deal of information; Monica Jenks, who provided copies of family letters in her possession; Davina Crookes and Colin Veitch, for taking photographs; and Clive and Heather Toomer, for the loan of a vast quantity of books.

I should also like to thank Alan Crookham and Ceri Brough of the National Gallery Archive; Suzanne Higgott and Carys Lewis of the Wallace Collection; Roger Ward, historian of Chicksands Priory; Brin Dunsire, archivist of the Diocese of Northampton; Simon Little of Lefays Fine Arts; Richard Peroni and Bob and Christine Branch of the church of Our Lady and the English Martyrs; and Father Bennie Noonan of the church of St Francis in Shefford.

I am grateful to Clare Owen and the Amberley team for their faith in this book, and to Lady Sarah Backhouse, Dr Hilary Custance Green, Dr Jean Shennan, Clive Toomer, and Professor Gareth Williams for reading the manuscript and for their many constructive comments. Finally – as always – my thanks to my husband Paul Beck for his support and encouragement, his help and company on most of my travels, and his tolerance as I immersed myself in the life of Yolande Lyne Stephens. I owe him far more than these words can express.

The author and publisher would like to thank the following people/ organisations for permission to use copyright material in this book: Her Majesty Queen Elizabeth II and the Royal Archives for permission to quote from Queen Victoria's Journals; Penguin Random House Canada (Alfred A. Knopf) and the Provost and Scholars of King's College, Cambridge, and the Society of Authors as the E. M. Forster Estate for permission to quote from *The Longest Journey* by E. M. Forster. Thanks are also due to Archives Nationales, Paris; Our Lady and the English Martyrs, Cambridge; Guildhall Library, Corporation of London; National Gallery Archive, London; North Devon Record Office; Northampton Diocesan Archives; University of Roehampton Archives and Special Collections; West Sussex Record Office; and Wiltshire and Swindon Archives. I am also grateful to Sir Henry Bedingfeld, Monica Jenks, Charles Lyne, Douglas Lyne, and John Lyne for permission to quote from letters and papers in their possession.

For permission to reproduce illustrations, I should like to thank AXA; Bibliotèque nationale de France; Friends of Chicksands Priory; John Hagger; Geoff Halsall; Bob Jones; John Lyne; National Portrait Gallery; Our Lady and the English Martyrs; Photography by Davina; Royal Collection Trust; Society of the Sacred Heart; Victoria and Albert Museum; and University of Roehampton.

Every attempt has been made to seek permission for copyright material used in this book. However, if we have inadvertently used copyright material without permission/acknowledgement we apologise and will make the necessary correction at the first opportunity.

ILLUSTRATION CREDITS

Image numbers not listed below belong to owners of private collections who wish to remain anonymous.

  1. © Bibliotèque nationale de France.
  3. © Bibliotèque nationale de France.
  4. Published in *Louis Véron* by Eugène de Mirecourt, Paris, 1855.
  5. © Robert Allen.
  6. © M. R. Lopez.
7–8. Royal Collection Trust/© Her Majesty Queen Elizabeth II 2015.
  9. © Victoria and Albert Museum, London.
 10. Royal Collection Trust/© Her Majesty Queen Elizabeth II 2015.
 12. © Friends of Chicksands Priory.
 13. © National Portrait Gallery, London.
14–16. © Victoria and Albert Museum, London.
 17. © Society of the Sacred Heart (England and Wales Provincial Archives).
18–19. © Archives and Special Collections, University of Roehampton.
 20. © Jenifer Roberts.
 21. © Jenifer Roberts, reproduced by permission of Sir Henry Bedingfeld.
 22. Published in *Select Views of London* by John B. Papworth, 1816.
 25. Reproduced by permission of Sir Henry Bedingfeld.
27–29. Reproduced by permission of AXA.
 30. © John Lyne.
33–34. Published in *Country Life* magazine, 28 November 1903.
 37. © Bibliotèque nationale de France.

INDEX